Workshop on Multiword Expressions: from Parsing and Generation to the Real World 2011

(MWE 2011)

Held at ACL HLT 2011

Portland, Oregon, USA
23 June 2011

ISBN: 978-1-61839-253-4

Printed from e-media with permission by:

Curran Associates, Inc.
57 Morehouse Lane
Red Hook, NY 12571

CURRAN ASSOCIATES INC. proceedings.com

Some format issues inherent in the e-media version may also appear in this print version.

Printed by Curran Associates, Inc. (2011)

Association for Computational Linguistics
209 N. Eighth Street
Stroudsburg, Pennsylvania 18360

Phone: 1-570-476-8006
Fax: 1-570-476-0860

acl@aclweb.org

Additional copies of this publication are available from:

Curran Associates, Inc.
57 Morehouse Lane
Red Hook, NY 12571 USA
Phone: 845-758-0400
Fax: 845-758-2634
Email: curran@proceedings.com
Web: www.proceedings.com

Introduction

The ACL 2011 Workshop on *Multiword Expressions: from Parsing and Generation to the Real World (MWE 2011)* took place on June 23, 2011 in Portland, Oregon, USA, in conjunction to the 49th Annual Meeting of the Association for Computational Linguistics: Human Language Technologies (ACL HLT 2011). The workshop has been held every year since 2003 in conjunction with ACL, EACL, COLING and LREC.

Multiword Expressions (MWEs) range over linguistic constructions such as idioms (a frog in the throat, kill some time), fixed phrases (per se, by and large, rock'n roll), noun compounds (telephone booth, cable car), compound verbs (give a presentation, go by [a name]), etc. While easily mastered by native speakers, their interpretation poses a major challenge for computational systems, due to their flexible and heterogeneous nature. Surprisingly enough, MWEs are not nearly as frequent in NLP resources (dictionaries, grammars) as they are in real-word text, where they have been reported to account for over 70% of the terms in a domain. Thus, MWEs are a key issue and a current weakness for tasks like Natural Language Parsing (NLP) and Generation (NLG), as well as real-life applications such as Machine Translation.

MWE 2011 is the 8th event in the series, and the time has come to move from basic preliminary research and theoretical results to actual applications in real-world NLP tasks. Therefore, following further the trend of previous MWE workshops, we have now turned our focus towards MWEs on NLP applications, specifically towards Parsing and Generation of MWEs, as there is a wide range of open problems that prevent MWE treatment techniques to be fully integrated in current NLP systems. We have thus asked our contributors for original research related (but not limited) to the following topics:

- **Lexical representations**: In spite of several proposals for MWE representation ranging along the continuum from words-with-spaces to compositional approaches connecting lexicon and grammar, to date, it remains unclear how MWEs should be represented in electronic dictionaries, thesauri and grammars. New methodologies that take into account the type of MWE and its properties are needed for efficiently handling manually and/or automatically acquired expressions in NLP systems. Moreover, strategies are also needed to represent deep attributes and semantic properties for these multiword entries.

- **Task and Application-oriented evaluation**: Evaluation is a crucial aspect for MWE research. Various evaluation techniques have been proposed, from manual inspection of top-n candidates to classic precision/recall measures. However, to get a clear indication of the effect of incorporating a treatment of MWEs in a particular context, task and application-oriented evaluations are needed. We have thus called for submissions that study the impact of MWE handling in the context of Parsing, Generation, Information Extraction, Machine Translation, Summarization, etc.

- **Type-dependent analysis**: While there is no unique definition or classification of MWEs, most researchers agree on some major classes such as named entities, collocations, multiword terminology and verbal expressions. These, though, are very heterogeneous in terms of syntactic and semantic properties, and should thus be treated differently by applications. Type-dependent analyses could shed some light on the best methodologies to integrate MWE knowledge in our analysis and generation systems.

- **MWE engineering**: Where do MWEs go after being extracted? Do they belong to the lexicon and/or to the grammar? In the pipeline of linguistic analysis and/or generation, where should we insert MWEs? And even more important: HOW? Because all the effort put in automatic MWE extraction will not be useful if we do not know how to employ these rich resources in our real-life NLP applications!

This year, we had three different submission types: long, short and demonstration papers. We received a total of 31 submissions, from which 16 were long papers, 9 were short papers and 6 were demo papers. Given our limited capacity as a one-day workshop, we were only able to accept 6 long papers for oral presentation and 4 long papers as posters: an acceptance rate of 62.5%. We further accepted 4 short papers for oral presentation and 2 short papers as posters (67% acceptance), as well as 5 out of the 6 proposed demonstrations. The oral presentations were distributed in three sessions: Short Papers, Identification and Representation, and Tasks and Applications. The workshop also featured two invited talks, by Timothy Baldwin and by Kenneth Church, and a panel discussion.

We would like to thank the members of the Program Committee for the timely reviews. We would also like to thank the authors for their valuable contributions.

Valia Kordoni, Carlos Ramisch, Aline Villavicencio
Co-Organizers

Organizers:

Valia Kordoni, DFKI GmbH and Saarland University, Germany
Carlos Ramisch, University of Grenoble, France and Federal University of Rio Grande do Sul, Brazil
Aline Villavicencio, Federal University of Rio Grande do Sul, Brazil

Consulting Body:

Su Nam Kim, University of Melbourne, Australia
Preslav Nakov, National University of Singapore, Singapore

Program Committee:

Iñaki Alegria, University of the Basque Country, Spain
Dimitra Anastasiou, University of Bremen, Germany
Timothy Baldwin, University of Melbourne, Australia
Srinivas Bangalore, AT&T Labs-Research, USA
Francis Bond, Nanyang Technological University, Singapore
Aoife Cahill, IMS University of Stuttgart, Germany
Paul Cook, University of Toronto, Canada
Béatrice Daille, Nantes University, France
Mona Diab, Columbia University, USA
Gaël Dias, Beira Interior University, Portugal
Stefan Evert, University of Osnabrueck, Germany
Roxana Girju, University of Illinois at Urbana-Champaign, USA
Chikara Hashimoto, National Institute of Information and Communications Technology, Japan
Ulrich Heid, Stuttgart University, Germany
Kyo Kageura, University of Tokyo, Japan
Adam Kilgarriff, Lexical Computing Ltd., UK
Ioannis Korkontzelos, University of Manchester, UK
Zornitsa Kozareva, University of Southern California, USA
Brigitte Krenn, Austrian Research Institute for Artificial Intelligence, Austria
Takuya Matsuzaki, University of Tokyo, Japan
Diana McCarthy, Lexical Computing Ltd., UK
Yusuke Miyao, National Institute of Informatics, Japan
Rosamund Moon, University of Birmingham, UK
Diarmuid Ó Séaghdha, University of Cambridge, UK
Jan Odijk, University of Utrecht, The Netherlands
Pavel Pecina, Dublin City University, Ireland
Scott Piao, Lancaster University, UK
Thierry Poibeau, CNRS and École Normale Supérieure, France

Elisabete Ranchhod, University of Lisbon, Portugal
Barbara Rosario, Intel Labs, USA
Agata Savary, Université François Rabelais Tours, France
Violeta Seretan, University of Edinburgh, UK
Ekaterina Shutova, University of Cambridge, UK
Suzanne Stevenson, University of Toronto, Canada
Sara Stymne, Linköping University, Sweden
Stan Szpakowicz, University of Ottawa, Canada
Beata Trawinski, University of Vienna, Austria
Vivian Tsang, Bloorview Research Institute, Canada
Kyioko Uchiyama, National Institute of Informatics, Japan
Ruben Urizar, University of the Basque Country, Spain
Gertjan van Noord, University of Groningen, The Netherlands
Tony Veale, University College Dublin, Ireland
Begoña Villada Moirón, RightNow, The Netherlands
Yi Zhang, DFKI GmbH and Saarland University, Germany

Invited Speakers:

Timothy Baldwin, University of Melbourne, Australia
Kenneth Church, Johns Hopkins University, USA

Table of Contents

Workshop Program

Thursday, June 23, 2011

08:15–08:30 Welcome

08:30–09:30 **Invited talk**
MWEs and Topic Modelling: Enhancing Machine Learning with Linguistics
Timothy Baldwin

Session I - Short Papers

09:30–09:45 *Automatic Extraction of NV Expressions in Basque: Basic Issues on Cooccurrence Techniques*
Antton Gurrutxaga and Iñaki Alegria

09:45–10:00 *Semantic Clustering: an Attempt to Identify Multiword Expressions in Bengali*
Tanmoy Chakraborty, Dipankar Das and Sivaji Bandyopadhyay

10:00–10:15 *Decreasing Lexical Data Sparsity in Statistical Syntactic Parsing - Experiments with Named Entities*
Deirdre Hogan, Jennifer Foster and Josef van Genabith

10:15–10:30 *Detecting Multi-Word Expressions Improves Word Sense Disambiguation*
Mark Finlayson and Nidhi Kulkarni

10:30–11:00 MORNING BREAK

Session II - Identification and Representation

11:00–11:25 *Tree-Rewriting Models of Multi-Word Expressions*
William Schuler and Aravind Joshi

11:25–11:50 *Learning English Light Verb Constructions: Contextual or Statistical*
Yuancheng Tu and Dan Roth

11:50–12:15 *Two Types of Korean Light Verb Constructions in a Typed Feature Structure Grammar*
Juwon Lee

12:15–13:50 LUNCH BREAK

Session III - Tasks and Applications

13:50–14:15 *MWU-Aware Part-of-Speech Tagging with a CRF Model and Lexical Resources*
Matthieu Constant and Anthony Sigogne

14:15–14:40 *The Web is not a PERSON, Berners-Lee is not an ORGANIZATION, and African-Americans are not LOCATIONS: An Analysis of the Performance of Named-Entity Recognition*
Robert Krovetz, Paul Deane and Nitin Madnani

14:40–15:05 *A Machine Learning Approach to Relational Noun Mining in German*
Berthold Crysmann

Thursday, June 23, 2011 (continued)

15:05–15:30 **Poster and Demo Session**
Long Papers

Identifying and Analyzing Brazilian Portuguese Complex Predicates
Magali Sanches Duran, Carlos Ramisch, Sandra Maria Aluísio and Aline Villavicencio

An N-gram Frequency Database Reference to Handle MWE Extraction in NLP Applications
Patrick Watrin and Thomas François

Extracting Transfer Rules for Multiword Expressions from Parallel Corpora
Petter Haugereid and Francis Bond

Identification and Treatment of Multiword Expressions Applied to Information Retrieval
Otavio Acosta, Aline Villavicencio and Viviane Moreira

Short Papers

Stepwise Mining of Multi-Word Expressions in Hindi
Rai Mahesh Sinha

Detecting Noun Compounds and Light Verb Constructions: a Contrastive Study
Veronika Vincze, István Nagy T. and Gábor Berend

Demo Papers

jMWE: A Java Toolkit for Detecting Multi-Word Expressions
Nidhi Kulkarni and Mark Finlayson

FipsCoView: On-line Visualisation of Collocations Extracted from Multilingual Parallel Corpora
Violeta Seretan and Eric Wehrli

The StringNet Lexico-Grammatical Knowledgebase and its Applications
David Wible and Nai-Lung Tsao

The Ngram Statistics Package (Text::NSP) : A Flexible Tool for Identifying Ngrams, Collocations, and Word Associations
Ted Pedersen, Satanjeev Banerjee, Bridget McInnes, Saiyam Kohli, Mahesh Joshi and Ying Liu

Fast and Flexible MWE Candidate Generation with the mwetoolkit
Vitor De Araujo, Carlos Ramisch and Aline Villavicencio

15:30–16:00 AFTERNOON BREAK

Invited talk

16:00–17:00 *How Many Multiword Expressions do People Know?*
Kenneth Church

17:00–18:00 **Panel: Toward a Special Interest Group for MWEs**

MWEs and Topic Modelling: Enhancing Machine Learning with Linguistics

Timothy Baldwin
University of Melbourne, Australia
tim@csse.unimelb.edu.au

Abstract

Topic modelling is a popular approach to joint clustering of documents and terms, e.g. via Latent Dirichlet Allocation. The standard document representation in topic modelling is a bag of unigrams, ignoring both macro-level document structure and micro-level constituent structure. In this talk, I will discuss recent work on consolidating the micro-level document representation with multiword expressions, and present experimental results which demonstrate that linguistically-richer document representations enhance topic modelling.

Biography

Tim Baldwin is an Associate Professor and Deputy Head of the Department of Computer Science and Software Engineering, University of Melbourne and a contributed research staff member of the NICTA Victoria Research Laboratories. He has previously held visiting positions at the University of Washington, University of Tokyo, University of Saarland, and NTT Communication Science Laboratories. His research interests cover topics including deep linguistic processing, multiword expressions, deep lexical acquisition, computer-assisted language learning, information extraction and web mining, with a particular interest in the interface between computational and theoretical linguistics. Current projects include web user forum mining, information personalisation in museum contexts, biomedical text mining, online linguistic exploration, and intelligent interfaces for Japanese language learners. He is President of the Australasian Language Technology Association in 2011-2012.

Tim completed a BSc(CS/Maths) and BA(Linguistics/Japanese) at the University of Melbourne in 1995, and an MEng(CS) and PhD(CS) at the Tokyo Institute of Technology in 1998 and 2001, respectively. Prior to commencing his current position at the University of Melbourne, he was a Senior Research Engineer at the Center for the Study of Language and Information, Stanford University (2001-2004).

Automatic extraction of NV expressions in Basque: basic issues on cooccurrence techniques

Antton Gurrutxaga
Elhuyar Foundation
a.gurrutxaga@elhuyar.com

Iñaki Alegria
IXA group/Univ. of the Basque Country
i.alegria@ehu.es

Abstract

Taking as a starting-point the development on cooccurrence techniques for several languages, we focus on the aspects that should be considered in a NV extraction task for Basque. In Basque, NV expressions are considered those combinations in which a noun, inflected or not, is co-occurring with a verb, as *erabakia hartu* ('to make a decision'), *kontuan hartu* ('to take into account') and *buruz jakin* ('to know by heart'). A basic extraction system has been developed and evaluated against two references: a) a reference which includes NV entries from several lexicographic works; and b) a manual evaluation by three experts of a random sample from the n-best lists.

1 Introduction

The last decade has witnessed great advances in the automatic identification and processing of MWEs. In the case of Basque, advances are limited to terminology extraction and the tagging in corpora of the MWEs represented in lexical databases.

Furthermore, the work on both theoretical and practical phraseology in Basque has been mainly focused on idiomatic expressions, leaving aside collocations (Pérez Gaztelu et al., 2004). As a consequence, Basque NLP and lexicography have not benefited from the approach that emphasized the importance of such units, and very important areas are underdeveloped.

With the aim of taking steps to turn this situation, we undertake the task of extracting NV combinations from corpora. As a preliminary step, we must face the morphosyntactic aspects of Basque that might influence the efficiency of the process.

2 MWE: basic definition and extraction techniques

As a basis for our work, we take idiomaticity as the key feature for the definition and classification of MWE. Idiomaticity could be described as a non-discrete magnitude, whose "value", according to recent investigations (Baldwin and Kim, 2010; Fazly and Stevenson, 2007; Granger and Paquot, 2008), has turned to depend on a complex combination of features such as institutionalization, non-compositionality and lexico-syntactic fixedness.

The idiomaticity of MWEs appears rather as a continuum than as a scale of discrete values (Sinclair, 1996; Wulff, 2010). Thus, the classification of MWEs into discrete categories is a difficult task. Taking Cowie's classification as an initial basis (Cowie, 1998), our work is focused on phrase-like units, aiming, at this stage, to differentiate MWEs (idioms and collocations) from free combinations. Specifically, NV combinations with the following characteristics are considered as MWEs:

- Idioms: non-compositional combinations, as opaque idioms (*adarra jo*: 'to pull somebody's leg'; lit: 'to play the horn') and figurative idioms (*burua hautsi*: 'to rack one's brain'; lit: 'to break one's head').
- Collocations:
  - Semicompositional combinations, in which the noun keeps its literal meaning,

whereas the verb acts as a support verb (*lan egin*: 'to work'; lit. 'to do work'), or has a meaning which is specific to that combination (*atentzioa eman*: 'to catch someone's eye'; lit. 'to give attention' (sth to sb)); *legea urratu*: 'to break the law'; lit. 'to tear the law').

- Compositional combinations with lexical restriction, in which it is not possible to substitute the verb with its synonyms, or that present a clear statistical idiosyncrasy in favor of a given synonym choice (*elkartasuna adierazi*: 'to express solidarity'; *konpromisoa berretsi*: 'to confirm a commitment').

Among the different techniques that have been proposed to extract and characterize MWEs, the cooccurrence of the components is the most used heuristic of institutionalization, and the use of association measures (AM) goes back to early research on this field (Church and Hanks, 1990; Smadja, 1993). In recent years, the comparative analysis of AMs has aroused considerable interest, as well as the possibility of obtaining better results by combining them (Pearce, 2002; Pecina, 2005). Cooccurrence techniques are usually used in combination with linguistic techniques, which allow the use of lemmatized and POS-tagged corpora, or even syntactic dependencies (Seretan, 2008).

3 Special features of Basque NV combinations

These are some characteristics of the NV combinations in Basque to be considered in order to design the extraction process efficiently:

- Basque being an agglutinative language, MWE extraction must work on tagged texts, in order to identify different surface forms with their corresponding lemma. Thus, pure statistical methods working with raw text are not expected to yield acceptable results.

- Some combinations with a noun as first lemma do not correspond to NV combinations in the sense that is usually understood in English. For example, the expression *kontuan hartu* can be translated as *take into account*, where *kontu* is a noun in the inessive case. We are interested in all types of combinations that a noun can form with verbs.

- Representing NV combinations as lemma-lemma pairs is by no means satisfactory; we would not be able to differentiate the aforementioned *kontuan hartu* from *kontu hartu* ("to ask for an explanation"). So it is necessary to deal with the form or type of every noun.

- In order to propose canonical forms for NV combinations, we need case and number annotations for nouns in bigram data. The next examples are different forms of the canonical *erabakia hartu* ('to make a decision'): *ez zuen erabakirik hartu* ('he did not make any decision'), *zenbait erabaki hartu behar ditugu* ('we have to make some decisions'). Canonical forms can be formulated by bigram normalization (see section 4.5 for details).

4 Experimental setup

4.1 Corpora resources

In our experiments, we use a journalistic corpus from two sources: (1) Issues published between 2001-2002 by the newspaper *Euskaldunon Egunkaria* (28 Mw); and (2) Issues published between 2006-2010 by the newspaper *Berria* (47 Mw). So, the overall size of the corpus is 75 Mw.

4.2 Corpus-processing

For linguistic tagging, we use EUSTAGGER by the IXA group of the University of the Basque Country (Aduriz et al., 1996). After linguistic processing, we obtain information about the lemma, part-of-speech, subcategory, case, number and other morphosyntactic features.

We used EUSTAGGER without the module to detect and annotate MWEs in order to evaluate the automatic extraction, regardless of wheter the candidates are in the lexical database.

4.3 Preparing tagged corpora for bigram generation

For bigram generation, we use the Ngram Statistics Package-NSP (Banerjee and Pedersen, 2010). In order to retain in the text sent to NSP the linguistic information needed according to section 3, we add different types of linguistic information to the tokens, depending on the POS of the components of the combination we are dealing with. In the case of NV combinations, the nouns are represented in the following form:

```
token_lemma_POS_subcategory_case_number
```

In the case of verbs, only lemma and POS are used, as verb inflection has no influence on the canonical form of the expression. In future work, verb inflection will be one of the parameters to measure syntactical flexibility. All other types of tokens are discarded and considered as 'non-token' for NSP processing.

Before this step, some surface-grammar rules are defined to detect and filter the participle forms that are not part of a NV combination, but must be analyzed as adjectives or nouns (eg. *herrialde aurreratuak* 'developed countries', and *gobernuaren aliatuak*, 'government's allies').

4.4 Bigram generation

We generated bigram sets for two different window spans: ± 1 and ± 5. In both sets, the frequency criterion for a bigram to be generated is $f > 30$. Also, the following punctuation marks are interpreted as a boundary for bigram generation: period, colon, semicolon, and question and exclamation marks. Then, all counts of bigrams in NV and VN order are combined using NSP, and reordered in NV order.

Additionally, a heuristic is used to filter some combinations. The first member of many "compound verbs" like *nahi izan* ('to want'), is a noun, and some of them combine usually with a verb, in VN order: *ikusi nahi (zuen)* ('he wanted to see'). In order to reduce this noise, the combinations occurring mostly in VN order are removed. The combinations generated from passive constructions (*hartutako erabakien ondorioak*, 'the consequences of the decisions made') are not affected by this filtering.

4.5 Bigram normalization

In order to get more representative statistics, and to get information that would enable us to propose a canonical form for each MWE candidate, different inflection forms of the same case in nouns are normalized to the most frequent form, and bigram counts are recalculated. I.e. $\left[\right.$ *erabakia / erabakiak / erabakiok / erabakirik / erabaki* $\left.\right]$ *hartu* are collapsed to *erabakia hartu* ('to make a decision'), because all the mentioned forms of the lemma *erabaki* appear in the absolutive case. In contrast, the combinations *kontu hartu* ("to ask for an explanation") and *kontuan hartu* ("take into account") are not normalized, as their noun forms correspond to different cases, namely, absolutive (*kontu*) and inessive (*kontuan*). A Perl script detects in the dataset the bigrams to be normalized, using the combined key noun_lemma/noun_case+verb_lemma, creates a single bigram with the most frequent form, and sums the frequencies of bigrams and those of the noun unigrams.

As an example, this is normalization data for *kalean ibili* ('to walk on the street'):

```
kalean_kale_IZE_ARR_INE_NUMS<>ibili_ADI<>223 3354 10880
kaleetan_kale_IZE_ARR_INE_NUMP<>ibili_ADI<>119 243 10880
→
kalean_kale_IZE_ARR_INE_NUMS<>ibili_ADI<>342 3597 10880
```

Besides, ergative-singular → absolutive-plural normalization is carried out when the ratio is greater than 1:5. This heuristic is used in order to repair some mistakes from the tagger. Finally, partitive case (PAR) is assimilated to absolutive (ABS) for bigram normalization; partitive is a case used in negative, interrogative and conditional sentences with subjects of intransitive verbs and objects of transitive verbs. I.e. *ez zuen erabakirik hartu* ('he did not make any decision').

Thus, this is the normalization of *erabakia hartu*:

```
erabakia_erabaki_IZE_ARR_ABS_NUMS<>hartu_ADI<>2658 6329 88447
erabakiak_erabaki_IZE_ARR_ABS_NUMP<>hartu_ADI<>1632 2397 88447
erabakiak_erabaki_IZE_ARR_ERG_NUMP<>hartu_ADI<>88 141 88447
erabakirik_erabaki_IZE_ARR_PAR_MG<>hartu_ADI<>211 211 88447
→
erabakia_erabaki_IZE_ARR_ABS_NUMS<>hartu_ADI<>4589 9361 88447
```

4.6 AM calculation

The statistical analysis of cooccurrence data is carried out using Stefan Evert's UCS toolkit (Evert, 2005). The most common association measures are calculated for each bigram: f, t-score (also t-test), log-likelihood ratio, MI, MI^3, and chi-square (χ^2).

4.7 Evaluation

In order to evaluate the results of the bigram extraction process, we use as a reference a collection of

NV expressions published in five Basque resources: a) *The Unified Basque Dictionary*, b) *Euskal Hiztegia* (Sarasola, 1996); c) *Elhuyar Hiztegia*; d) *Intza* project; and e) EDBL (Aldezabal et al., 2001).

The total number for NV expressions is 3,742. Despite the small size of the reference, we believe that it may be valid for a comparison of the performance of different AMs. Nevertheless, even a superficial analysis reveals that the reference is mostly made up of two kinds of combinations, idioms and typical "compound verbs"[1].

Every evaluation against a dictionary depends largely on its recall and quality, and we envisage, as recommended by Krenn (1999), to build a handmade gold standard. To this end, we extract an evaluation sample merging the 2,000-best candidates of each AM ranking from the w = ±1 extraction set. There are 4,334 different bigrams in this set. This manual evaluation is an ongoing work by a group of three experts (one of them is an author of this paper). Annotators were provided with an evaluation manual, with explanatory information about the evaluation task and the guidelines that must be followed to differentiate MWEs from free combinations, based on the criteria mentioned in section 2. Illustrative examples are included.

At present, a random sample of 600 has been evaluated (13.8%), with a Fleiss kappa of 0.46. Even though some authors have reported lower agreements on this task (Street et al., 2010), this level of agreement is comparatively low (Fazly and Stevenson, 2007; Krenn et al., 2004), and by no means satisfactory. It is necessary to make further efforts to improve the discriminatory criteria, and achieve a better "tuning" between the annotators.

5 Results

Figure 1 shows the precision curves obtained for each AM in the automatic evaluation. Frequency yields the best precision, followed by t-score, log-likelihood and MI^3. MI and χ^2 have a very low performance, even below the baseline[2]. These results are consistent with those reported by Krenn and Evert (2001) for support-verbs (FVG). Accordingly, this is the type of combination which is very much present in our dictionary reference.

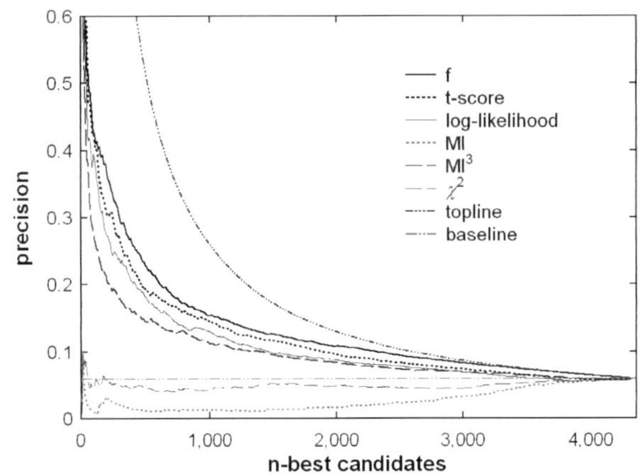

Figure 1: Precision results for the extraction set with w = ±1 and $f > 30$.

Figure 2 offers an evaluation of the influence of window span and bigram normalization. The best results are obtained by the f ranking with a narrow window and without bigram normalization. Regarding bigram normalization, it could be concluded, at first sight, that the canonical forms included in the dictionary are not the most frequent forms of their corresponding MWEs. Thus, the frequency criteria used to normalize different forms of the same case and assign canonical forms must be reviewed. As for window span, the hypothesis that, since Basque is largely a free-word-order language, a wider window would yield more significant cooccurrence statistics, is not confirmed at the moment. Further analysis is needed to interpret these results from a deeper linguistic point of view.

Even though the manually evaluated random sample is small (600 combinations), some provisional conclusions can be drawn from the results. The amount of candidates validated by at least two of the three evaluators is 153, whereas only 29 of them are included in the dictionary reference. Even though MWE classification has not yet been undertaken by the annotator's team, a first analysis by the authors shows that most of the manually validated combina-

[1]Support verbs with syntactic idiosyncrasy (anomalous use of the indefinite noun), as *lan egin* ('to work') and *min hartu* ('to get hurt').

[2]Following Evert (2005), our baseline corresponds to the precision yielded by a random ranking of the n candidates from thedata set"; and our topline is "the precision achieved by an "ideal" measure that ranks all TPs at the top of the list".

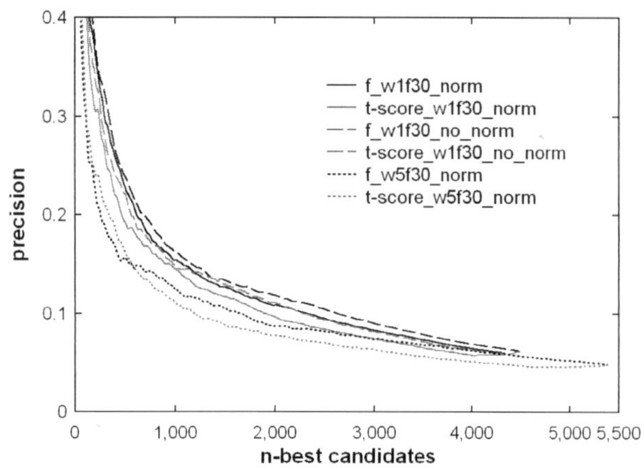

Figure 2: Precision results of f and t-score for three different extraction sets ($f > 30$): a) w = ± 1 with bigram normalization; b) w = ± 1 without bigram normalization; and c) w = ± 5 with bigram normalization.

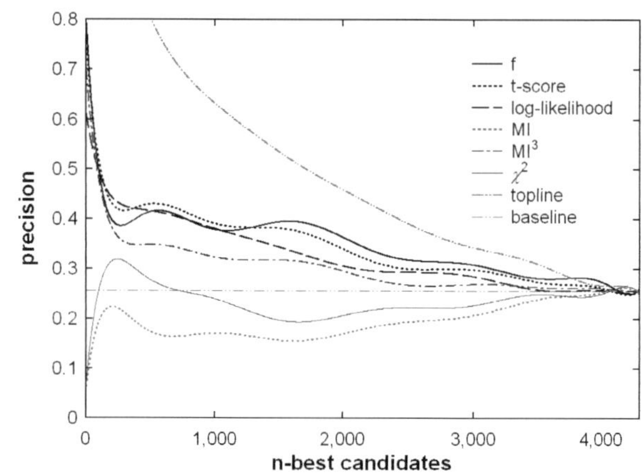

Figure 3: Precision results estimated from a 13.8% randon sample manually evaluated (600 conbinations).

tions not included in the dictionary (108 out of 124) are restricted collocations (mainly support-verb constructions that are not "compound verbs") or statistically idiosyncratic units. This is the first clue that confirms our suspicions about the limited coverage and representativeness of the reference. At the same time, it could be one of the possible explanations for the low inter-annotator agreement achieved, as far as those types of MWEs are the most difficult to differentiate from free combinations.

Figure 3 presents the precision curves for the complete evaluation set estimated from the manually evaluated random sample using the technique proposed by Evert and Krenn (2005). As expected, precision results increase compared with the evaluation against the dictionary. Frequency and t-score outperform the other AMs, but frequency is not the best measure in the whole range, as it is overtaken by t-score in the first 1,200 candidates.

6 Conclusions and Future work

The first results for the extraction of NV expressions in Basque are similar to the figures in Krenn and Evert (2001). Frequency and t-score are good measures and it seems difficult to improve upon them. Nevertheless, in light of the results, it is essential to complete the manual evaluation and build a representative gold standard in order to have a more precise idea of the coverage of the reference, and get a more accurate view of the behaviour of AMs in function of several factors such as the type of combination, corpus size, frequency range, window span, etc. Bigram normalization is, in principle, a reasonable procedure to formulate representative canonical forms, but requires a deeper analysis of the silence that it seems to generate in the results. Finally, the first evaluation using a small gold-standard is encouraging, because it suggests that using AMs it is possible to find new expressions that are not published in Basque dictionaries.

In the near future, we want to carry out a more comprehensive evaluation of the AMs, and study how to combine them in order to improve the results (Pecina and Schlesinger, 2006). In addition of this, we want to detect lexical, syntactic and semantic features of the expressions, and use this information to characterize them (Fazly et al., 2009).

Acknowledgments

This research was supported in part by the Spanish Ministry of Education and Science (OpenMT-2, TIN2009-14675-C03-01) and by the Basque Government (Berbatek: Tools and Technologies to promote Language Industry. Etortek - IE09-262). Our colleagues Ainara Estarrona and Larraitz Uria are kindly acknowledged for providing their expertise as linguists in the manual evaluation process.

References

Aduriz, I., I. Aldezabal, I. Alegria, X. Artola, N. Ezeiza, and R. Urizar (1996). EUSLEM: A lemmatiser/tagger for Basque. *Proc. of EURALEX'96*, 17–26.

Aldezabal, I., O. Ansa, B. Arrieta, X. Artola, A. Ezeiza, G. Hernández, and M. Lersundi (2001). EDBL: A general lexical basis for the automatic processing of Basque. In *IRCS Workshop on linguistic databases*, pp. 1–10.

Baldwin, T. and S. Kim (2010). Multiword expressions. *Handbook of Natural Language Processing, second edition. Morgan and Claypool.*

Banerjee, S. and T. Pedersen (2010). The design, implementation, and use of the Ngram Statistics Package. *Computational Linguistics and Intelligent Text Processing*, 370–381.

Church, K. and P. Hanks (1990). Word association norms, mutual information, and lexicography. *Computational linguistics 16*(1), 22–29.

Cowie, A. (1998). *Phraseology: Theory, analysis, and applications.* Oxford University Press, USA.

Evert, S. (2005). *The statistics of word cooccurrences: Word pairs and collocations.* Ph. D. thesis, University of Stuttgart.

Evert, S. and B. Krenn (2005). Using small random samples for the manual evaluation of statistical association measures. *Computer Speech & Language 19*(4), 450–466.

Fazly, A., P. Cook, and S. Stevenson (2009). Unsupervised type and token identification of idiomatic expressions. *Computational Linguistics 35*(1), 61–103.

Fazly, A. and S. Stevenson (2007). Distinguishing subtypes of multiword expressions using linguistically-motivated statistical measures. In *Proceedings of the Workshop on A Broader Perspective on Multiword Expressions*, pp. 9–16. Association for Computational Linguistics.

Granger, S. and M. Paquot (2008). Disentangling the phraseological web. *Phraseology. An interdisciplinary perspective*, 27–50.

Krenn, B. (1999). *The usual suspects: Data-oriented models for identification and representation of lexical collocations.* German Research Center for Artificial Intelligence.

Krenn, B. and S. Evert (2001). Can we do better than frequency? A case study on extracting PP-verb collocations. In *Proceedings of the ACL Workshop on Collocations*, pp. 39–46.

Krenn, B., S. Evert, and H. Zinsmeister (2004). Determining intercoder agreement for a collocation identification task. In *Proceedings of KONVENS*, pp. 89–96.

Pearce, D. (2002). A comparative evaluation of collocation extraction techniques. In *Proc. of LREC 2002*, pp. 1530–1536.

Pecina, P. (2005). An extensive empirical study of collocation extraction methods. In *Proceedings of the ACL Student Research Workshop*, pp. 13–18. Association for Computational Linguistics.

Pecina, P. and P. Schlesinger (2006). Combining association measures for collocation extraction. pp. 651–658.

Pérez Gaztelu, E., I. Zabala, and L. Grácia (2004). *Las fronteras de la composición en lenguas románicas y en vasco.* San Sebastián: Universidad de Deusto.

Sarasola, I. (1996). *Euskal Hiztegia.* Kutxa Fundazioa / Fundación Kutxa.

Seretan, V. (2008). *Collocation extraction based on syntactic parsing.* Ph. D. thesis, University of Geneva.

Sinclair, J. (1996). The search for units of meaning. *Textus 9*(1), 75–106.

Smadja, F. (1993). Retrieving collocations from text: Xtract. *Computational linguistics 19*(1), 143–177.

Street, L., N. Michalov, R. Silverstein, M. Reynolds, L. Ruela, F. Flowers, A. Talucci, P. Pereira, G. Morgon, S. Siegel, M. Barousse, A. Anderson, T. Carroll, and A. Feldman (2010). Like finding a needle in a haystack: Annotating the american national corpus for idiomatic expressions. In *Proc. of LREC 2010*, Valletta, Malta.

Wulff, S. (2010). *Rethinking Idiomaticity.* Corpus and Discourse. New York: Continuum International Publishing Group Ltd.

Semantic Clustering: an Attempt to Identify Multiword Expressions in Bengali

Tanmoy Chakraborty **Dipankar Das** **Sivaji Bandyopadhyay**
Department of Computer Science and Engineering
Jadavpur University, Kolkata 700 032, India
its_tanmoy@yahoo.co.in, dipankar.dipnil2005@gmail.com
sivaji_cse_ju@yahoo.com

Abstract

One of the key issues in both natural language understanding and generation is the appropriate processing of Multiword Expressions (MWEs). MWE can be defined as a semantic issue of a phrase where the meaning of the phrase may not be obtained from its constituents in a straightforward manner. This paper presents an approach of identifying bigram noun-noun MWEs from a medium-size Bengali corpus by clustering the semantically related nouns and incorporating a vector space model for similarity measurement. Additional inclusion of the English WordNet::Similarity module also improves the results considerably. The present approach also contributes to locate clusters of the synonymous noun words present in a document. Experimental results draw a satisfactory conclusion after analyzing the Precision, Recall and F-score values.

1 Introduction

Over the past two decades or so, Multi-Word Expressions (MWEs) have been identified with an increasing amount of interest in the field of Computational linguistics and Natural Language Processing (NLP). The term MWE is used to refer the various types of linguistic units and expressions including idioms (*kick the bucket,* 'to die'), noun compounds (*village community*), phrasal verbs (*find out,* 'search') and other habitual collocations like conjunction (*as well as),* institutionalized phrases (*many thanks*) etc. They can also be grossly defined as "idiosyncratic interpretations that cross the word boundaries" (Sag *et al.*, 2002).

MWE is considered as a special issue of semantics where the individual components of an expression often fail to keep their meanings intact within the actual meaning of the expression. This opaqueness in meaning may be partial or total depending on the degree of compositionality of the whole expression. In Bengali, an analogous scenario can be observed when dealing with the expressions like compound nouns (*taser ghar*, 'house of cards', 'fragile'), complex predicates such as conjunct verbs (*anuvab kara*, 'to feel') and compound verbs (*uthe para*, 'to arise'), idioms (*matir manus*, 'down to the earth'), Named Entities (NEs) (*Rabindranath Thakur*, 'Rabindranath Tagore') etc.

In this paper, we analyze MWEs from the perspective of semantic interpretation. We have focused mainly on the fact that the individual meanings of the components are totally or partially diminished in order to form the actual semantics of the expression. A constellation technique has been employed to group all nouns that are somehow related to the meaning of the component of any expression in the corpus and hence to build cluster for that component. Two types of vector space based similarity techniques are applied to make a binary classification of the candidate nouns. The intuition was that more the similarity of the components of an expression, less the probability of the candidate to become a MWE. We have also shown the results using WordNet::Similarity module.

The remainder of the paper is organized as follows. In the next section, we review the related work on MWE and graph-clustering approach for detecting compositionality. Section 3 proposes a brief description of the semantic clustering approach. The system framework is elaborated in Section 4. Experimental results and the various observations derived from our research are discussed in Section 5. Finally, Section 6 concludes the paper.

2 Related Work

A number of research activities regarding MWE identification have been carried out in various languages like English, German and many other European languages. The statistical co-occurrence measurements such as Mutual Information (MI) (Church and Hans, 1990), Log-Likelihood (Dunning, 1993) and Salience (Kilgarriff and Rosenzweig, 2000) have been suggested for identification of MWEs. An unsupervised graph-based algorithm to detect the compositionality of MWEs has been proposed in (Korkontzelos and Manandhar 2009).

In case of Indian languages, an approach in compound noun MWE extraction (Kunchukuttan and Damani, 2008) and a classification based approach for Noun-Verb collocations (Venkatapathy and Joshi, 2009) have been reported. In Bengali, the works on automated extraction of MWEs are limited in number. One method of automatic extraction of Noun-Verb MWE in Bengali (Agarwal *et al.*, 2004) has been carried out using significance function. In contrast, we have proposed a clustering technique to identify Bengali MWEs using semantic similarity measurement. It is worth noting that the conducted experiments are useful for identifying MWEs for the electronically resource constrained languages.

3 Semantic Clustering Approach

Semantic clustering aims to cluster semantically related tokens present in a document. Identifying semantically related words for a particular token is carried out by looking the surrounding tokens and finding the synonymous words within a fixed context window. Statistical idiomaticity demands frequent occurrence of a particular expression as one or few occurrences of a particular word cannot infer all its meaning. However, the semantics of a word may be obtained by analyzing its similarity sets called *synset*. Higher value of the similarity coefficient between two synonymous sets of the multi-word components indicates more affinity of the components to each other.

For individual component of a bigram expression, semantically related words of the documents are extracted by using a monolingual dictionary (as discussed in Section 4.4). Count of elements in an intersection of two synsets indicates the commonality of the two sets and its absolute value stands for their commonality measure. Considering the common elements as the dimensions of the vector space, similarity based techniques are applied to measure the semantic affection of the two components present in a bigram.

4 System Framework

4.1 Corpus Preparation and Candidate Selection

The system uses a large number of Bengali articles written by the noted Indian Nobel laureate Rabindranath Tagore[1]. We are primarily interested in single document term affinity rather than document information and document length normalization. Merging all of the articles, a medium size raw corpus consisting of 393,985 tokens and 283,533 types has been prepared. Basic pre-processing of the crawled corpus is followed by parsing with the help of an open source shallow parser[2] developed for Bengali. Parts-of-Speech (POS), chunk, root, inflection and other morphological information for each token have been retrieved. Bigram noun sequence within a noun chunk is extracted and treated as candidates based on their POS, chunk categories and the heuristics described as follows.

1. **POS**: POS of each token is either 'NN' or 'NNP'
2. **Chunk**: w1 and w2 must be in the same 'NP' chunk
3. **Inflection**: Inflection [3] of w1 must be '- শুন্য'*(null)*, '-র'(-*r*), '-এর'(-*er*), '-এ'(-*e*), '-য়'(-*y*) or '-য়ের'(-*yr*) and for w2, any inflection is considered.

4.2 Dictionary Restructuring

To the best of our knowledge, no full-fledged WordNet resource is available for Bengali. Hence, the building of Bengali synsets from a monolingual Bengali dictionary not only aims to identify the meaning of a token, but also sets up the framework towards the development of Bengali WordNet. Each word present in the monolingual dictionary (Samsada Bengali Abhidhana)[4] contains its POS,

---

[1] http://www.rabindra-rachanabali.nltr.org
[2] http://ltrc.iiit.ac.in/analyzer/bengali
[3] Linguistic study (Chattopadhyay, 1992) reveals that for compound noun MWE, considerable inflections of first noun are only those which are mentioned above.
[4] http://dsal.uchicago.edu/dictionaries/biswas-bangala/

phonetics and synonymous sets. An automatic technique has been devised to identify the synsets of a particular word based on the clues (“,” comma and “;” semi-colon) provided in the dictionary to distinguish words of similar and different sense from the synonymous sets. The symbol tilde (~) indicates that the suffix string followed by the tilde (~) notation makes another new word concatenating with the original entry word. A partial snapshot of the synsets for the Bengali word “অংশু” (Angshu) is shown in Figure 1. In Table 1, the frequencies of different synsets according to their POS are shown.

<u>Dictionary Entry:</u>
অংশু [aṃśu] বি. 1 কিরণ, রশ্মি, প্রভা; ~ ক বি. বস্ত্র , সূক্ষ্ম বস্ত্র ; রেশম পাট ইত্যাদিতে প্রস্তুত বস্ত্র। ~ জাল বি. কিরণরাশি, কিরণমালা।
<u>Synsets:</u>
অংশু কিরণ/রশ্মি/প্রভা_বি.#25_1_1
অংশুক বস্ত্র/সূক্ষ্ম_বস্ত্র_বি.#26_1_1
অংশুক রেশম_পাট_ইত্যাদিতে_প্রস্তুত_বস্ত্র_বি.#26_2_2
অংশুজাল কিরণরাশি/কিরণমালা_বি.#27_1_1

Figure 1: A partial snapshot of the Bengali monolingual dictionary entry (word and synsets)

Total #Word	Total #Synset	Noun	Adjective	Pronoun	Verb
33619	63403	28485	11023	235	1709

Table 1: Total number of words, synsets and Frequencies of different POS based synsets

4.3 Generating Semantic Clusters of Nouns

In the first phase, we have generated the synonymous sets for all nouns present in the corpus using the synset based dictionary whereas in the second phase, the task is to identify the semantic distance between two nouns. The format of the dictionary can be thought of as follows:

$W^1 = n_1^1, n_2^1, n_3^1, \ldots\ldots\ldots\ldots\ldots\ldots = \{n_i^1\}$

.

.

$W^m = n_1^m, n_2^m, n_3^m, \ldots\ldots\ldots\ldots\ldots = \{n_p^m\}$

where, W^1, W^2, ..., W^m are the dictionary word entries and n_j^m (for all j) are the elements of the synsets of W^m. Now, each noun entry identified by the shallow parser in the document is searched in the dictionary. For example, if a noun N present the corpus becomes an entry of the synsets, W^1, W^3 and W^5, the synset of N is as follows,

$$SynSet(N) = \{W^1, W^3, W^5\} \ldots\ldots\ldots (1)$$

To identify the semantic similarity between two nouns, we have applied simple intersection rule. The number of common elements between the synsets of the two noun words denotes the similarity between them. If N_i and N_j are the two noun words in the document and W^i and W^j are their corresponding synsets, the similarity of the two words can be defined as,

$$Similarity(N_i, N_j) = |W^i \cap W^j| \ldots\ldots\ldots (2)$$

We have clustered all the nouns present in the document for a particular noun and have identified the similarity score for every pair of nouns obtained using equation 2.

4.4 Checking of Candidate Bigram as MWE

The identification of candidates as MWE is done using the results obtained from the previous phase. The algorithm to identify the noun-noun bigram <M1 M2> as MWE is discussed below with an example shown in Figure 2.

ALOGRITHM: MWE-CHECKING

INPUT: Noun-noun bigram <*M1 M2*>

OUTPUT: Return true if MWE, or return false.

1. Extract semantic clusters of *M1* and *M2*
2. Intersection of the clusters of both *M1* and *M2* (Figure 2.1 shows the common synset entries of *M1* and *M2* using rectangle).
3. For measuring the semantic similarity between *M1* and *M2*:
   3.1. In an *n*-dimensional vector space (here *n*=2), the common entries act as the axes. Put *M1* and *M2* as two vectors and associated weights as their co-ordinates.
   3.2. Calculate cosine-similarity measurement and Euclidean distance (Figure 2.2).
4. Final decision taken individually for two different measurements-
   4.1 If cosine-similarity > *m*, return false; Else return true;
   4.2 If Euclidean-distance > *p*, return false; Else return true;

(Where *m* and *p* are the pre-defined cut-off values)

We have also employed English WordNet[5] to measure the semantic similarity between two

[5] http://www.d.umn.edu/tpederse/similarity.html

Cut-off	Cosine-Similarity			Euclidean Distance			WordNet Similarity		
	P	R	FS	P	R	FS	P	R	FS
0.6	70.75	64.87	67.68	70.57	62.23	66.14	74.60	61.78	67.58
0.5	**78.56**	**59.45**	**67.74**	72.97	58.79	65.12	**80.90**	**58.75**	**68.06**
0.4	73.23	56.97	64.08	**79.78**	**53.03**	**63.71**	75.09	52.27	61.63

Table 3: Precision (P), Recall (R) and F-score (FS) (in %) for various measurements

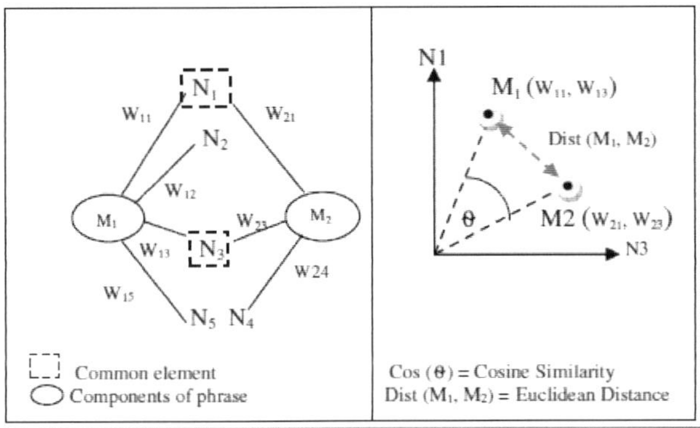

Figure 2.1: Intersection of the clusters of the constituents (left side); Figure 2.2: Similarity between two constituents Evaluation (right side)

Bengali words translated into English. WordNet::Similarity is an open-source package for calculating the lexical similarity between word (or sense) pairs based on various similarity measures. Basically, WordNet measures the relative distance between two nodes denoted by two words in the WordNet tree which can vary from -1 to 1 where -1 indicates total dissimilarity between two nodes. The equation used to calculate this distance is mentioned below-

Normalized_Distance= minDistToCommonParent / (DistFromCommonParentToRoot + minDistToCommonParent) ....(3)

We have translated the root of the two components of a Bengali candidate into their English equivalents using a Bengali to English bilingual dictionary. They are passed into the WordNet based similarity module for measuring similarity between the components.

If we take an example of a Bengali idiom *hater panch* (*remaining resource*) to describe our intuition, we have seen that the WordNet defines two components of the idiom *hat* (*hand*) as 'a part of a limb that is farthest from the torso' and *panch* (*five*) as 'a number which is one more than four'. So from these two glosses it is quite clear that they are not at all semantically related in any sense.

The synonymous sets for these two components extracted from the formatted dictionary are shown below –

Synset (হাত *'hat'*) = { হস্ত, কর, পাণি, বাহু, ভুজ, কৌশল, হস্তক্ষেপ, ধারণ, রেখা, লিখিত, হস্তাক্ষর, হস্তান্তর, হাতা }

Synset (পাঁচ *'panch'*) = {পঞ্চ, সংখ্যা, কর্ম, গঙ্গা, গব্য, কন্যা, গুণ, গৌড়, তন্ত্র, তীর্থ, পঞ্চত্ব, পনেরো, পূর্ণিমা, পঞ্চাশ }

It is clearly seen from the above synonymous sets that there is no common element and hence its similarity score is obviously zero. In this case, the vector space model cannot be drawn using zero dimensions. For them, a marginal weight is assigned to show them as completely non-compositional phrase. To identify their non-compositionality, we have to show that their occurrence is not certain only in one case; rather they can occur side by side in several occasions. But this statistical proof can be determined better using a large corpus. Here, for those candidate phrases, which show zero similarity, we have seen their existence more than one time in the corpus. Taking any decision using single occurrence may give incorrect result because they can be unconsciously used by the authors in their writings. That is why, the more the similarity between two components in a bigram, the less the probability to be a MWE.

4.5 Annotation Agreement

Three annotators identified as A1, A2 and A3 were engaged to carry out the annotation. The annotation agreement of 628 candidate phrases is measured using standard Cohen's *kappa* coefficient (κ) (Cohen, 1960). It is a statistical measure of inter-rater agreement for qualitative (categorical) items. In addition to this, we also choose the measure of agreements on set-valued items (*MASI*) (Passonneau, 2006) that was used for measuring agreement in the semantic and pragmatic annotation. Annotation results as shown in Table 2 are satisfactory.

The list of noun-noun collocations are extracted from the output of the parser for manual checking. It is observed that 39.39% error occurs due to wrong POS tagging or extracting invalid collocations by considering the bigrams in a n-gram chunk where n > 2. We have separated these phrases from the final list.

MWEs [# 628]	Agreement between pair of annotators			
	A1-A2	A2-A3	A1-A3	Avg
KAPPA	87.23	86.14	88.78	87.38
MASI	87.17	87.02	89.02	87.73

Table 2: Inter-Annotator Agreement (in %)

4.6 Experimental Results

We have used the standard IR matrices like Precision (P), Recall (R) and F-score (F) for evaluating the final results obtained from three modules. Human annotated list is used as the gold standard for the evaluation. The present system results are shown in Table 3. These results are compared with the statistical baseline system described in (Chakraborty, 2010). Our baseline system is reported with the precision of 39.64%. The predefined threshold has been varied to catch individual results in each case. Increasing Recall in accordance with the increment of cut-off infers that the maximum numbers of MWEs are identified in a wide range of threshold. But the Precision does not increase considerably. It shows that the higher cut-off degrades the performance. The reasonable results for Precision and Recall have been achieved in case of cosine-similarity at the cut-off value of 0.5 where Euclidean distance and WordNet Similarity give maximum precision at cut-off values of 0.4 and 0.5 respectively. In all cases, our system outperforms the baseline system.

It is interesting to observe that English WordNet becomes a very helpful tool to identify Bengali MWEs. WordNet detects maximum MWEs correctly at the cut-off of 0.5. Baldwin *et al.*, (2003) suggested that WordNet::Similarity measure is effective to identify empirical model of Multiword Expression Decomposability. This is also proved in this experiment as well and even for Bengali language. There are also candidates with very low value of similarity between their constituents (for example, *ganer gajat* (*earth of song, affectionate of song*), yet they are discarded from this experiment because of their low frequency of occurrence in the corpus which could not give any judgment regarding collocation. Whether such an unexpectedly low frequent high decomposable elements warrant an entry in the lexicon depends on the type of the lexicon being built.

5 Conclusions

We hypothesized that sense induction by analyzing synonymous sets can assist the identification of Multiword Expression. We have introduced an unsupervised approach to explore the hypothesis and have shown that clustering technique along with similarity measures can be successfully employed to perform the task. This experiment additionally contributes to the following scenarios - (i) Clustering of words having similar sense, (ii) Identification of MWEs for resource constraint languages and (iii) Reconstruction of Bengali monolingual dictionary towards the development of Bengali WordNet. However, in our future work, we will apply the present techniques for other type of MWEs (e.g., adjective-noun collocation, verbal MWEs) as well as for other languages.

Acknowledgement

The work reported in this paper is supported by a grant from the "Indian Language to Indian Language Machine Translation (IL-ILMT) System Phrase II", funded by Department of Information and Technology (DIT), Govt. of India.

References

Agarwal, Aswini, Biswajit Ray, Monojit Choudhury, Sudeshna Sarkar and Anupam Basu. 2004. Automatic Extraction of Multiword Expressions in Bengali: An Approach for Miserly Resource Scenario. In *Proceedings of International Conference on Natural Language Processing (ICON)*, pp. 165-174.

Baldwin, Timothy, Colin Bannard, Takaaki Tanaka and Dominic Widdows. 2003. An Empirical Model of Multiword Expression Decomposability. *Proceedings of the Association for Computational Linguistics-2003, Workshop on Multiword Expressions: Analysis, Acquisition and Treatment*, Sapporo, Japan, pp. 89–96.

Ckakraborty, Tanmoy, 2010, Identification of Noun-Noun (N-N) Collocations as Multi-Word Expressions in Bengali Corpus. *Student Session, International Conference of Natural Language Processing (ICON)*, IIT Kharagpur, India

Chakraborty, Tanmoy and Sivaji Bandyopadhyay. 2010. Identification of Reduplication in Bengali Corpus and their Semantic Analysis: A Rule Based Approach. In *proceedings of the Workshop on Multiword Expressions: from Theory to Applications (MWE 2010), 23rd International Conference on Computational Linguistics (COLING 2010)*, pp.73-76, Beijing, China.

Chattopadhyay Suniti K. 1992. *Bhasa-Prakash Bangala Vyakaran*, Third Edition.

Church, Kenneth Wrad and Patrick Hans. 1990. Word Association Norms, Mutual Information and Lexicography. *Proceedings of 27th Association for Computational Linguistics (ACL)*, 16(1). pp. 22-29.

Cohen, J. 1960. A coefficient of agreement for nominal scales. *Educational and Psychological Measurement*, vol. 20, pp. 37–46.

Dunning, T. 1993. Accurate Method for the Statistic of Surprise and Coincidence. In *Computational Linguistics*, pp. 61-74.

Kilgarriff, Adam and Joseph Rosenzweig. 2000. Framework and results for English SENSEVAL. *Computers and the Humanities*. Senseval Special Issue, 34(1-2). pp. 15-48.

Korkontzelos,Ioannis and Suresh Manandhar. 2009. Detecting Compositionality in Multi-Word Expressions. *Proceedings of the Association for Computational Linguistics-IJCNLP*, Singapore, pp. 65-68.

Kunchukuttan F. A. and Om P. Damani. 2008. A System for Compound Noun Multiword Expression Extraction for Hindi. *Proceeding of 6th International Conference on Natural Language Processing (ICON)*. pp. 20-29.

Passonneau, R.J. 2006. Measuring agreement on set-valued items (MASI) for semantic and pragmatic annotation. *Language Resources and Evaluation.*

Sag, Ivan A., Timothy Baldwin, Francis Bond, Ann Copestake and Dan Flickinger. 2002. Multiword Expressions: A Pain in the Neck for NLP. In *Proceedings of Conference on Intelligent Text Processing and Computational Linguistics (CICLING),* pp. 1-15.

Venkatapathy, Sriram and Aravind Joshi. 2005. Measuring the relative compositionality of verb-noun (V-N) collocations by integrating features. *Proceedings of Human Language Technology Conference and Conference on Empirical Methods in Natural Language Processing (HLT/EMNLP), Association for Computational Linguistics.* pp. 899 - 906.

Decreasing lexical data sparsity in statistical syntactic parsing - experiments with named entities

Deirdre Hogan, Jennifer Foster and Josef van Genabith
National Centre for Language Technology
School of Computing
Dublin City University
Dublin 9, Ireland
dhogan,jfoster,josef@computing.dcu.ie

Abstract

In this paper we present preliminary experiments that aim to reduce lexical data sparsity in statistical parsing by exploiting information about named entities. Words in the WSJ corpus are mapped to named entity clusters and a latent variable constituency parser is trained and tested on the transformed corpus. We explore two different methods for mapping words to entities, and look at the effect of mapping various subsets of named entity types. Thus far, results show no improvement in parsing accuracy over the best baseline score; we identify possible problems and outline suggestions for future directions.

1 Introduction

Techniques for handling lexical data sparsity in parsers have been important ever since the lexicalisation of parsers led to significant improvements in parser performance (Collins, 1999; Charniak, 2000). The original treebank set of non-terminal labels is too general to give good parsing results. To overcome this problem, in lexicalised constituency parsers, non-terminals are enriched with lexical information. Lexicalisation of the grammar vastly increases the number of parameters in the model, spreading the data over more specific events. Statistics based on low frequency events are not as reliable as statistics on phenomena which occur regularly in the data; frequency counts involving words are typically sparse.

Word statistics are also important in more recent unlexicalised approaches to constituency parsing such as latent variable parsing (Matsuzaki et al., 2005; Petrov et al., 2006). The basic idea of latent variable parsing is that rather than enrich the non-terminal labels by augmenting them with words, a set of enriched labels which can encapsulate the syntactic behaviour of words is automatically learned via an EM training mechanism.

Parsers need to be able to handle both low frequency words and words occurring in the test set which were unseen in the training set (unknown words). The problem of rare and unknown words is particularly significant for languages where the size of the treebank is small. Lexical sparseness is also critical when running a parser on data that is in a different domain to the domain upon which the parser was trained. As interest in parsing real world data increases, a parsers ability to adequately handle out-of-domain data is critical.

In this paper we examine whether clustering words based on their named entity category can be useful for reducing lexical sparsity in parsing. Intuitively word tokens in the corpus such as, say, 'Dublin' and 'New York' should play similar syntactic roles in sentences. Likewise, it is difficult to see how different people names could have different discriminatory influences on the syntax of sentences. This paper describes experiments at replacing word tokens with special named entity tokens (person names are mapped to PERSON tokens and so on). Words in the original WSJ treebank are mapped to entity types extracted from the BBN corpus (Weischedel and Brunstein, 2005) and a latent variable parser is trained and tested on the mapped corpus. Ultimately, the motivation behind grouping words together in this fashion is to make it easier for the parser to recognise regularities in the data.[1]

The structure of paper is as follows: A brief summary of related work is given in Section 2. This includes an outline of a common treatment of low frequency and rare words in constituency parsing, involving a mapping process that is similar to the named entity mappings. Section 3 presents the experiments carried out, starting with a short introduction of the named entity resource used in our experiments and a description of the types of basic entity mappings we examine. In §3.1 and §3.2 we describe the two different types of mapping technique. Results are presented in Section 4, followed by a brief discussion in Section 5 indicating possible problems and avenues worth pursuing. Finally, we conclude.

2 Related Work

Much previous work on parsing and multiword units (MWUs) adopts the words-with-spaces approach which treats MWUs as one token (by concatenating the words together) (Nivre and Nilsson, 2004; Cafferkey et al., 2007; Korkontzelos and Manandhar, 2010). Alternative approaches are that of Finkel and Manning (2009) on joint parsing and named entity recognition and the work of (Wehrli et al., 2010) which uses collocation information to rank competing hypotheses in a symbolic parser. Also related is work on MWUs and grammar engineering, such as (Zhang et al., 2006; Villavicencio et al., 2007) where automatically detected MWUs are added to the lexicon of a HPSG grammar to improve coverage.

Our work is most similar to the words-with-spaces approach. Our many-to-one experiments (see §3.1) in particular are similar to previous work on parsing words-with-spaces, except that we map words to entity types rather than concatenated words. Results are difficult to compare however, due to different parsing methodologies, different types of MWUs, as well as different evaluation methods.

Other relevant work is the integration of named entity types in a surface realisation task by Rajkumar et al. (2009) and the French parsing experiments of (Candito and Crabbé, 2009; Candito and Seddah, 2010) which involve mapping words to clusters based on morphology as well as clusters automatically induced via unsupervised learning on a large corpus.

2.1 Parsing unknown words

Most state-of-the-art constituency parsers (e.g. (Petrov et al., 2006; Klein and Manning, 2003)) take a similar approach to rare and unknown words. At the beginning of the training process very low frequency words in the training set are mapped to special UNKNOWN tokens. In this way, some probability mass is reserved for occurrences of UNKNOWN tokens and the lexicon contains productions for such tokens ($X \rightarrow$ UNKNOWN), with associated probabilities. When faced with a word in the test set that the parser has not seen in its training set - the unknown word is mapped to the special UNKNOWN token.

In syntactic parsing, rather than map all low frequency words to one generic UNKNOWN type, it is useful to have several different clusters of unknown words, grouped according to morphological and other 'surfacey' clues in the original word. For example, certain suffixes in English are strong predictors for the part-of-speech tag of the word (e.g. 'ly') and so all low frequency words ending in 'ly' are mapped to 'UNKNOWN-ly'. As well as suffix information, UNKNOWN words are commonly grouped based on information on capitalisation and hyphenation. Similar techniques for handling unknown words have been used for POS tagging (e.g. (Weischedel et al., 1993; Tseng et al., 2005)) and are used in the Charniak (Charniak, 2000), Berkeley (Petrov et al., 2006) and Stanford (Klein and Manning, 2003) parsers, as well as in the parser used for the experiments in this paper, an in-house implementation of the Berkeley parser.

3 Experiments

The BBN Entity Type Corpus (Weischedel and Brunstein, 2005) consists of sentences from the Penn WSJ corpus, manually annotated with named entities. The Entity Type corpus includes annota-

[1] It is true that latent variable parsers automatically induce categories for similar words, and thus might be expected to induce a category for say names of people if examples of such words occurred in similar syntactic patterns in the data. Nonetheless, the problem of data sparsity remains - it is difficult even for latent variable parsers to learn accurate patterns based on words which only occur say once in the training set.

type	count	examples
PERSON	11254	Kim Cattrall
PER_DESC	21451	president,chief executive officer,
FAC	383	office, Rockefeller Center
FAC_DESC	2193	chateau ,stadiums, golf course
ORGANIZATION	24239	Securities and Exchange Commission
ORG_DESC	15765	auto maker, college
GPE	10323	Los Angeles,South Africa
GPE_DESC	1479	center, nation, country
LOCATION	907	North America,Europe, Hudson River
NORP	3269	Far Eastern
PRODUCT	667	Maxima, 300ZX
PRODUCT_DESC	1156	cars
EVENT	296	Vietnam war,HUGO ,World War II
WORK_OF_ART	561	Revitalized Classics Take..
LAW	300	Catastrophic Care Act,Bill of Rights
LANGUAGE	62	Latin
CONTACT_INFO	30	555 W. 57th St.
PLANT	172	crops, tree
ANIMAL	355	hawks
SUBSTANCE	2205	gold,drugs, oil
DISEASE	254	schizophrenia,alcoholism
GAME	74	football senior tennis and golf tours

Table 1: Name expression entity types (sections 02-21)

tion for three classes of named entity: name expressions, time expressions and numeric expressions (in this paper we focus on name expressions). These are further broken down into types. Table 1 displays name expression entity types, their frequency in the training set (sections 02-21), as well as some illustrative examples from the training set data.

We carried out experiments with different subsets of entity types. In one set of experiments, all name expression entities were mapped, with no restriction on the types (ALL_NAMED). We also carried out experiments on a reduced set of named entities - where only entities marked as *PERSON*, *ORGANIZATION*, or *GPE* and *LOCATION* were mapped ($REDUCED$). Finally, we ran experiments where only one type of named entity was mapped at a time. In all cases the words in the named entities were replaced by their entity type.

3.1 Many-to-one Mapping

In the many-to-one mapping all words in a named entity were replaced with one named entity type token. This approach is distinct from the words-with-spaces approach previously pursued in parsing where, for example, 'New York' would be replaced with 'New_York'. Instead, in our experiments 'New York' is replaced with 'GPE' (geo-political entity). In both approaches, the parser is forced to respect the multiword unit boundary (and analyses which contain constituents that cross the MWU boundary will not be considered by the parser). Intuitively, this should help parser accuracy and speed. The advantage of mapping the word tokens to their entity type rather than to a words-with-spaces token is that in addition we will be reducing data sparsity.

unk map	NE map	#unks	*f*-score	POS
generic	**none (baseline 1)**	**2966 (4.08%)**	**88.69**	**95.57**
	ALL_NAMED	1908 (2.73%)	89.21	95.49
	$REDUCED$	2122 (3.02%)	89.43	96.08
	$Person$	2671 (3.68%)	88.98	95.55
	$Organisation$	2521 (3.55%)	89.38	95.92
	$Location$	2945 (4.05%)	89.00	95.62
sigs	**none (baseline 2)**	**2966 (4.08%)**	**89.72**	**96.51**
	ALL_NAMED	1908 (2.73%)	89.67	95.99
	$REDUCED$	2122 (3.02%)	89.53	96.65
	$Person$	2671 (3.68%)	89.32	96.47
	$Organisation$	2521 (3.55%)	89.53	96.64
	$Location$	2945 (4.05%)	89.20	96.52

Table 2: Many-to-One Parsing Results.

One issue with the many-to-one mapping is that in evaluation exact comparison with a baseline result is difficult because the tokenisation of test and gold sets is different. When named entities span more than one word, we are reducing the number of words in the sentences. As parsers tend to do better on short sentences than on long sentences, this could make parsing somewhat easier. However, we found that the average number of words in a sentence before and after this mapping does not change by much. The average number of words in the development set is 23.9. When we map words to named entity tokens (ALL_NAMED), the average drops by just one word to 22.9.[2]

3.2 One-to-one Mapping

In the one-to-one experiments we replaced each word in named entity with a named entity type token (e.g. Ada Lovelace → pperson pperson).[3] The motivation was to measure the effect of reducing word sparsity using named entities without altering the original tokenisation of the data.[4]

[2] A related issue is that the resulting parse tree will lack an analysis for the named entity.

[3] The entity type was given an extra letter where needed (e.g. 'pperson') to avoid the conflation of a mapped entity token with an original word (e.g. 'person') in the corpus.

[4] Note, where there is punctuation as part of a named entity we do not map the punctuation.

unk map	NE map	#unks	*f*-score	POS
generic	**none (baseline 1)**	**2966 (4.08%)**	**88.69**	**95.57**
	ALL_NAMED	1923 (2.64%)	89.28	94.99
	REDUCED	2122 (2.90%)	88.76	95.76
	Person	2654(3.65%)	88.95	95.57
	Organisation	2521 (3.45%)	88.80	95.59
	Location	2945 (4.04%)	88.88	95.66
sigs	**none (baseline 2)**	**2966 (4.08%)**	**89.72**	**96.51**
	ALL_NAMED	1923 (2.64%)	89.36	95.64
	REDUCED	2122 (2.90%)	89.01	96.32
	Person	2654(3.65%)	89.30	96.52
	Organisation	2521 (3.45%)	89.29	96.30
	Location	2945 (4.04%)	89.55	96.54

Table 3: One-to-One Parsing Results

In an initial experiment, where the mapping was simply the word to the named entity type, many sentences received no parse. This happened often when a named entity consisted of three or more words and resulted in a sentence such as 'But while the Oorganization Oorganization Oorganization Oorganization did n't fall apart Friday'. We found that refining the named entity by adding the number of the word in the entity to the mapping resolved the coverage problem. The example sentence is now: 'But while the Oorganization1 Oorganization2 Oorganization3 Oorganization4 did n't fall apart Friday'. See §5 for a possible explanation for the parser's difficulty with one-to-one mappings to coarse grained entity types.

4 Results

Table 2 and Table 3 give the results for the many-to-one and one-to-one experiments respectively. Results are given against a baseline where unknowns are given a 'generic' treatment (baseline 1) - i.e. they are not clustered according to morphological and surface information - and for the second baseline (baseline 2), where morphological or surface feature markers (sigs) are affixed to the unknowns.[5]

The results indicate that though lexical sparsity is decreasing, insofar as the number of unknown words ($\#unks$ column) in the development set decreases with all named entity mappings, the named entity clusters are not informative enough and parser accuracy falls short of the previous best result. For all experiments, a pattern that emerges is that mapping words to named entities improves results when low frequency words are mapped to a generic UNKNOWN token. However, when low frequency words are mapped to more fine-grained UNKNOWN tokens, mapping words to named entities decreases accuracy marginally.

If a particular named entity occurs often in the text then data sparsity is possibly not a problem for this word. Rather than map all occurrences of a named entity to its entity type, we experimented with mapping only low frequency entities. These named entity mapping experiments now mirror more closely the unknown words mappings - low frequency entities are mapped to special entity types, then the parser maps all remaining low frequency words to UNKNOWN types. Table 4 shows the effect of mapping only entities that occur less than 10 times in the training set, to the *person* type and the *reduced* set of entity types. Results somewhat improve for all but one of the one-to-one experiments, but nonetheless remain below the best baseline result. There is still no advantage in mapping low frequency person name words to, say, the *person* cluster, rather than to an UNKNOWN-plus-signature cluster.

5 Discussion

Our results thus far suggest that clusters based on morphology or surface clues are more informative than the named entity clusters.

For the one-to-one mappings one obvious problem that emerged is that all words in entities (including function words for example) get mapped to a generic named entity token. A multi-word named entity has its own internal syntactic structure, reflected for example in its sequence of part-of-speech tags. By replacing each word in the entity with the generic entity token we end up loosing information about words, conflating words that take different part-of-speech categories, and in fact make parsing more difficult. The named entity clusters in this case are too coarse-grained and words with different syntactic properties are merged into the one cluster, something we would like to avoid.

In future work, as well as avoiding mapping more complex named entities, we will refine the named entity clusters by attaching to the entity type signatures similar to those attached to the UNKNOWN

[5]For all experiments, a split-merge cycle of 5 was used. Following convention, sections 02-21 were used for training. Sections 22 and 24 (sentences less than or equal to 100 words) were used for the development set. As experiments are ongoing we do not report results on a test set.

unk map	NE map	one2one *f*-score	many2one *f*-score
generic	*Person*	88.95	88.98
	Person < 10	88.97	89.05
	Reduced	88.76	89.43
	Reduced < 10	89.51	88.85
sigs	*Person*	89.30	89.32
	Person < 10	89.49	89.33
	Reduced	89.01	89.53
	Reduced < 10	89.42	89.15

Table 4: Measuring the effect of mapping only low frequency named entities.

types. It would also be interesting to examine the effect of mapping other types of named entities, such as dates and numeric expressions. Finally, we intend trying similar experiments on out-of-domain data, such as social media text where unknown words are more problematic.

6 Conclusion

We have presented preliminary experiments which test the novel technique of mapping word tokens to named entity clusters, with the aim of improving parser accuracy by reducing data sparsity. While our results so far are disappointing, we have identified possible problems and outlined future experiments, including suggestions for refining the named entity clusters so that they become more syntactically homogenous.

References

Conor Cafferkey, Deirdre Hogan, and Josef van Genabith. 2007. Multi-word units in treebank-based probabilistic parsing and generation. In *Proceedings of the 10th International Conference on Recent Advances in Natural Language Processing (RANLP-07)*, Borovets, Bulgaria.

Marie Candito and Benoit Crabbé. 2009. Improving generative statistical parsing with semi-supervised word clustering. In *Proceedings of the International Workshop on Parsing Technologies (IWPT-09)*.

Marie Candito and Djamé Seddah. 2010. Lemmatization and statistical lexicalized parsing of morphologically-rich languages. In *Proceedings of the NAACL/HLT Workshop on Statistical Parsing of Morphologically Rich Languages (SPMRL)*.

Eugene Charniak. 2000. A maximum entropy-inspired parser. In *Proceedings of the 1st North American Chapter of the Association for Computational Linguistics (NAACL)*.

Michael Collins. 1999. *Head-Driven Statistical Models for Natural Language Parsing*. Ph.D. thesis, University of Pennsylvania.

Jenny Rose Finkel and Christopher D. Manning. 2009. Joint parsing and named entity recognition. In *Proceedings of the North American Chapter of the Association for Computational Linguistics (NAACL-2009)*.

Dan Klein and Christopher D. Manning. 2003. Accurate unlexicalized parsing. In *Proceedings of the 41st Annual Meeting of the Association of Computational Linguistics (ACL)*.

Ioannis Korkontzelos and Suresh Manandhar. 2010. Can recognising multiword expressions improve shallow parsing? In *Proceedings of the Conference of the North American Chapter of the ACL (NAACL-10)*, Los Angeles, California.

Takuya Matsuzaki, Yusuke Miyao, and Jun'ichi Tsujii. 2005. Probabilistic cfg with latent annotations. In *Proceedings of the 43rd Annual Meeting of the ACL*, pages 75–82, Ann Arbor, June.

Joakim Nivre and Jens Nilsson. 2004. Multiword units in syntactic parsing. In *Workshop on Methodologies and Evaluation of Multiword Units in Real-World Applications*.

Slav Petrov, Leon Barrett, Romain Thibaux, and Dan Klein. 2006. Learning accurate, compact and interpretable tree annotation. In *Proceedings of the 21st International Conference on Computational Linguistics and the 44th Annual Meeting of the ACL*, Sydney, Australia, July.

Rajakrishnan Rajkumar, Michael White, and Dominic Espinosa. 2009. Exploiting named entity classes in ccg surface realisation. In *Proceedings of the North American Chapter of the Association for Computational Linguistics (NAACL-09)*.

Huihsin Tseng, Daniel Jurafsky, and Christopher Manning. 2005. Morpholgical features help pos tagging of unknown words across language varieties. In *Proceedings of the Fourth SIGHAN Workshop on Chinese Language Processing*.

Aline Villavicencio, Valia Kordoni, Yi Zhang, Marco Idiart, and Carlos Ramisch. 2007. Validation and evaluation of automatically acquired multiword expressions for grammar engineering. In *Proceedings of the Joint Conference on Empirical Methods in Natural Language Processing and Computational Natural Language Learning (EMNLP-CoNLL)*.

Eric Wehrli, Violeta Seretan, and Luke Nerima. 2010. Sentence analysis and collocation identification. In *Proceedings of the Workshop on Multiword Expression: From Theory to Applications (MWE)*.

Ralph Weischedel and Ada Brunstein. 2005. BBN pronoun coreference and entity type corpus. In *Tehcnical Report*.

Ralph Weischedel, Richard Schwartz, Jeff Palmucci, Marie Meteer, and Lance Ramshaw. 1993. Coping with ambiguity and unknown words through probabilistic models. *Computational Linguistics*, 19(2).

Yi Zhang, Valia Kordoni, Aline Villavicencio, and Marco Idiart. 2006. Automated multiword expression prediction for grammar engineering. In *Proceedings of the Workshop on Multiword Expressions: Identifying and Exploiting Underlying Properties*.

Detecting Multi-Word Expressions improves Word Sense Disambiguation

Mark Alan Finlayson & Nidhi Kulkarni
Computer Science and Artificial Intelligence Laboratory
Massachusetts Institute of Technology
Cambridge, MA, 02139, USA
{markaf,nidhik}@mit.edu

Abstract

Multi-Word Expressions (MWEs) are prevalent in text and are also, on average, less polysemous than mono-words. This suggests that accurate MWE detection should lead to a non-trivial improvement in Word Sense Disambiguation (WSD). We show that a straightforward MWE detection strategy, due to Arranz *et al.* (2005), can increase a WSD algorithm's baseline f-measure by 5 percentage points. Our measurements are consistent with Arranz's, and our study goes further by using a portion of the Semcor corpus containing 12,449 MWEs - over 30 times more than the approximately 400 used by Arranz. We also show that perfect MWE detection over Semcor only nets a total 6 percentage point increase in WSD f-measure; therefore there is little room for improvement over the results presented here. We provide our MWE detection algorithms, along with a general detection framework, in a free, open-source Java library called jMWE.

Multi-word expressions (MWEs) are prevalent in text. This is important for the classic task of Word Sense Disambiguation (WSD) (Agirre and Edmonds, 2007), in which an algorithm attempts to assign to each word in a text the appropriate entry from a sense inventory. A WSD algorithm that cannot correctly detect the MWEs that are listed in its sense inventory will not only miss those sense assignments, it will also spuriously assign senses to MWE constituents that themselves have sense entries, dealing a double-blow to WSD performance.

Beyond this penalty, MWEs listed in a sense inventory also present an opportunity to WSD algorithms - they are, on average, less polysemous than mono-words. In Wordnet 1.6, multi-words have an average polysemy of 1.07, versus 1.53 for mono-words. As a concrete example, consider sentence *She broke the world record*. In Wordnet 1.6 the lemma *world* has nine different senses and *record* has fourteen, while the MWE *world record* has only one. If a WSD algorithm correctly detects MWEs, it can dramatically reduce the number of possible senses for such sentences.

Measure	**Us**	**Arranz**
Number of MWEs	12,449	382
Fraction of MWEs	7.4%	9.4%
WSD impr. (Best v. Baseline)	0.016_{F_1}	0.012_{F_1}
WSD impr. (Baseline v. None)	0.033_{F_1}	-
WSD impr. (Best v. None)	$\mathbf{0.050}_{F_1}$	-
WSD impr. (Perfect v. None)	$\mathbf{0.061}_{F_1}$	-

Table 1: Improvement of WSD f-measures over an MWE-unaware WSD strategy for various MWE detection strategies. *Baseline*, *Best*, and *Perfect* refer to the MWE detection strategy used in the WSD preprocess.

With this in mind, we expected that accurate MWE detection will lead to a small yet non-trivial improvement in WSD performance, and this is indeed the case. Table 1 summarizes our results. In particular, a relatively straightforward MWE detection strategy, here called the 'best' strategy and due to Arranz *et al.* (2005), yielded a 5 percentage point improvement[1] in WSD f-measure. We also measured an improvement similar to that of Arranz when

[1]For example, if the WSD algorithm has an f-measure of

moving from a Baseline MWE detection strategy to the Best strategy, namely, 1.6 percentage points to their 1.2.

We performed our measurements over the *brown1* and *brown2* concordances[2] of the Semcor corpus (Fellbaum, 1998), which together contain 12,449 MWEs, over 30 times as many as the approximately 400 contained in the portion of the XWN corpus used by Arranz. We also measured the improvement for WSD f-measure for Baseline and Perfect MWE detection strategies. These strategies improved WSD f-measure by 3.3 and 6.1 percentage points, respectively, showing that the relatively straightforward Best MWE detection strategy, at 5.0 percentage points, leaves little room for improvement.

1 MWE Detection Algorithms by Arranz

Arranz *et al.* describe their TALP Word Sense Disambiguation system in (Castillo et al., 2004) and (Arranz et al., 2005). The details of the WSD procedure are not critical here; what is important is that their preprocessing system attempted to detect MWEs that could later be disambiguated by the WSD algorithm. This preprocessing occurred as a pipeline that tokenized the text, assigned a part-of-speech tag, and finally determined a lemma for each stemmable word. This information was then passed to a MWE candidate identifier[3] whose output was then filtered by an MWE selector. The resulting list of MWEs, along with all remaining tokens, were then passed into the WSD algorithm for disambiguation.

The MWE identifier-selector pair determined what combinations of tokens were marked as MWEs. It considered only continuous (i.e., unbroken) sequences of tokens whose order matched the order of the constituents of the associated MWE entry in Wordnet. Because of morphological variation, not all sequences of tokens are in base form; the main function of the candidate identifier, therefore, was to determine what morphological variation was allowed for a particular MWE entry. They identified and tested four different strategies:

1. **None** - no morphological variation allowed, all MWEs must be in base form
2. **Pattern** - allows morphological variation according to a set of pre-defined patterns
3. **Form** - a morphological variant is allowed if it is observed in Semcor
4. **All** - all morphological variants allowed

The identification procedure produced a list of candidate MWEs. These MWEs were then filtered by the MWE selection process, which used one of two strategies:

1. **Longest Match, Left-to-Right** - starting from the left to right, selects the longest multi-word expression found
2. **Semcor** - selects the multi-word expression whose tokens have the maximum probability of participating in an MWE, according to measurements over Semcor

Arranz identified the *None/Longest-Match-Left-to-Right* strategy as the Baseline, noting that this was the most common strategy for MWE-aware WSD algorithms. For this strategy the only MWE candidates allowed were those already in base form (*None*), followed by resolution of conflicts by selecting the MWEs that started farthest to the left, choosing the longest in case of ties (*Longest-Match-Left-to-Right*);

Arranz's Best strategy was *Pattern/Semcor*, namely, allowing candidate MWEs to vary morphologically according to a pre-defined set of syntactic patterns (*Pattern*), followed by selecting the most likely MWE based on examination of token frequencies in the Semcor corpus (*Semcor*). They ran their detection strategies over a subset of the sense-disambiguated glosses of the eXtended WordNet (XWN) corpus (Moldovan and Novischi, 2004). They selected all glosses whose sense-disambiguated words were all marked as 'gold' quality, namely, reviewed by a human annotator. Over this set of words, their WSD system achieved 0.617_{F_1} ($0.622_p/0.612_r$) when using the Baseline MWE detection strategy, and 0.629_{F_1} ($0.638_p/0.620_r$) when using the Best strategy.

0.6, then a 5 percentage point increase yields an f-measure of 0.65.

[2]The third concordance, *brownv*, only has verbs marked, so we did not test on it.

[3]Arranz calls the candidate identification stage the MWE *detector*; we have renamed it because we take 'detection' to be the end-to-end process of marking MWEs.

2 Extension of Results

We implemented both the Baseline and Best MWE-detection strategies, and used them as preprocessors for a simple WSD algorithm, namely, the Most-Frequent Sense algorithm. This algorithm simply chooses, for each identified base form, the most frequent sense in the sense inventory. We chose this strategy, instead of re-implementing Arranz's strategy, for two reasons. First, our purpose was to study the improvement MWE-detection provides to WSD in general, not to a specific WSD algorithm. We wished to show that, to the first order, MWE detection improves WSD irrespective of the WSD algorithm chosen. Using a different algorithm than Arranz's supports this claim. Second, for those wishing to further this work, or build upon it, the Most-Frequent-Sense strategy is easily implemented.

We used JSemcor (Finlayson, 2008a) to interface with the Semcor data files. We used Wordnet version 1.6 with the original version of Semcor[4]. Each token in each sentence in the *brown1* and *brown2* concordances of Semcor was assigned a part of speech tag calculated using the Stanford Java NLP library (Toutanova et al., 2003), as well as a set of lemmas calculated using the MIT Java Wordnet Interface (Finlayson, 2008b). This data was the input to each MWE detection strategy.

There was one major difference between our detector implementations and Arranz, stemming from a major difference between XWN and Semcor: Semcor contains a large number of proper nouns, whereas XWN glosses contain almost none. Therefore our detector implementations included a simple proper noun MWE detector, which marked all unbroken runs of tokens tagged as proper nouns as a proper noun MWE. This proper noun detector was run first, before the Baseline and Best detectors, and the proper noun MWEs detected took precedence over the MWEs detected in later stages.

Baseline MWE Detection This MWE detection strategy was called *None/Longest-Match-Left-to-Right* by Arranz; we implemented it in four stages. First, we detected proper nouns, as described. Second, for each sentence, the strategy used the part of speech tags and lemmas to identify all possible consecutive MWEs, using a list extracted from WordNet 1.6 and Semcor 1.6. The only restriction was that at least one token identified as part of the MWE must share the basic part of speech (e.g., noun, verb, adjective, or adverb) with the part of speech of the MWE. As noted, tokens that were identified as being part of a proper noun MWE were not included in this stage. In the third stage, we removed all non-proper-noun MWEs that were inflected–this corresponds to Arranz's *None* stage. In our final stage, any conflicts were resolved by choosing the MWE with the leftmost token. For two conflicting MWEs that started at the same token, the longest MWE was chosen. This corresponds to Arranz's *Longest-Match-Left-to-Right* selection.

Best MWE Detection This MWE detection strategy was called *Pattern/Semcor* by Arranz, and we also implemented this strategy in four stages. The first and second stages were the same as the Baseline strategy, namely, detection of proper nouns followed by identification of continuous MWEs. The third stage kept only MWEs whose morphological inflection matched one of the inflection rules described by Arranz (*Pattern*). The final stage resolved any conflicts by choosing the MWE whose constituent tokens occur most frequently in Semcor as an MWE rather than a sequence of monowords (Arranz's *Semcor* selection).

Word Sense Disambiguation No special technique was required to chain the Most-Frequent Sense WSD algorithm with the MWE detection strategies. We measured the performance of the WSD algorithm using no MWE detection, the Baseline detection, the Best detection, and Perfect detection[5]. These results are shown in Table 2.

Our improvement from Baseline to Best was approximately the same as Arranz's: 1.7 percentage points to their 1.2. We attribute the difference to the much worse performance of our Baseline detection algorithm: our Baseline MWE detection f-measure was 0.552, compared their 0.740. The reason for this

[4]The latest version of Wordnet is 3.0, but Semcor has not been manually updated for Wordnet versions later than 1.6. Automatically updated versions of Semcor are available, but they contain numerous errors resulting from deleted sense entries, and the sense assignments and multi-word identifications have not been adjusted to take into account new entries. Therefore we decided to use versions 1.6 for both Wordnet and Semcor.

[5]Perfect detection merely returned the MWEs identified in Semcor

Measure	Arranz *et al.* (2005)	Finlayson & Kulkarni
Corpus	eXtended WordNet (XWN) 2.0	Semcor 1.6 (`brown1` & `brown2`)
Number of Tokens (non-punctuation)	8,493	376,670
Number of Open-Class Tokens	5,133	196,852
Number of Open-Class Monowords	4,332	168,808
Number of Open-Class MWEs	382	12,449
Number of Tokens in Open-Class MWEs	801	28,044
Number of Open-Class Words (mono & multi)	4,714	181,257
Fraction MWEs	9.4%	7.4%
MWE Detection, Baseline	0.740_{F_1} $(0.765_p/0.715_r)$	0.552_{F_1} $(0.452_p/0.708_r)$
MWE Detection, Best	0.811_{F_1} $(0.806_p/0.816_r)$	0.856_{F_1} $(0.874_p/0.838_r)$
WSD, MWE-unaware	-	0.579_{F_1} $(0.572_p/0.585_r)$
WSD, Baseline MWE Detection	0.617_{F_1} $(0.622_p/0.612_r)$	0.612_{F_1} $(0.614_p/0.611_r)$
WSD, Best MWE Detection	0.629_{F_1} $(0.638_p/0.620_r)$	0.629_{F_1} $(0.630_p/0.628_r)$
WSD, Perfect MWE Detection	-	0.640_{F_1} $(0.642_p/0.638_r)$
WSD Improvement, Baseline vs. Best	0.012_{F_1} $(0.016_p/0.008_r)$	0.016_{F_1} $(0.016_p/0.017_r)$
WSD Improvement, Baseline vs. None	-	$\mathbf{0.033}_{F_1}$ $\mathbf{(0.042_p/0.025_r)}$
WSD Improvement, Best vs. None	-	$\mathbf{0.050}_{F_1}$ $\mathbf{(0.058_p/0.043_r)}$
WSD Improvement, Perfect vs. None	-	$\mathbf{0.061}_{F_1}$ $\mathbf{(0.070_p/0.053_r)}$

Table 2: All the relevant numbers for the study. For purposes of comparison we recalculated the token counts for the gold-annotated portion of the XWN corpus, and found discrepancies with Arranz's reported values. They reported 1300 fully-gold-annotated glosses containing 397 MWEs; we found 1307 glosses containing 382 MWEs. The table contains our token counts, but Arranz's actual MWE detection and WSD f-measures, precisions, and recalls.

striking difference in Baseline performance seems to be that, in the XWN glosses, a much higher fraction of the MWEs are already in base form (e.g., nouns in glosses are preferentially expressed as singular).

To encourage other researchers to build upon our results, we provide our implementation of these two MWE detection strategies, along with a general MWE detection framework and numerous other MWE detectors, in the form of a free, open-source Java library called jMWE (Finlayson and Kulkarni, 2011a). Furthermore, to allow independent verification of our results, we have placed all the source code and data required to run these experiments in an online repository (Finlayson and Kulkarni, 2011b).

3 Contributions

We have shown that accurately detecting multiword expressions allows a non-trivial improvement in word sense disambiguation. Our Baseline, Best, and Perfect MWE detection strategies show a 3.3, 5.1, and 6.1 percentage point improvement in WSD f-measure. Our Baseline-to-Best improvement is comparable with that measured by Arranz, the difference being due to more prevalent base-form MWEs between XWN glosses and Semcor. The very small improvement of the Perfect strategy over the Best shows that, at least for Wordnet over texts with an MWE distribution similar to Semcor, there is little to be gained even from a highly-sophisticated MWE detector. We have provided these two MWE detection algorithms in a free, open-source Java library called jMWE.

Acknowledgments

This work was supported in part by the Air Force Office of Scientific Research under grant number A9550-05-1-0321, and the Defense Advanced Research Projects Agency under contract number FA8750-10-1-0076. Thanks to Michael Fay for helpful comments.

References

Eneko Agirre and Philip Edmonds. 2007. *Word Sense Disambiguation*. Text, Speech, and Language Technology. Springer-Verlag, Dordrecht, The Netherlands.

Victoria Arranz, Jordi Atserias, and Mauro Castillo. 2005. Multiwords and word sense disambiguation. In Alexander Gelbukh, editor, *Proceedings of the Sixth International Conference on Intelligent Text Processing and Computational Linguistics (CICLING)*, volume 3406 of Lecture Notes in Computer Science (LNCS), pages 250–262, Mexico City, Mexico. Springer-Verlag.

Mauro Castillo, Francis Real, Jordi Asterias, and German Rigau. 2004. The TALP systems for disambiguating WordNet glosses. In Rada Mihalcea and Phil Edmonds, editors, *Proceedings of Senseval-3: Third International Workshop on the Evaluation of Systems for the Semantic Analysis of Text*, pages 93–96. Association for Computational Linguistics.

Christiane Fellbaum. 1998. *Wordnet: An Electronic Lexical Database*. MIT Press, Cambridge, MA.

Mark Alan Finlayson and Nidhi Kulkarni. 2011a. jMWE, version 1.0.0. `http://projects.csail.mit.edu/jmwe` `http://hdl.handle.net/1721.1/62793`.

Mark Alan Finlayson and Nidhi Kulkarni. 2011b. Source code and data for MWE'2011 papers. `http://hdl.handle.net/1721.1/62792`.

Mark Alan Finlayson. 2008a. JSemcor, version 1.0.0. `http://projects.csail.mit.edu/jsemcor`.

Mark Alan Finlayson. 2008b. JWI: The MIT Java Wordnet Interface, version 2.1.5. `http://projects.csail.mit.edu/jwi`.

Dan Moldovan and Adrian Novischi. 2004. Word sense disambiguation of WordNet glosses. *Computer Speech and Language*, 18:301–317.

Kristina Toutanova, Daniel Klein, Christopher D. Manning, and Yoram Singer. 2003. Feature-rich part-of-speech tagging with a cyclic dependency network. pages 252–259. Proceedings of the Human Language Technology Conference of the North American Chapter of the Association for Computational Linguistics (HLT-NAACL).

Tree-Rewriting Models of Multi-Word Expressions

William Schuler
Department of Linguistics
The Ohio State University
schuler@ling.osu.edu

Aravind K. Joshi
Dept. Computer and Information Science
University of Pennsylvania
joshi@linc.cis.upenn.edu

Abstract

Multi-word expressions (MWEs) account for a large portion of the language used in day-to-day interactions. A formal system that is flexible enough to model these large and often syntactically-rich non-compositional chunks as single units in naturally occurring text could considerably simplify large-scale semantic annotation projects, in which it would be undesirable to have to develop internal compositional analyses of common technical expressions that have specific idiosyncratic meanings. This paper will first define a notion of functor-argument decomposition on phrase structure trees analogous to graph coloring, in which the tree is cast as a graph, and the elementary structures of a grammar formalism are colors. The paper then presents a formal argument that tree-rewriting systems, a class of grammar formalism that includes Tree Adjoining Grammars, are able to produce a proper superset of the functor-argument decompositions that string-rewriting systems can produce.

1 Introduction

Multi-word expressions (MWEs), whose structure and meaning cannot be derived from their component words as they occur independently, account for a large portion of the language used in day-to-day interactions. Indeed, the relatively low frequency of comparable single-word paraphrases for elementary spatial relations like 'in front of' (compare to 'before') or 'next to' (compare to 'beside') suggest a fundamentality of expressions, as opposed to words, as a basic unit of meaning in language (Becker, 1975; Fillmore, 2003). Other examples of MWEs are idioms such as 'kick the bucket' or 'spill the beans', which have figurative meanings as expressions that sometimes even allow modification ('spill some of the beans') and variation in sentence forms ('which beans were spilled?'), but are not available when the component words of the MWE occur independently. A formal system that is flexible enough to model these large and often syntactically-rich non-compositional chunks as single units in naturally occurring text could considerably simplify large-scale semantic annotation projects, in which it would be undesirable to have to develop internal compositional analyses of common technical expressions that have specific idiosyncratic meanings.

Models have been proposed for MWEs based on string-rewriting systems such as HPSG (Sag et al., 2002), which model compositionality as string adjacency of a functor and an argument substring. This string-rewriting model of compositionality essentially treats each projection of a head word as a functor, each capable of combining with an argument to yield a higher-level projection or functor. The set of projections from a lexical head can therefore be thought of as a single elementary structure: an n-ary functor, subsuming the arguments of the individual functors at each projection. This kind of approach is intuitive for fully-compositional analyses (e.g. in which a transitive verb like 'hold' is a functor and a NP complement like 'the basket' is an argument), but is less natural when applied to substrings of MWEs (e.g. treating *pick* as a functor and *up* as an argument in the verb-particle MWE *pick ... up*), since some of these arguments do not have any semantic significance (in the *pick ... up* example , there is no coherent meaning for *Up* such that $[\![\text{pick } X \text{ up}]\!] = \mathit{Pick}([\![X]\!], \mathit{Up})$).

This paper will argue that tree-rewriting systems, a class of grammar formalisms that includes Tree Adjoining Grammars (Joshi, 1985; Joshi and Schabes, 1997), are a more natural candidate for modeling MWEs since they can model entire fragments of phrase structure trees as elementary (locally non-compositional) semantic building blocks, in addition to the set of head-projections used in string-rewriting

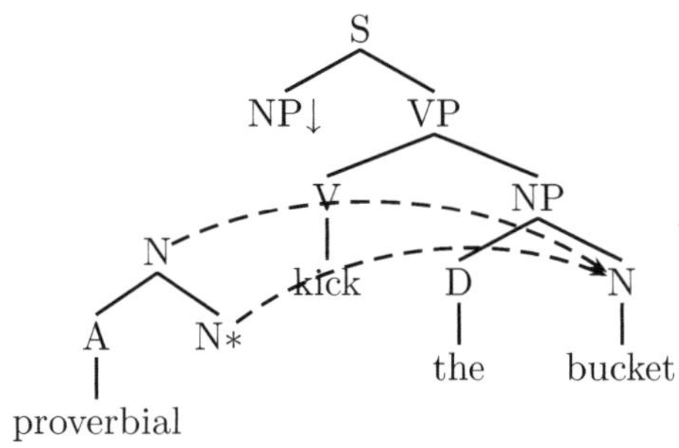

Figure 1: Composition of elementary trees for idiom MWE 'kick the bucket' and adjective 'proverbial,' with the same semantics as an adverb 'proverbially' adjoining at the VP.

systems. This allows more flexibility in defining the functor-argument decomposition of a given phrase structure tree.

This will be demonstrated by reducing the functor-argument decompositions (compositional accounts of semantics assigned to portions of phrase structure trees) of string-rewriting systems to a special case of functor-argument decompositions of tree-rewriting systems. Discussion in this paper will focus on string-rewriting systems augmented with unification (such as HPSG) because in this framework the issue of multi-word expressions has been discussed (Sag et al., 2002). The arguments in this paper also apply to other string rewriting systems such as categorial grammars (Ajdukiewicz, 1935; Bar-Hillel, 1953; Steedman, 2000), but in these formalisms the issues concerning MWEs have not been extensively developed. Essentially, this paper formalizes the intuition (Abeillé, 1993) that the extended domain of locality of tree-rewriting systems allows them to provide a compositional account of the semantics assigned to multi-word or idiomatic portions of phrase structure trees using elementary units that, after composition, may end up partially discontinuous in these trees. For example, a portion of a phrase structure tree for 'kick the bucket' with a single interpretation equivalent to 'die' can be modified through adjunction of the adjective 'proverbial' at the noun constituent 'bucket' without postulating separate semantics for 'kick' (see Figure 1).

2 Definitions

String rewriting systems are sets of rules for replacing symbols with other symbols in strings. A rewriting of some start symbol into a set of lexical symbols is called a derivation. Rewrite rules in a string rewriting system can be defined to have designated functor and argument symbols. Any derivation τ can therefore yield a functor-argument decomposition $\mathcal{D}(\tau)$, essentially defining a set of semantic functor-argument dependencies among structured elementary categories.

For simplicity, a functor-argument decomposition will be defined as a mapping from the constituent nodes in a phrase structure tree to the nodes in the elementary structures used to derive that tree. This can be thought of as a coloring of phrase structure nodes, in which colors correspond to elementary structures in the rewriting system. The elementary structures used in such a decomposition may then be considered n-ary functors, which may take several arguments, each of a different color.

In string-rewriting systems such as HPSG, these n-ary functors consist of a head word and its projections, and the arguments of the functor are the non-projecting child of each such projection. Figure 2 shows feature-based and categorial analyses for the MWE '*... to the ... power*' (as in '*raise Y to the X power*') which is taken here to have unambiguous meaning (in a technical context) as Y^X or $Pow(Y, X)$, and is analyzed here to wrap around an ordinal number argument X and then adjoin onto a verb phrase '*raise Y*' as a modifier.[1] Because their elementary structures are projected up from individual head words, these systems prohibit an analysis of this MWE as a single wrapping functor. Instead, MWEs like this must be decomposed into individual functor words (e.g. *power*) and argument words (e.g. *the*, and *to*).

Tree-rewriting systems, on the other hand, allow elementary structures to contain nodes which are neither projections nor argument sites. This permits an analysis of '*to the ... power*' as a single functor wrapped around its argument (see Figure 3), without having to specify functor-argument relations between *power*, *to*, and *the*.

More generally, string-rewriting systems use elementary structures (n-ary functors) that originate at the lexical item and exhibit a bottom-up branching structure, branching to an argument site and a higher level projection at each step. In contrast, tree-rewriting systems use elementary structures that originate at a phrasal or clausal node and exhibit

[1] We are using the MWE '... to the ... power' as a simple example with an unambiguous meaning in the domain of mathematics to illustrate our main points in the context of both adjunction and substitution operations. Alternative analyses are possible (e.g. with '*the*' or additional modifiers adjoining in, to allow variations like '*to every even power under six*'), but in any case the words '*to*' and '*power*' on either side of the X argument are taken to be idiosyncratic to this expression of Y^X. Since it is analyzed as a modifier, this example can be used to demonstrate coindexation of structure in a tree-rewriting system.

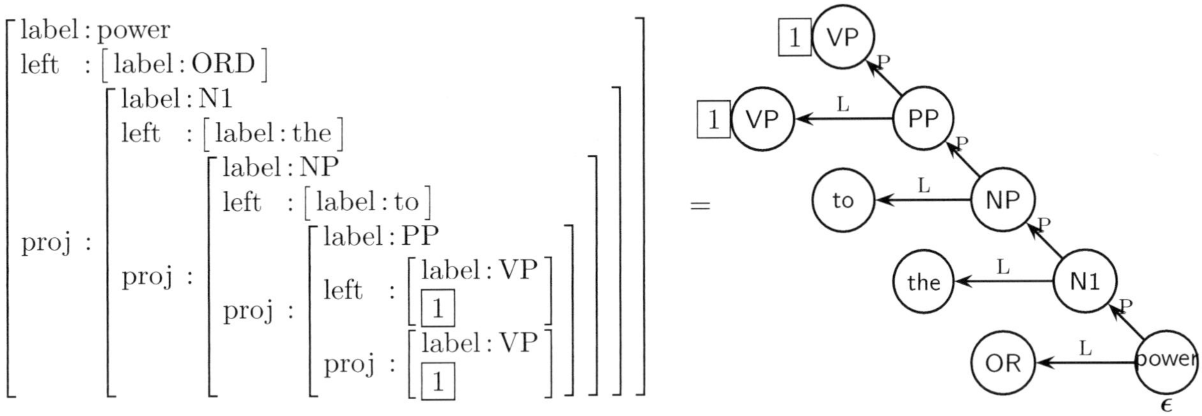

Figure 2: Elementary structures for a verb-phrase-modifying preposition in a functor-argument analysis derived from a feature structure grammar. Here, ϵ indicates the origin node and boxed numbers indicate coindexations.

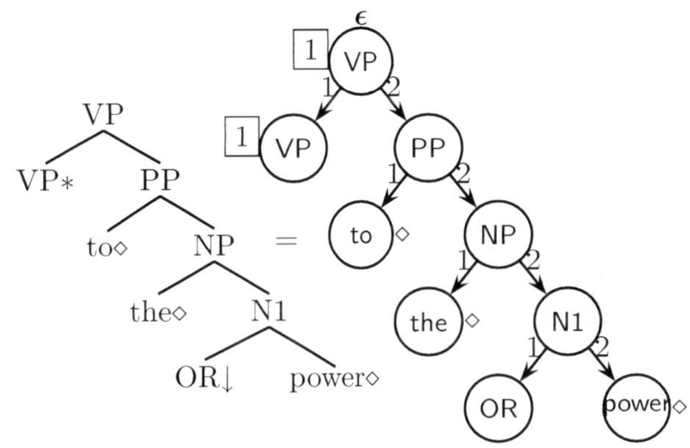

Figure 3: Elementary structure for a verb-phrase-modifying prepositional phrase *'to the ... power'* in a tree-rewriting system, derived from a tree-adjoining grammar. Here, ϵ indicates the origin node, ◇ indicates a non-argument node (or lexical 'anchor'), and boxed numbers indicate coindexations.

a top-down branching structure that mirrors that of a phrase structure tree. As one might expect, there are tree-rewriting systems (namely those whose elementary structures contain multiple lexical items) that can produce functor-argument decompositions ('colorings') of a phrase structure tree which cannot be produced by a string-rewriting system. More surprisingly however, this paper will show that the converse is not true: in other words, for any string-rewriting system there always exists a tree-rewriting system that can produce the same functor-argument decomposition of a phrase structure tree. Thus, the set of functor-argument decompositions that can be produced by tree-rewriting systems is a proper superset of those that can be produced by string-rewriting systems.

This is surprising because, taken as a class, there is no inherent difference in recognition complexity between string-rewriting systems and tree-rewriting systems (as may be the case between specific members of these classes, say between CGs and TAGs), since both are worst-case exponential if unconstrained coindexation of structure is allowed (as in unification grammars). This is also surprising because, since they branch upward, the elementary structures of string-rewriting systems can specify complex functors as arguments, which the downward-branching elementary structures of tree-rewriting systems cannot. However, this paper will show that this ability to specify complex functors as arguments does not confer any additional flexibility in calculating functor-argument decompositions of phrase structure trees, and can be factored out with no loss in expressivity.

3 Reduction of string-rewriting systems to tree-rewriting systems

The first step will be to define an n-ary functor in a string-rewriting system as a kind of elementary structure α (a tree in fact), whose nodes α_μ branch 'upward' into sub-structure nodes (connected by departing arcs labeled L, R, or P,) specifying a left or right argument category ($\alpha_{\mu\cdot\text{L}}$ or $\alpha_{\mu\cdot\text{R}}$) and a projected category ($\alpha_{\mu\cdot\text{P}}$), rather than branching 'downward' into left and right child constituents as in an ordinary phrase structure tree.[2] In order to extend this reduction to feature-based systems, these elementary structures will also be augmented with coindexation sets I of elementary structure nodes that must be identical (in terms of labels and departing arcs) in any functor-argument decomposition of a phrase structure tree.

[2]Here, a node α_μ is defined by the path of concatenated arcs μ that lead to it from the origin or root α_ϵ.

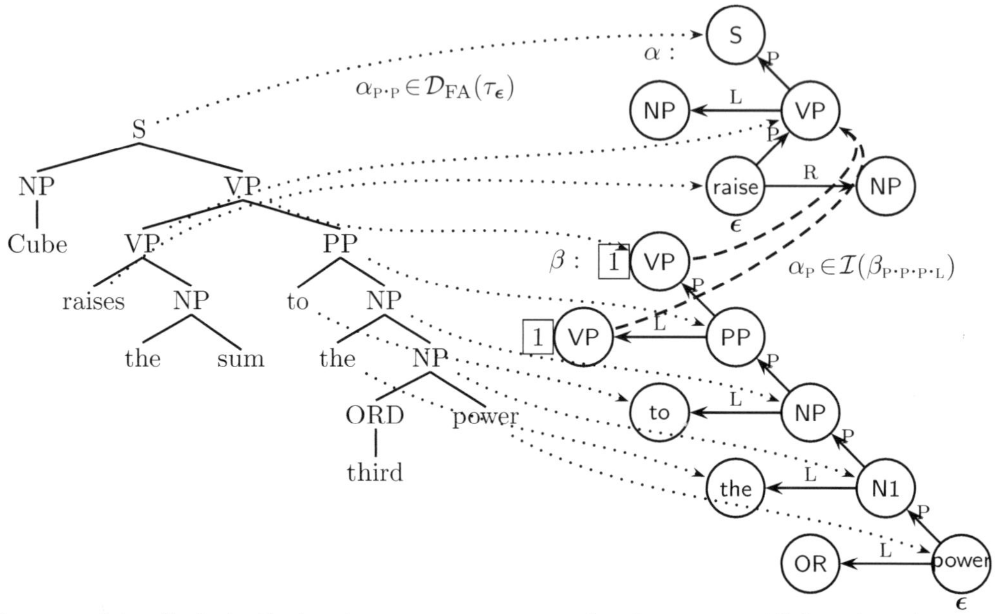

Figure 4: Decomposition ('coloring') of a phrase structure tree τ for the sentence 'Cube raises the sum to the third power', using elementary structures α and β shown at right. Dotted lines from phrase structure tree nodes τ_η to elementary structure nodes α_μ indicate that α_μ generates τ_η in the functor-argument decomposition: $\alpha_\mu \in \mathcal{D}_{\text{FA}}(\tau_\eta)$. Dashed lines from elementary structure nodes β_ν to other elementary structure nodes α_μ indicate that α_μ is among the nodes identified with β_ν as arguments of β in the decomposition. Boxed identifiers indicated coindices between nodes β_ν and $\beta_{\nu'}$ in β such that $\exists I \in \beta\ .\ \beta_\nu, \beta_{\nu'} \in I$.

Figure 4 shows a functor-argument decomposition (or 'coloring') of a phrase structure tree using these upward-branching elements.

The upward-branching elementary structures used in any such decomposition can then be converted into a normal form in which all argument nodes are *atomic* (have no departing arcs), using the following transformations of elementary structures to equivalent structures that fit together generate the same functor-argument decomposition. This is done by simultaneously excising 'matched' material from both the argument branch of an elementary structure and the top of the elementary structure that is its argument in the given decomposition.

The use of coindexation sets complicates this transformation somewhat. Initial configurations of coindexation sets in upward-branching elementary structures can be exhaustively partitioned into three classes, defined with respect to the 'trunk' of the elementary structure, which is the set of nodes connected to the origin by paths containing only P arcs. These classes are:

1. coindexations with more than one coindexed node on the trunk,
2. coindexations with fewer than one coindexed node on the trunk, and
3. coindexations with exactly one coindexed node on the trunk.

Elementary structures in the first class, with more than one coindexed node on the trunk, are equivalent to graphs with directed cycles, and are ordinarily excluded from feature-based analyses, so they will be ignored here.

Elementary structures in the second class, with fewer than one coindexed node on the trunk, can be converted to equivalent structures with no coindices (which trivially satisfies the above argument-atomicity requirement), using the simultaneous excision of 'matched' structure in functor and argument structures described above, by simply extending this to cover the portion of the argument elementary structure that extends all the way to the top of the trunk.

Elementary structures in the third class, with exactly one coindexed node on the trunk, can be converted to equivalent structures that satisfy argument-atomicity using a three-step process. First, the upward-branching sub-structures above these coindexed nodes (if any) are unified, so the arcs departing from each coindexed node will be recursively identical (this must be possible in any feature-based grammar, or the coindexation would be ill-formed, and should therefore be excluded). The coindexation is then recursively slid up along the P arc departing from each such node, until the coindexation set contains nothing but atomic categories (with no departing arcs). Finally, the argument nodes are made to be atomic using the simultaneous excision of 'matched' structure in functor and argument structures described above, leaving an (atomic) coindexation at each (atomic) argument position in each affected branch.

Elementary structures with multiple class 3 coindexation sets I and I' (which cannot be deleted as described above for class 2 sets) can be transformed into structures with a single coindexation set I by copying the portion of the trunk between the (unique) on-trunk members of each initial set I and I' onto every other node in the set I' that contains the lower trunk node (this copy should include the coindex belonging to I). The coindexation set I' containing the lower on-trunk node is then simply deleted.

The normal-form upward-branching structures resulting from this transformation can now be converted into downward-branching elementary trees in a tree-rewriting system (with coindexed nodes corresponding to 'root' and 'foot' nodes as defined for tree-adjoining grammars) by simply replacing each pair of argument and conclusion arcs with a pair of left-child and right-child arcs departing the conclusion node. Since the normal form for upward-branching elementary structures allows only atomic arguments, this re-drawing of arcs must result in well-formed downward-branching elementary trees in every case.[3]

In particular, this conversion results in a subset of tree-rewriting systems in which each (binary) branch of every elementary tree must have exactly one argument position and one non-argument position among its two children. This is a special case of a more general class of tree-rewriting systems, which may have two argument positions or no argument positions among the children at each binary branch. Such trees are not equivalent to trees with a single argument position per branch, because they will result in different functor-argument decompositions ('colorings') of a target phrase structure tree. Moreover, it is precisely these non-string-rewriting-equivalent elementary trees that are needed to model the local non-compositionality of larger multi-word expressions like 'threw X to the lions' (see Figure 5), because only downward branches with multiple non-

[3]Recognition and parsing of feature-based grammars, and of tree-rewriting systems whose elementary trees contain multiple foot nodes, are both exponential in the worst case. However, both types of grammars are amenable to regular-from restrictions which prohibit recursive adjunction at internal (non-root, non-foot) tree nodes, and thereby constrain recognition and parsing complexity to cubic time for most kinds of natural language grammars (Rogers, 1994).

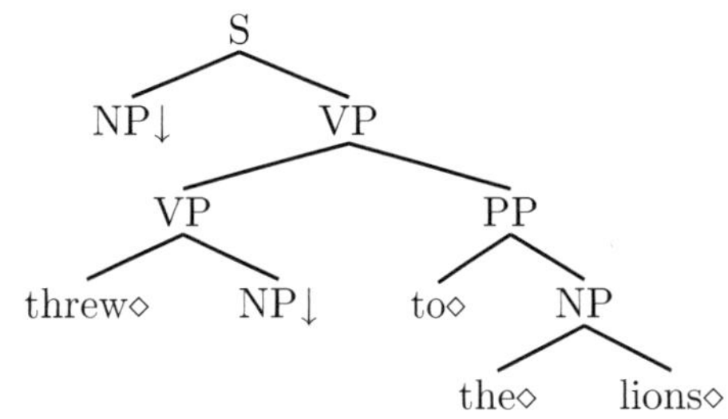

Figure 5: Elementary structure for MWE idiom '*threw ... to the lions*,' allowing modification to both VP, PP and NP sub-constituents (e.g. '*threw your friends today right to the proverbial lions*).

argument children can produce the multi-level subtrees containing the word 'threw' and the word 'lions' in the same elementary unit.

4 Conclusion

This paper has shown that tree-rewriting systems are able to produce a superset of the functor-argument decompositions that can be produced by string-rewriting systems such as categorial grammars and feature-structure grammars such as HPSG. This superset additionally allows elementary units to contain multiple (lexical) leaves, which a string-rewriting system cannot. This makes tree-rewriting systems ideally suited to the analysis of natural language texts that contain many multi-word expressions with idiosyncratic (non-compositional) meanings. Although neither the tree-rewriting nor the string-rewriting analyses defined above can be generated in guaranteed polynomial time (since they may require the construction of unbounded stacks of unrecognized structure during bottom-up recognition), they can both be made polynomial (indeed, cubic) by the introduction of 'regular form' constraints (Rogers, 1994), which limit this stack in the same way in both cases.

In contrast with representations like that of (Villavicencio et al., 2004), in which concepts are distributed over several lexical entries, a tree-rewriting representation such as the one described in this paper allows only a single lexical entry to be listed for each concept. For example:

... throw ... to the lions:
(s(np0!)(vp(v)(np1!)(pp(p)(np(d)(n)))))
... to the ... power:
(vp(vp0*)(pp(p)(np(d)(n(a1!)(n)))))

(using the notation '!' and '*' for substitution sites and foot nodes, respectively). It is anticipated that this will simplify the organization of lexical resources for multi-word expressions.

References

Abeillé, Anne. 1993. The flexibility of french idioms: a representation with lexicalized tree adjoining grammar. In A. Schenk and E. van der Linden, editors, *Idioms*. Erlbaum.

Ajdukiewicz, Kazimierz. 1935. Die syntaktische konnexitat. In S. McCall, editor, *Polish Logic 1920-1939*. Oxford University Press, pages 207–231. Translated from Studia Philosophica 1: 1–27.

Bar-Hillel, Yehoshua. 1953. A quasi-arithmetical notation for syntactic description. *Language*, 29:47–58.

Becker, Joseph D. 1975. The phrasal lexicon. In *Proceedings of the Workshop on Theoretical Issues in Natural Language Processing, Workshop in Computational Linguisitcs, Psychology, and AI*, Cambridge, MA.

Fillmore, Charles J. 2003. Multiword expressions, November. Invited talk at the Institute for Research in Cognitive Science (IRCS), University of Pennsylvania. http://www.cis.upenn.edu/~ircs/colloq/2003/fall/fillmore.html.

Joshi, Aravind and Yves Schabes. 1997. Tree-adjoning grammars. In G. Rozenberg and A. Salomaa, editors, *Handbook of Formal Languages*. Springer-Verlag, Berlin, pages 69–123.

Joshi, Aravind K. 1985. How much context sensitivity is necessary for characterizing structural descriptions: Tree adjoining grammars. In L. Karttunen D. Dowty and A. Zwicky, editors, *Natural language parsing: Psychological, computational and theoretical perspectives*. Cambridge University Press, Cambridge, U.K., pages 206–250.

Rogers, James. 1994. Capturing CFLs with tree adjoining grammars. In *Proceedings of the 32nd Annual Meeting of the Association for Computational Linguistics (ACL'94)*.

Sag, Ivan, Timothy Baldwin, Francis Bond, Ann Copestake, and Dan Flickinger. 2002. Multiword expressions: a pain in the neck for nlp. In *Proceedings of the Third International Conference on Intelligent Text Processing and Computational Linguistics (CICLING'02)*, pages 1–15, Mexico City, Mexico.

Steedman, Mark. 2000. *The syntactic process*. MIT Press/Bradford Books, Cambridge, MA.

Villavicencio, Aline, Ann Copestake, Benjamin Waldron, and Fabre Lambeau. 2004. Lexical encoding of mwes. In Takaaki Tanaka, Aline Villavicencio, Francis Bond, and Anna Korhonen, editors, *Second ACL Workshop on Multiword Expressions: Integrating Processing*, pages 80–87, Barcelona, Spain, July. Association for Computational Linguistics.

Learning English Light Verb Constructions: Contextual or Statistical

Yuancheng Tu
Department of Linguistics
University of Illinois
ytu@illinois.edu

Dan Roth
Department of Computer Science
University of Illinois
danr@illinois.edu

Abstract

In this paper, we investigate a supervised machine learning framework for automatically learning of English **L**ight **V**erb **C**onstructions (LVCs). Our system achieves an 86.3% accuracy with a baseline (chance) performance of 52.2% when trained with groups of either contextual or statistical features. In addition, we present an in-depth analysis of these contextual and statistical features and show that the system trained by these two types of cosmetically different features reaches similar performance empirically. However, in the situation where the surface structures of candidate LVCs are identical, the system trained with contextual features which contain information on surrounding words performs 16.7% better.

In this study, we also construct a balanced benchmark dataset with 2,162 sentences from BNC for English LVCs. And this data set is publicly available and is also a useful computational resource for research on MWEs in general.

1 Introduction

Multi-**W**ord **E**xpressions (MWEs) refer to various types of linguistic units or expressions, including idioms, noun compounds, named entities, complex verb phrases and any other habitual collocations. MWEs pose a particular challenge in empirical Natural Language Processing (NLP) because they always have idiosyncratic interpretations which cannot be formulated by directly aggregating the semantics of their constituents (Sag et al., 2002).

The study in this paper focuses on one special type of MWEs, i.e., the **L**ight **V**erb **C**onstructions (LVCs), formed from a commonly used verb and usually a noun phrase (NP) in its direct object position, such as *have a look* and *make an offer* in English. These complex verb predicates do not fall clearly into the discrete binary distinction of compositional or non-compositional expressions. Instead, they stand somewhat in between and are typically semi-compositional. For example, consider the following three candidate LVCs: *take a wallet*, *take a walk* and *take a while*. These three complex verb predicates are cosmetically very similar. But a closer look at their semantics reveals significant differences and each of them represents a different class of MWEs. The first expression, *take a wallet* is a literal combination of a verb and its object noun. The last expression *take a while* is an idiom and its meaning *cost a long time to do something*, cannot be derived by direct integration of the literal meaning of its components. Only the second expression, *take a walk* is an LVC whose meaning mainly derives from one of its components, namely its noun object (*walk*) while the meaning of its main verb is somewhat bleached (Butt, 2003; Kearns, 2002) and therefore *light* (Jespersen, 1965).

LVCs have already been identified as one of the major sources of problems in various NLP applications, such as automatic word alignment (Samardžić and Merlo, 2010) and semantic annotation transference (Burchardt et al., 2009), and machine translation. These problems provide empirical grounds for distinguishing between the bleached and full meaning of a verb within a given sentence, a task that is often difficult on the basis of surface structures since they always exhibit identical surface properties. For example, consider the following sentences:

1. He *had a look* of childish bewilderment on his face.
2. I've arranged for you to *have a look* at his file in our library.

In sentence 1, the verb *have* in the phrase *have a look* has its full fledged meaning "*possess, own*" and therefore it is *literal* instead of *light*. However, in sentence 2, *have a look* only means *look* and the meaning of the verb *have* is impoverished and is thus *light*.

In this paper, we propose an in-depth case study on LVC recognition, in which we investigate machine learning techniques for automatically identifying the impoverished meaning of a verb given a sentence. Unlike the earlier work that has viewed all verbs as possible light verbs (Tan et al., 2006), We focus on a half dozen of broadly documented and most frequently used English light verbs among the small set of them in English.

We construct a token-based data set with a total of 2,162 sentences extracted from British National Corpus (BNC)[1] and build a learner with L2-loss SVM. Our system achieves a 86.3% accuracy with a baseline (chance) performance of 52.2%. We also extract automatically two groups of features, statistical and contextual features and present a detailed ablation analysis of the interaction of these features. Interestingly, the results show that the system performs similarly when trained independently with either groups of these features. And the integration of these two types of features does not improve the performance. However, when tested with all sentences with the candidate LVCs whose surface structures are identical in both negative and positive examples, for example, the aforementioned sentence 1 (negative) and 2 (positive) with the candidate LVC "*have a look*", the system trained with contextual features which include information on surrounding words performs more robust and significantly better. This analysis contributes significantly to the understanding of the functionality of both contextual and statistical features and provides empirical evidence to guide the usage of them in NLP applications.

In the rest of the paper, we first present some related work on LVCs in Sec. 2. Then we describe our model including the learning algorithm and statistical and contextual features in Sec. 3. We present our experiments and analysis in Sec. 4 and conclude our paper in Sec. 5.

2 Related Work

LVCs have been well-studied in linguistics since early days (Jespersen, 1965; Butt, 2003; Kearns, 2002). Recent computational research on LVCs mainly focuses on type-based classification, i.e., statistically aggregated properties of LVCs. For example, many works are about direct measuring of the compositionality (Venkatapathy and Joshi, 2005), compatibility (Barrett and Davis, 2003), acceptability (North, 2005) and productivity (Stevenson et al., 2004) of LVCs. Other works, if related to token-based identification, i.e., identifying idiomatic expressions within context, only consider LVCs as one small subtype of other idiomatic expressions (Cook et al., 2007; Fazly and Stevenson, 2006).

Previous computational works on token-based identification differs from our work in one key aspect. Our work builds a learning system which systematically incorporates both informative statistical measures and specific local contexts and does in-depth analysis on both of them while many previous works, either totally rely on or only emphasize on one of them. For example, the method used in (Katz and Giesbrecht, 2006) relies primarily on local co-occurrence lexicon to construct feature vectors for each target token. On the other hand, some other works (Fazly and Stevenson, 2007; Fazly and Stevenson, 2006; Stevenson et al., 2004), argue that linguistic properties, such as canonical syntactic patterns of specific types of idioms, are more informative than local context.

Tan et.al. (Tan et al., 2006) propose a learning approach to identify token-based LVCs. The method is only similar to ours in that it is a supervised framework. Our model uses a different data set annotated from BNC and the data set is larger and more balanced compared to the previous data set from WSJ. In addition, previous work assumes all verbs as potential LVCs while we intentionally exclude those verbs which linguistically never tested as light verbs, such as *buy* and *sell* in English and only focus on a half dozen of broadly documented English light

[1]http://www.natcorp.ox.ac.uk/XMLedition/

verbs, such as *have*, *take*, *give*, *do*, *get* and *make*.

The lack of common benchmark data sets for evaluation in MWE research unfortunately makes many works incomparable with the earlier ones. The data set we construct in this study hopefully can serve as a common test bed for research in LVCs or MWEs in general.

3 Learning English LVCs

In this study, we formulate the context sensitive English LVC identification task as a supervised binary classification problem. For each target LVC candidate within a sentence, the classifier decides if it is a true LVC. Formally, given a set of n labeled examples $\{x_i, y_i\}_{i=1}^{n}$, we learn a function $f : \mathcal{X} \rightarrow \mathcal{Y}$ where $\mathcal{Y} \in \{-1, 1\}$. The learning algorithm we use is the classic soft-margin SVM with L2-loss which is among the best "off-the-shelf" supervised learning algorithms and in our experiments the algorithm indeed gives us the best performance with the shortest training time. The algorithm is implemented using a modeling language called Learning Based Java (LBJ) (Rizzolo and Roth, 2010) via the LIBSVM Java API (Chang and Lin, 2001).

Previous research has suggested that both local contextual and statistical measures are informative in determining the class of an MWE token. However, it is not clear to what degree these two types of information overlap or interact. Do they contain similar knowledge or the knowledge they provide for LVC learning is different? Formulating a classification framework for identification enables us to integrate all contextual and statistical measures easily through features and test their effectiveness and interaction systematically.

We focus on two types of features: contextual and statistical features, and analyze in-depth their interaction and effectiveness within the learning framework. Statistical features in this study are numerical features which are computed globally via other big corpora rather than the training and testing data used in the system. For example, the *Cpmi* and *Deverbal v/n Ratio* (details in sec. 3.1) are generated from the statistics of Google n-gram and BNC corpus respectively. Since the *phrase size* feature is numerical and the selection of the candidate LVCs in the data set uses the canonical length information[2], we include it into the statistical category. Contextual features are defined in a broader sense and consist of all local features which are generated directly from the input sentences, such as word features within or around the candidate phrases. We describe the details of the used contextual features in sec. 3.2.

Our experiments show that arbitrarily combining statistic features within our current learning system does not improve the performance. Instead, we provide systematic analysis for these features and explore some interesting empirical observations about them within our learning framework.

3.1 Statistical Features

Cpmi: *C*ollocational *p*oint-wise *m*utual *i*nformation is calculated from Google n-gram dataset whose n-gram counts are generated from approximately one trillion words of text from publicly accessible Web pages. We use this big data set to overcome the data sparseness problem.

Previous works (Stevenson et al., 2004; Cook et al., 2007) show that one canonical surface syntactic structure for LVCs is *V + a/an Noun*. For example, in the LVC *take a walk*, "take" is the verb (V) and "walk" is the deverbal noun. The typical determiner in between is the indefinite article "a". It is also observed that when the indefinite article changes to definite, such as "the", "this" or "that", a phrase is less acceptable to be a true LVC. Therefore, the direct collocational pmi between the verb and the noun is derived to incorporate this intuition as shown in the following[3]:

$$Cpmi = 2I(v, aN) - I(v, theN)$$

Within this formula, $I(v, aN)$ is the point-wise mutual information between "v", the verb, and "aN", the phrase such as "a walk" in the aforementioned example. Similar definition applies to $I(v, theN)$. PMI of a pair of elements is calculated as (Church et al., 1991):

$$I(x, y) = \log \frac{N_{x+y} f(x, y)}{f(x, *) f(*, y)}$$

[2]We set an empirical length constraint to the maximal length of the noun phrase object when generating the candidates from BNC corpus.

[3]The formula is directly from (Stevenson et al., 2004).

N_{x+y} is the total number of verb and a/the noun pairs in the corpus. In our case, all trigram counts with this pattern in N-gram data set. $f(x, y)$ is the frequency of x and y co-occurring as a v-a/theN pair where $f(x, *)$ and $f(*, y)$ are the frequency when either of x and y occurs independent of each other in the corpus. Notice these counts are not easily available directly from search engines since many search engines treat articles such as "a" or "the" as stop words and remove them from the search query[4].

Deverbal v/n Ratio: the second statistical feature we use is related to the verb and noun usage ratio of the noun object within a candidate LVC. The intuition here is that the noun object of a candidate LVC has a strong tendency to be used as a verb or related to a verb via derivational morphology. For example, in the candidate phrase "have a look", "look" can directly be used as a verb while in the phrase "make a transmission", "transmission" is derivationally related to the verb "transmit". We use frequency counts gathered from British National Corpus (BNC) and then calculate the ratio since BNC encodes the lexeme for each word and is also tagged with parts of speech. In addition, it is a large corpus with 100 million words, thus, an ideal corpus to calculate the verb-noun usage for each candidate word in the object position.

Two other lexical resources, WordNet (Fellbaum, 1998) and NomLex (Meyers et al., 1998), are used to identify words which can directly be used as a noun and a verb and those that are derivational related. Specifically, WordNet is used to identify the words which can be used as both a noun and a verb and NomLex is used to recognize those derivationally related words. And the verb usage counts of these nouns are the frequencies of their corresponding derivational verbs. For example, for the word "transmission", its verb usage frequency is the count in BNC with its derivationally related verb "transmit".

Phrase Size: the third statistical feature is the actual size of the candidate LVC phrase. Many modifiers can be inserted inside the candidate phrases to generate new candidates. For example, "take a look" can be expanded to "take a *close* look", "take an *extremely* close look" and the expansion is in theory infinite. The hypothesis behind this feature is that regular usage of LVCs tends to be short. For example, it is observed that the canonical length in English is from 2 to 6.

3.2 Contextual Features

All features generated directly from the input sentences are categorized into this group. They consists of features derived directly from the candidate phrases themselves as well as their surrounding contexts.

Noun Object: this is the noun head of the object noun phrase within the candidate LVC phrase. For example, for a verb phrase "take a quick look", its noun head "look" is the active *Noun Object* feature. In our data set, there are 777 distinctive such nouns.

LV-NounObj: this is the bigram of the light verb and the head of the noun phrase. This feature encodes the collocation information between the candidate light verb and the head noun of its object.

Levin's Class: it is observed that members within certain groups of verb classes are legitimate candidates to form acceptable LVCs (Fazly et al., 2005). For example, many sound emission verbs according to Levin (Levin, 1993), such as *clap*, *whistle*, and *plop*, can be used to generate legitimate LVCs. Phrases such as *make a clap/plop/whistle* are all highly acceptable LVCs by humans even though some of them, such as *make a plop* rarely occur within corpora. We formulate a vector for all the 256 Levin's verb classes and turn the corresponding class-bits on when the verb usage of the head noun in a candidate LVC belongs to these classes. We add one extra class, *other*, to be mapped to those verbs which are not included in any one of these 256 Levin's verb classes.

Other Features: we construct other local contextual features, for example, the part of speech of the word immediately before the light verb (titled *posBefore*) and after the whole phrase (*posAfter*). We also encode the determiner within all candidate LVCs as another lexical feature (*Determiner*). We examine many other combinations of these contextual features. However, only those features that contribute positively to achieve the highest performance of the classifier are listed for detailed analysis in the next section.

[4]Some search engines accept "quotation strategy" to retain stop words in the query.

4 Experiments and Analysis

In this section, we report in detail our experimental settings and provide in-depth analysis on the interactions among features. First, we present our motivation and methodology to generate the new data set. Then we describe our experimental results and analysis.

4.1 Data Preparation and Annotation

The data set is generated from BNC, a balanced synchronic corpus containing 100 million words collected from various sources of British English. We begin our sentence selection process with the examination of a handful of previously investigated verbs (Fazly and Stevenson, 2007; Butt, 2003). Among them, we pick the 6 most frequently used English light verbs: *do*, *get*, *give*, *have*, *make* and *take*.

To identify potential LVCs within sentences, we first extract all sentences where one or more of the six verbs occur from BNC (XML Edition) and then parse these sentences with Charniak's parser (Charniak and Johnson, 2005). We focus on the "*verb + noun object*" pattern and choose all the sentences which have a direct NP object for the target verbs. We then collect a total of $207,789$ sentences.

We observe that within all these chosen sentences, the distribution of true LVCs is still low. We therefore use three resources to filter out trivial negative examples. Firstly, We use WordNet (Fellbaum, 1998) to identify the head noun in the object position which can be used as both a noun and a verb. Then, we use frequency counts gathered from BNC to filter out candidates whose verb usage is smaller than their noun usage. Finally, we use NomLex (Meyers et al., 1998) to recognize those head words in the object position whose noun forms and verb forms are derivationally related, such as *transmission* and *transmit*. We keep all candidates whose object head nouns are derivationlly related to a verb according to a gold-standard word list we extract from NomLex[5]. With this pipeline method, we filter out approximately 55% potential negative examples. This leaves us with $92,415$ sentences which we sample about 4% randomly to present to annotators. This filtering method successfully improves the recall of the positive examples and ensures us a corpus with balanced examples.

A website[6] is set up for annotators to annotate the data. Each potential LVC is presented to the annotator in a sentence. The annotator is asked to decide whether this phrase within the given sentence is an LVC and to choose an answer from one of these four options: *Yes*, *No*, *Not Sure*, and *Idiom*.

Detailed annotation instructions and LVC examples are given on the annotation website. When facing difficult examples, the annotators are instructed to follow a general "*replacing*" principle, i.e, if the candidate light verb within the sentence can be replaced by the verb usage of its direct object noun and the meaning of the sentence does not change, that verb is regarded as a light verb and the candidate is an LVC. Each example is annotated by two annotators and We only accept examples where both annotators agree on positive or negative. We generate a total of $1,039$ positive examples and $1,123$ negative examples. Among all these positive examples, there are 760 distinctive LVC phrases and 911 distinctive verb phrases with the pattern "*verb + noun object*" among negative examples. The generated data set therefore gives the classifier the 52.2% chance baseline if the classifier always votes the majority class in the data set.

4.2 Evaluation Metrics

For each experiment, we evaluate the performance with three sets of metrics. We first report the standard accuracy on the test data set. Since accuracy is argued not to be a sufficient measure of the evaluation of a binary classifier (Fazly et al., 2009) and some previous works also report F1 values for the positive classes, we therefore choose to report the precision, recall and F1 value for both positive and negative classes.

		True Class +	True Class -
Predicted Class	+	**tp**	**fp**
	-	**fn**	**tn**

Table 1: Confusion matrix to define *true positive (tp)*, *true negative (tn)*, *false positive (fp)* and *false negative (fn)*.

[5]We do not count those nouns ending with *er* and *ist*

[6]http://cogcomp.cs.illinois.edu/~ytu/test/LVCmain.html

Based on the classic confusion matrix as shown in Table 1, we calculate the precision and recall for the positive class in equation 1:

$$P^{+} = \frac{tp}{tp + fp} \qquad R^{+} = \frac{tp}{tp + fn} \qquad (1)$$

And similarly, we use equation 2 for negative class. And the F1 value is the harmonic mean of the precision and recall of each class.

$$P^{-} = \frac{tn}{tn + fn} \qquad R^{-} = \frac{tn}{tn + fp} \qquad (2)$$

4.3 Experiments with Contextual Features

In our experiments, We aim to build a high performance LVC classifier as well as to analyze the interaction between contextual and statistical features. We randomly sample 90% sentences for training and the rest for testing. Our chance baseline is 52.2%, which is the percentage of our majority class in the data set. As shown in Table 2, the classifier reaches an 86.3% accuracy using all contextual features described in previous section 3.2. Interestingly, we observe that adding other statistical features actually hurts the performance. The classifier can effectively learn when trained with discrete contextual features.

Label	Precision	Recall	F1
+	86.486	84.211	85.333
-	86.154	88.189	87.160
Accuracy	**86.307**		
Chance Baseline	52.2		

Table 2: By using all our contextual features, our classifier achieves overall 86.307% accuracy.

In order to examine the effectiveness of each individual feature, we conduct an ablation analysis and experiment to use only one of them each time. It is shown in Table 3 that *LV-NounObj* is found to be the most effective contextural feature since it boosts the baseline system up the most, an significant increase of 31.6%.

We then start from this most effective feature, *LV-NounObj* and add one feature each step to observe the change of the system accuracy. The results are listed in Table 4. Other significant features are features within the candidate LVCs themselves such as *Determiner*, *Noun Object* and *Levin's Class* related

Features Baseline (chance)	Accuracy 52.2	Diff(%)
LV-NounObj	83.817	**+31.6**
Noun Object	79.253	+27.1
Determiner	72.614	+20.4
Levin's Class	69.295	+17.1
posBefore	53.112	+0.9
posAfter	51.037	-1.1

Table 3: Using only one feature each time. *LV-NounObj* is the most effective feature. Performance gain is associated with a plus sign and otherwise a negative sign.

to the object noun. This observation agrees with previous research that the acceptance of LVCs is closely correlated to the linguistic properties of their components. The part of speech of the word after the phrase seems to have negative effect on the performance. However, experiments show that without this feature, the overall performance decreases.

Features Baseline (chance)	Accuracy 52.2	Diff(%)
+ LV-NounObj	83.817	*+31.6*
+ Noun Object	84.232	*+0.4*
+ Levin's Class	84.647	*+0.4*
+ posBefore	84.647	0.0
+ posAfter	83.817	-0.8
+ Determiner	86.307	*+2.5*

Table 4: Ablation analysis for contextual features. Each feature is added incrementally at each step. Performance gain is associated with a plus sign otherwise a negative sign.

4.4 Experiments with Statistical Features

When using statistical features, instead of directly using the value, we discretize each value to a binary feature. On the one hand, our experiments show that this way of transformation achieves the best performance. On the other hand, the transformation plays an analogical role as a kernel function which maps one dimensional non-linear separable examples into an infinite or high dimensional space to render the data linearly separable.

In these experiments, we use only numerical features described in section 3.1. And it is interesting to observe that those features achieve very similar

Label	Precision	Recall	F1
+	86.481	85.088	86.463
-	86.719	87.402	87.059
Accuracy	**86.307**		

Table 5: Best performance achieved with statistical features. Comparing to Table 2, the performance is similar to that trained with all contextual features.

Features BaseLine (chance)	Accuracy 52.2	Diff(%)
+ Cpmi	83.402	**+31.2**
+ Deverbal v/n Ratio	85.892	+2.5
+ Phrase Size	86.307	+0.4

Table 6: Ablation analysis for statistical features. Each feature is added incrementally at each step. Performance gain is associated with a plus sign.

performance as the contextual features as shown in Table 5.

To validate that the similar performance is not incidental. We then separate our data into 10-fold training and testing sets and learn independently from each fold of these ten split. Figure 1, which shows the comparison of accuracies for each data fold, indicates the comparable results for each fold of the data. Therefore, we conclude that the similar effect achieved by training with these two groups of features is not accidental.

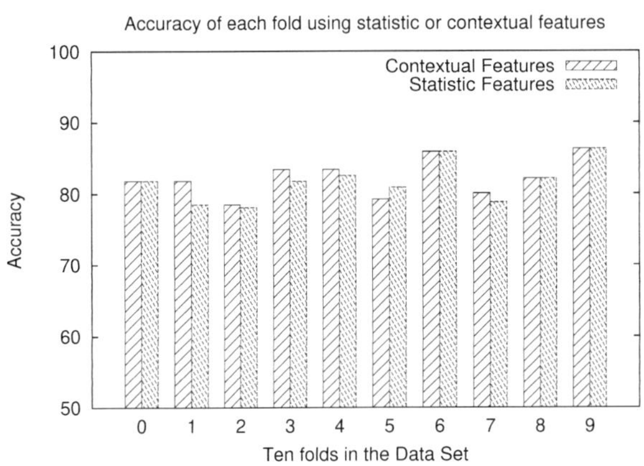

Figure 1: Classifier Accuracy of each fold of all 10 fold testing data, trained with groups of statistical features and contextual features separately. The similar height of each histogram indicates the similar performance over each data separation and the similarity is not incidental.

We also conduct an ablation analysis with statistical features. Similar to the ablation analyses for contextual features, we first find that the most effective statistical feature is *Cpmi*, the collocational based point-wise mutual information. Then we add one feature at each step and show the increasing performance in Table 6. *Cpmi* is shown to be a good indicator for LVCs and this observation agrees with many previous works on the effectiveness of point-wise mutual information in MWE identification tasks.

4.5 Interaction between Contextual and Statistical Features

Experiments from our previous sections show that two types of features which are cosmetically different actually achieve similar performance. In the experiments described in this section, we intend to do further analysis to identify further the relations between them.

4.5.1 Situation when they are similar

Our ablation analysis shows that *Cpmi* and *LV-NounObj* features are the most two effective features since they boost the baseline performance up more than 30%. We then train the classifier with them together and observe that the classifier exhibits similar performance as the one trained with them independently as shown in Table 7. This result indicates that these two types of features actually provide similar knowledge to the system and therefore combining them together does not provide any additional new information. This observation also agrees with the intuition that point-wise mutual information basically provides information on word collocations (Church and Hanks, 1990).

Feature	Accuracy	F1+	F1-
LV-NounObj	83.817	82.028	85.283
Cpmi	83.402	81.481	84.962
Cpmi+LV-NounObj	83.817	82.028	85.283

Table 7: The classifier achieves similar performance trained jointly with *Cpmi* and *LV-NounObj* features, comparing with the performance trained independently.

4.5.2 Situation when they are different

Token-based LVC identification is a difficult task on the basis of surface structures since they always exhibit identical surface properties. However, candidate LVCs with identical surface structures in both positive and negative examples provide an ideal test bed for the functionality of local contextual features. For example, consider again these two aforementioned sentences which are repeated here for reference:

1. He *had a look* of childish bewilderment on his face.
2. I've arranged for you to *have a look* at his file in our library.

The system trained only with statistic features cannot distinguish these two examples since their type-based statistical features are exactly the same. However, the classifier trained with local contextual features is expected to perform better since it contains feature information from surrounding words. To verify our hypothesis, we extract all examples in our data set which have this property and then select same number of positive and negative examples from them to formulate our test set. We then train out classifier with the rest of the data, independently with contextual features and statistical features. As shown in Table 8, the experiment results validate our hypothesis and show that the classifier trained with contextual features performs significantly better than the one trained with statistical features. The overall lower system results also indicate that indeed the test set with all ambiguous examples is a much harder test set.

One final observation is the extremely low F1 value for negative class and relatively good performance for positive class when trained with only statistical features. This may be explained by the fact that statistical features have stronger bias toward predicting examples as positive and can be used as an unsupervised metric to acquire real LVCs in corpora.

Classifier	Accuracy	F1+	F1-
Contextual	**68.519**	75.362	56.410
Statistical	51.852	88.976	27.778
Diff (%)	+16.7	-13.6	+28.3

Table 8: Classifier trained with local contextual features is more robust and significantly better than the one trained with statistical features when the test data set consists of all ambiguous examples.

5 Conclusion and Further Research

In this paper, we propose an in-depth case study on LVC recognition, in which we build a supervised learning system for automatically identifying LVCs in context. Our learning system achieves an 86.3% accuracy with a baseline (chance) performance of 52.2% when trained with groups of either contextual or statistical features. In addition, we exploit in detail the interaction of these two groups of contextual and statistical features and show that the system trained with these two types of cosmetically different features actually reaches similar performance in our learning framework. However, when it comes to the situation where the surface structures of candidate LVCs are identical, the system trained with contextual features which include information on surrounding words provides better and more robust performance.

In this study, we also construct a balanced benchmark dataset with 2,162 sentences from BNC for token-based classification of English LVCs. And this data set is publicly available and is also a useful computational resource for research on MWEs in general.

There are many aspects for further research of the current study. One direction for further improvement would be to include more long-distance features, such as parse tree path, to test the sensitivity of the LVC classifier to those features and to examine more extensively the combination of the contextual and statistical features. Another direction would be to adapt our system to other MWE types and to test if the analysis on contextual and statistical features in this study also applies to other MWEs.

Acknowledgments

The authors would like to thank all annotators who annotated the data via the web interface and four annonymous reviewers for their valuable comments. The research in this paper was supported by the Multimodal Information Access & Synthesis Center at

UIUC, part of CCICADA, a DHS Science and Technology Center of Excellence.

References

L. Barrett and A. Davis. 2003. Diagnostics for determing compatibility in english support verb nominalization pairs. In *Proceedings of CICLing-2003*, pages 85–90.

A. Burchardt, K. Erk, A. Frank, A. Kowalski, S. Pado, and M. Pinkal. 2009. Using framenet for semantic analysis of german: annotation, representation and automation. In Hans Boas, editor, *Multilingual FrameNets in Computational Lexicography: methods and applications*, pages 209–244. Mouton de Gruyter.

M. Butt. 2003. The light verb jungle. In *Harvard Working Paper in Linguistics*, volume 9, pages 1–49.

C. Chang and C. Lin, 2001. *LIBSVM: a library for support vector machines*. Software available at http://www.csie.ntu.edu.tw/~cjlin/libsvm.

E. Charniak and M. Johnson. 2005. Coarse-to-fine n-best parsing and maxent discriminative reranking. In *Proceedings of ACL-2005*.

K. Church and P. Hanks. 1990. Word association norms, mutual information, and lexicography. *Computational Linguistics*, 16(1), March.

K. Church, W. Gale, P. Hanks, and D. Hindle. 1991. Using statistics in lexical analysis. In *Lexical Acquisition: Exploiting On-Line Resources to Build a Lexicon*, pages 115–164. Erlbaum.

P. Cook, A. Fazly, and S. Stevenson. 2007. Pulling their weight: Exploiting syntactic forms for the automatic identification of idiomatic expressions in context. In *Proceedings of the Workshop on A Broader Perspective on Multiword Expressions*, pages 41–48, Prague, Czech Republic, June. Association for Computational Linguistics.

A. Fazly and S. Stevenson. 2006. Automatically constructing a lexicon of verb phrase idiomatic combinations. In *Proceedings of EACL-2006*.

A. Fazly and S. Stevenson. 2007. Distinguishing subtypes of multiword expressions using linguistically-motivated statistical measures. In *Proceedings of the Workshop on A Broader Perspective on Multiword Expressions*, pages 9–16, Prague, Czech Republic, June.

A. Fazly, R. North, and S. Stevenson. 2005. Automatically distinguishing literal and figurative usages of highly polysemous verbs. In *Proceedings of the ACL-SIGLEX Workshop on Deep Lexical Acquisition*, pages 38–47, Ann Arbor, Michigan, June. Association for Computational Linguistics.

A. Fazly, P. Cook, and S. Stevenson. 2009. Unsupervised type and token identification of idiomatic expression. *Comutational Linguistics*.

C. Fellbaum, editor. 1998. *WordNet: An Electronic Lexical Database*. MIT Press.

O. Jespersen. 1965. *A Modern English Grammar on Historical Principles, Part VI, Morphology*. Aeorge Allen and Unwin Ltd.

G. Katz and E. Giesbrecht. 2006. Automatic identification of non-compositional multi-word expressions using latent semantic analysis. In *Proceedings of the Workshop on Multiword Expressions: Identifying and Exploiting Underlying Properties*, pages 12–19.

K. Kearns. 2002. Light verbs in english. In *http://www.ling.canterbury.ac.nz/documents*.

B. Levin. 1993. *English Verb Classes and Alternations, A Preliminary Investigation*. University of Chicago Press.

A. Meyers, C. Macleod, R. Yangarber, R. Grishman, L. Barrett, and R. Reeves. 1998. Using nomlex to produce nominalization patterns for information extraction. In *Proceedings of COLING-ACL98 Workshop:the Computational Treatment of Nominals*.

R. North. 2005. Computational measures of the acceptability of light verb constructions. University of Toronto, Master Thesis.

N. Rizzolo and D. Roth. 2010. Learning based java for rapid development of nlp systems. In *Proceedings of the International Conference on Language Resources and Evaluation (LREC)*.

I. Sag, T. Baldwin, F. Bond, and A. Copestake. 2002. Multiword expressions: A pain in the neck for nlp. In *In Proc. of the 3rd International Conference on Intelligent Text Processing and Computational Linguistics (CICLing-2002*, pages 1–15.

T. Samardžić and P. Merlo. 2010. Cross-lingual variation of light verb constructions: Using parallel corpora and automatic alignment for linguistic research. In *Proceedings of the 2010 Workshop on NLP and Linguistics: Finding the Common Ground*, pages 52–60, Uppsala, Sweden, July.

S. Stevenson, A. Fazly, and R. North. 2004. Statistical measures of the semi-productivity of light verb constructions. In *Proceedings of ACL-04 workshop on Multiword Expressions: Integrating Processing*, pages 1–8.

Y. Tan, M. Kan, and H. Cui. 2006. Extending corpus-based identification of light verb constructions using a supervised learning framework. In *Proceedings of EACL-06 workshop on Multi-word-expressions in a multilingual context*, pages 49–56.

S. Venkatapathy and A. Joshi. 2005. Measuring the relative compositionality of verb-noun (v-n) collocations by integrating features. In *Proceedings of HLT and EMNLP05*, pages 899–906.

Two Types of Korean Light Verb Constructions in a Typed Feature Structure Grammar

Juwon Lee
Department of Linguistics, The University of Texas at Austin
juwonlee@utexas.edu

Abstract

In this paper, I present a lexical representation of the light verb *ha* 'do' used in two types of Korean *light verb constructions* (LVCs). These two types of the constructions have the typical theoretical and implementation problems as *multiword expressions* (MWEs): lexical proliferation of the possible light verb senses in the lexicon, potential overgeneration of ill-formed LVCs, and the semantic compositionality issue. Adopting and adapting the idea of qualia structure (Pustejovsky, 1991) into a typed-feature structure grammar (Copestake, 1993; Copestake, 2002; Sag et al., 2003), I suggest that some Korean common nouns have their associated predicate information in their lexical entries (e.g., the predicate meaning *cook* is included in the lexical entry of the common noun *pap* 'rice'). Thus such common nouns provide an appropriate predicate meaning to the light verb. The lexical constraints on the light verb and common nouns, and relevant phrase structure rules allow me to capture the generalizations and idiosyncrasies regarding LVCs in a systematic way.

1 Two Types of LVCs

A particular type of Korean LVCs, exemplified in (1), has been much studied (Chae, 1996, 2002; Choi and Wechsler, 2001; Kim et al., 2004; Kim et al., 2007, inter alia, and similar Japanese examples in Miyagawa, 1989; Matsumoto, 1996; Yokota, 2005, among others):

(1)a. ku-ka [swuhak-ul **kongpwu-lul**]
he-Nom math-Acc study-Acc
ha-yess-ta.[1]
do-Pst-Dec
'He *studied* mathematics.'

b. ku-ka [Mary-wa **tayhwa-lul**] **ha**-yess-ta.
he-Nom Mary-with talk-Acc do-Pst-Dec
'He *talked* with Mary.'

In (1a), the light verb *ha-yess-ta* 'do-Pst-Dec' requires as its complement the *verbal noun* (VN) phrase, *swuhak-ul kongpwu-lul* 'math-Acc study-Acc', and thus the types of LVCs in (1) are called VN-LVC in this paper, but see different syntactic analyses in Choi and Wechsler, 2001; Kim et al., 2004. Although the light verbs are the syntactic heads of the VN-LVCs, the core meanings of the sentences come from the verbal nouns. The mixed properties of VN in VN-LVC (that is, a VN can assign verbal cases to its arguments, but at the same time it can be modified by an adjective) have attracted much research on VN-LVCs (Grimshaw and Mester, 1988 on Japanese; Cho and Sells, 1991; Manning, 1993; Choi and Wechsler, 2001; Kim et al., 2007, among others).

However, there are many other usages of the Korean light verb *ha* 'do', which are almost ignored in the literature. In this paper, I investigate the two frequently-used, but less-studied types of Korean LVCs.

In the first type of the LVCs, the light verb requires a phrase headed by a *common noun* (CN) as its object (so, it is named CN-LVC here):

(2)a. ku-ka **pap-ul** **ha**-yess-ta.
he-Nom rice-Acc do-Pst-Dec
'He *cooked*/**ate* the rice (result product).'

b. ku-ka **khephi-lul/*mwul-ul** **ha**-yess-ta.
he-Nom coffee-Acc/water-Acc do-Pst-Dec
'He *brewed /drank* the coffee/*water.'

In (2), we can see that the meaning of the light verb is determined by the object as with the VN-LVCs in (1).[2] Almost every VN seems possible to

[1] Abbreviations: Nom = Nominative, Acc = Accusative, Pst = Past, Dec = Declarative, Pass = Passive, Que = Question, Comp = Complementizer, Top = Topicalization, Rel = Relative marker

[2] Similar examples in English (Pustejovsky, 1991):

appear as the object in a VN-LVC. However, not every common noun can be the object of a CN-LVC.

The questions that naturally arise are 1) how to represent the light verbs of the CN-LVCs in the lexicon, and 2) how to formally and efficiently describe the way the predicate meanings (e.g., *brew* and *drink*) are derived from the objects (e.g., *khephi-lul* 'coffee-Acc').

If we treat CN-LVCs as words-with-spaces, then they suffer from a lexical proliferation in describing all possible meanings of the light verb expressions (e.g., *do_drink_coffee*, *do_brew_coffee*, *do_drink_tea*, *do_brew_tea*, etc.) (see Sag et al., 2002). On the other hand, a fully compositional analysis would overgenerate (e.g licensing **mwul-ul ha-yess-ta* 'water-Acc do-Pst-Dec' in (2b)) and would not be able to explain the problem of the semantic compositionality (that is, exactly where and how does the predicate meaning of the light verb phrase in a CN-LVC come from?) (see Sag et al., 2002). These problems of the CN-LVCs are not properly treated yet.

English LVCs have almost the same problems as the Korean CN-LVCs: idiosyncrasies on which light verb combines with a given noun (Abeille, 1988) (e.g., *make a mistake, give a demo*). A fully compositional account, on the other hand, would be unable to block alternative light verb combinations (e.g., **give a mistake*, **make a demo*) (see Sag et al., 2002).

Moreover, in Korean *serial verb constructions* (SVCs) the situation gets more complicated:

(3)a. ku-ka **pap-ul** **hay** **mek**-ess-ta.
he-Nom rice-Acc do eat-Pst-Dec
'He *cooked* the rice and *ate* it.'
b. ku-ka **khephi-lul*mwul-ul/** **hay**
he-Nom coffee-Acc/ water-Acc do
masi-ess-ta.
drink-Pst-Dec
'He *brewed/*drank* the coffee and *drank* it.'

---

i) Mary **finished** the cigarette.
ii) Mary **finished** her beer.
iii) John **finished** the book.

The exact meaning of the verb is determined by the object: *finish smoking* for i), *finish drinking* for ii) and *finish writing* for iii). The verb, however, has also its own meaning: *finishing* X. So, in this case, the verb seems to be an intermediate type between light and heavy verbs.

In (3), the specific meanings of the light verbs depend on the common noun objects, which is parallel with the CN-LVCs. The difference, however, is that there is more restriction on the appropriate choice from the associated predicate(s) for the determination of the light verb meaning: e.g., only *brew* (creation sense) is allowed in (3b). I return to this semantic restriction in Section 3. The type of the constructions in (3) is called *serial verb-light verb construction* (SV-LVC) in this paper.

SV-LVCs have the same problems as CN-LVCs, including lexical proliferation of every possible senses of the serial light verb expressions with the words-with-spaces approach, the potential overgeneration, and the question of semantic compositionality.

These issues of the Korean LVCs as MWEs are crucial problems in *natural language processing* (NLP) like the disambiguation problems (see Sag et al., 2002). The goal of this paper is to solve the problems and to present an efficient formal account for CN- and SV-LVCs that is suitable for applications to linguistically precise NLP.

2 Grammatical Properties of CN-LVCs

CN-LVCs are very productive: the light verb *ha*- 'do' can combine with many (but not all) different common nouns to constitute CN-LVCs. The basic semantic and syntactic properties of CN-LVCs are discussed below.

2.1 Semantic Constraints of CN-LVCs

As is already illustrated in (2), there are two kinds of idiosyncratic restrictions on CN-LVCs. The first one is about what common noun can appear as the object in a CN-LVC:

(4)a. ku-ka **pap-ul/*khwukhi-lul** **ha**-yess-ta.
he-Nom rice-Acc/*cookie-Acc do-Pst-Dec
'He *cooked* the rice/(int.) *baked* the cookie.'
b. ku-ka **khemphwuthe-lul/*kaysanki-lul**
he-Nom computer-Acc/*calculator-Acc
ha-yess-ta.
do-Pst-Dec
'He *used* the computer/*calculator.'

The examples in (4) show that only certain food products or machines can occur as the objects in the CN-LVCs. The loan word *khwukhi-lul* 'cookie-

Acc' in (4a) is not allowed, but other loan words, such as *khephi-lul* 'coffee-Acc' in (2b) and *khemphwuthe-lul* 'computer-Acc' in (4b), are fine. There seems to be no natural semantic class of common nouns that can appear in CN-LVCs, which leads me to attribute the idiosyncratic property to the individual common nouns.

The second idiosyncratic property is about what predicate is associated with what common noun. For instance, in (4a) the CN-LVC has only one reading, 'He *cooked* the rice', not other interpretations like 'He *ate* the rice,' although 'cook' and 'eat' are (at least semantically and maybe also statistically) plausible candidates for the associated predicates of the common noun *pap* 'rice'. Lapata (2001) uses a large corpus to acquire the meanings of polysemous adjectives (e.g., *fast*). However, such corpus findings only tell us the possible interpretations, but not impossible interpretations.

It seems intuitive that common nouns have such information about their related predicates since without a specific predicate given, we can normally guess what predicate might come after a common noun object in an incomplete sentence (at least in Korean whose word order is SOV) (see similar combinatoric information related with Korean VN of VN-LVCs in Cho and Sells, 1991 and Japanese VN in Manning, 1993).

In short, only some common nouns have such information about certain related predicates. Pustejovsky (1991) refers to this kind of relation as *cospecification*: i.e. like verb can select for its argument type, an argument also can select its associated predicates. The associated predicate information is included in the qualia structure of a lexical item (Pustejovsky, 1991). Among the four basic roles in qualia structure, the telic role has values about purpose and function of the object (e.g., *read* for *novel*), and the agentive role has values on factors involved in the origin or "bringing about" of an object (e.g., *write* for *novel*).

Building on the qualia structure, I propose that Korean common nouns have dual semantic components, the first of which is the meaning of the common noun itself, and second of which is the qualia structure. Details of the semantic feature structures of such common nouns are introduced in Section 5.

2.2 Syntactic Constraints of CN-LVCs

The CN-LVCs allow internal adverb modification:

(5)a. ku-ka pap-ul **ppalli** **ha**-yess-ta.
he-Nom rice-Acc quickly do-Pst-Dec
'He *quickly cooked* the rice.'
b. ku-ka khemphwuthe-lul **ppalli** **ha**-yess-ta.
he-Nom computer-Acc quickly do-Pst-Dec
'He *quickly used* the computer.'

So, the CN-LVCs are like Syntactically-Flexible Expressions (see Sag et al., 2002). I treat the CN-LVCs as a normal transitive verb phrase construction (generated by the general head-complement phrase rule) in syntax.

Since the light verb *ha* 'do' is syntactically a transitive verb, the passive counterparts of the CN-LVCs are predicted to be generated. However, only (4a) allows its passive:

(6)a. ku-eyuyhay **pap-i** **toy**-ess-ta.
he-by rice-Nom do.Pass-Pst-Dec
'The *rice* (product, not raw material) *was cooked* by him.'
b. *ku-eyuyhay **khemphwuthe-ka**
he-by computer-Nom
toy-ess-ta.
do.Pass-Pst-Dec

The passive light verb *toy* has the *become* meaning (i.e. creation sense). The associated predicate of *pap* 'rice' is *cook* (an agentive role predicate). Thus in (6a) *toy* is compatible with *be cooked*, which is also a "bringing about" predicate, but in the passive form. However, *khemphuthe* 'computer' has as its associated predicate *use* (a telic role predicate) and its passive form *be used* is also a telic role predicate. So, the creation meaning of *toy* is not compatble with the common noun subject *khemphwuthe-ka* 'computer-Nom' in (6b).

In sum, CN-LVCs are basically transitive phrases, but they are constrained by the semantic relations between common nouns and the light verb.

3 Grammatical Properties of SV-LVCs

As CN-LVCs are highly productive, SV-LVCs are accordingly very productive. The two types of the LVCs have similar semantic and syntactic constraints. But SV-LVCs are more restricted.

3.1 Semantic Constraints of SV-LVCs

As noted in (3), there are lexical constraints on the meanings of SV-LVCs. Consider (7):

(7)a. ku-ka **pap-ul** **hay** **ponay**-ess-ta.
he-Nom rice-Acc do send-Pst-Dec
(lit.) 'He *cooked* the rice and *sent* it (to me).'
b. ku-ka **khephi-lul** **hay** **ponay**-ess-ta.
he-Nom coffee-Acc do send-Pst-Dec
(lit.) 'He *brew* the coffee and *sent* it (to me).'

Since the common noun *pap* 'rice' has only one associated predicate, *cook* as shown in (2a), (7a) has only one reading. Although *khephi* 'coffee' has two associated predicates, *drink* and *brew* as evidenced in (2b), (7b) also has only one interpretation with *brewed* (the reading that he drank the coffee and sent it somewhere is implausible). Here, two hypotheses on the interpretations are possible: 1) any associated predicate that is plausible and available is chosen for the V1 light verb meaning, or 2) the V1 light verb meaning must be a creation (that is, an agentive role predicate).

The second hypothesis predicts that if a common noun has only a telic role predicate whose meaning is plausible in an SV-LVC, then the SV-LVC must be ill-formed. This is confirmed below:

(8) *ku-ka **khemphwuthe-lul** **hay**
he-Nom computer-Acc do
ponay-ess-ta.
send-Pst-Dec

The common noun *khemphuthe* 'computer' has the associated predicate *use*. The meaning of the telic role is plausible before the *sending* relation. So, the ungrammaticality of (8) rejects the first hypothesis.

Thus I suggest that certain common nouns have certain associated predicates information, and then in an SV-LVC, an available predicate of *bringing about* meaning must be chosen as the meaning of the V1 light verb *hay* in the construction. If such a predicate is not available, then the SV-LVC is ill-formed. Also, I have already illustrated that the agentive role predicate of a common noun is required for the generation of the passive CN-LVCs like (6a). Then how about passive SV-LVCs? I discuss this question in the following section.

3.2 Syntactic Constraints of SV-LVCs

First, adverbs can modify the serial verbs in the SV-LVCs:

(9)a. ku-ka pap-ul **ppalli** **hay** **mek**-ess-ta.
he-Nom rice-Acc quickly do eat-Pst-Dec
'He *quickly cooked* the rice and *ate* it.'
b. ku-ka khephi-lul **ppalli** **hay**
he-Nom coffee-Acc quickly do
masi-ess-ta.
drink-Pst-Dec
'He *quickly brew* the coffee and *drank* it.'

SV-LVCs are also categorized into Syntactically-Flexible Expressions. However, unlike CN-LVCs, the serial verbs (e.g., *hay mek-ess-ta* 'do eat-Pst-Dec') are complex predicates that need a special phrase (like (23) in Section 5).

As predicted, a common noun must have an agentive role predicate to license a well-formed passive SV-LVC. In other words, only if an SV-LVC is allowed, its passive SV-LVC is licensed:

(10)a. pap-i/khephi-ka **toy-e**
rice-Nom/coffee-Nom do.Pass-Comp
ponay-e **ci**-ess-ta.
send-Comp Pass-Pst-Dec
(lit.) 'The rice *was cooked* and *sent* (to me).'
(lit.) 'The coffee *was brewed* and *sent* (to me).'
b. *khemphwuthe-ka **toy-e**
computer-Nom do.Pass-Comp
ponay-e **ci**-ess-ta.
send-Comp Pass-Pst-Dec

Just like the passive CN-LVCs, the exact meaning of *toy* depends on the common noun subject.

So, SV-LVCs are complex predicate structures in syntax, but they are also constrained by the semantics of common nouns and the light verb.

4 Pragmatic Factors

If a rich context is given, some ill-formed LVCs can be saved:

(11)a. ku-ka ***chayk-ul** **ha**-yess-ta.
he-Nom book-Acc do-Pst-Dec
b. ku-ka sayngil **senmwul-lo** **chayk-ul**
he-Nom birthday present-as book-Acc
ha-yess-ta.

do-Pst-Dec
'he *gave* a book as a birthday *present*.'

The telic role of *senmwul* 'present' is *give* and this telic role seems to be passed to the object *chayk-ul* 'book-Acc' in (11b).

The grammaticality depends on what sense of a word is used in the sentence:

(12)a. *ku-ka **haksayng**-ul **ha**-yess-ta.
he-Nom student-Acc do-Pst-Decl
b. nwu-ka **haksayng** **ha**-lay?
who-Nom student do-Que?
'Who told you to *be* a student?'
(from the Korean TV show, *Hot Brothers*)

The ill-formed CN-LVC in (12a) can be saved in a special context where *haksayng-ul* 'student-Acc' is interpreted as a student role of a play (then the telic role *play* for the light verb), or in a colloquial context like (12b). Being a student (or lawyer, teacher, doctor, etc.) means that the person *performs* (telic role) the tasks of the position.

The object of the light verb can be implicit:

(13) **ce** **ken** twu-ko kan-ta. ne **hay**.
that thing leave-and go-Dec. you do.
'Let me leave that thing for you. You *have* it.'
(from the Korean movie, *Hello Ghost*)

The common noun object *ce ken* 'that thing' of the light verb is dropped from the second sentence of (13). The associated predicate of the common noun object is linked to the light verb across the sentence boundary. The abandonment of the possession of *that thing* seems to enforce the light verb to have the meaning of *have*. Such verbs as *write*, *cook*, *build* are related with physical creations, but *buy*, *have*, *possess* are related with relational creations.

Leaving the detailed formal analysis of the pragmatic factors for future research, I focus on the representations of the semantic and syntactic constraints.

5 Typed-feature Structure Grammar

In this section, I present the formal analyses of the CN- and SV-LVCs in a typed-feature structure system (Copestake, 2002) based on the framework of the Head-driven Phrase Structure Grammar (Pollard and Sag, 1994; Sag et al., 2003).

5.1 Type Hierarchy of Korean

First, I adopt the following type hierarchy of the KPSG (Korean Phrase Structure Grammar) (Kim, 2004; Kim et al., 2004):

(14) Type hierarchy of linguistic expressions[3]:

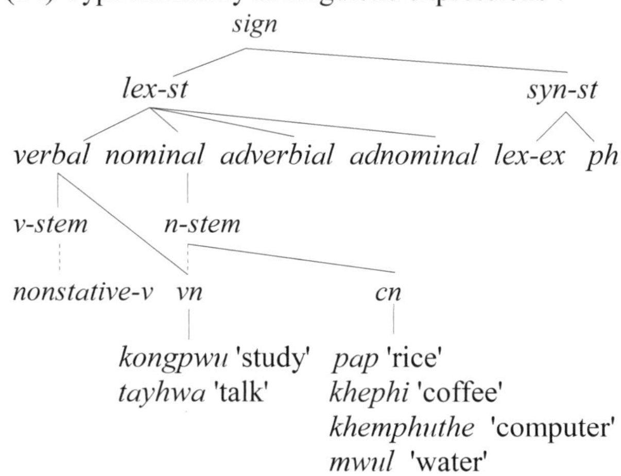

The type *vn* has the mixed properties inherited from its supertypes, *verbal* and *n-stem* (see Malouf, 1998, 2000; Choi and Wechsler, 2001). The type *cn* also inherits its constraints from its supertypes: for instance, nominal properties from the type *n-stem* (see Kim et al., 2004).

Briscoe et al. (1990) and Copestake (1993) illustrate some lexical entries with the qualia structure following Pustejovsky and Aniek (1988), Pustejovsky (1989, 1991). For example, *autobiography* has its associated predicates, *write* (the value of the agentive role) and *read* (the value of the telic role). They are represented in the lexical entry of *autobiography*.

I declare that Korean common nouns have both the RESTR(ICTION) for normal semantics and the QUALIA-ST(RUCTURE), which in turn has the AGENTIVE and TELIC attributes, adopting the basic idea from Pustejovsky (1991) and adapting the feature structure from Copestake (1993). Moreover, I posit the QUALIA attribute whose value is the sum of the values of the AGENTIVE and TELIC. Based on this feature structure, I propose the following representations of the Korean common nouns:

[3] The dashed line here means that there are intermediate types between the types that are connected with it.

(15)a. Lexical entry for *pap* 'rice'

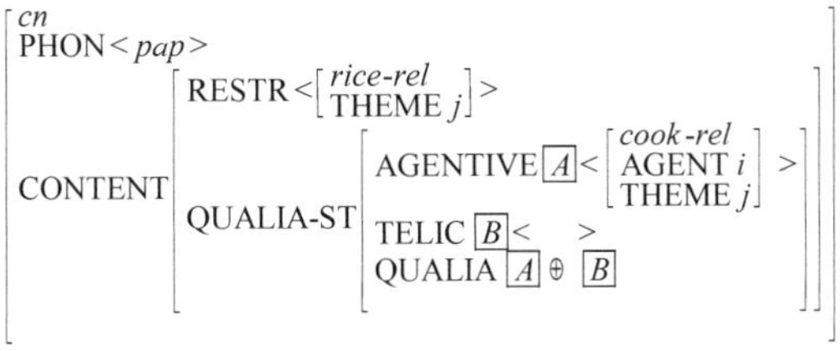

b. Lexical entry for *khephi* 'coffee'

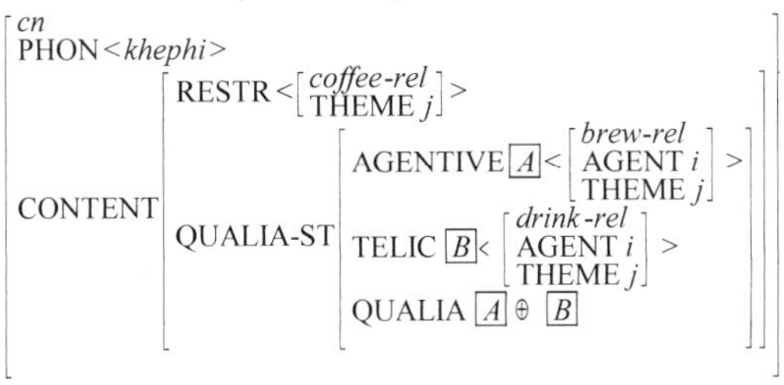

c. Lexical entry for *khemphuthe* 'computer'

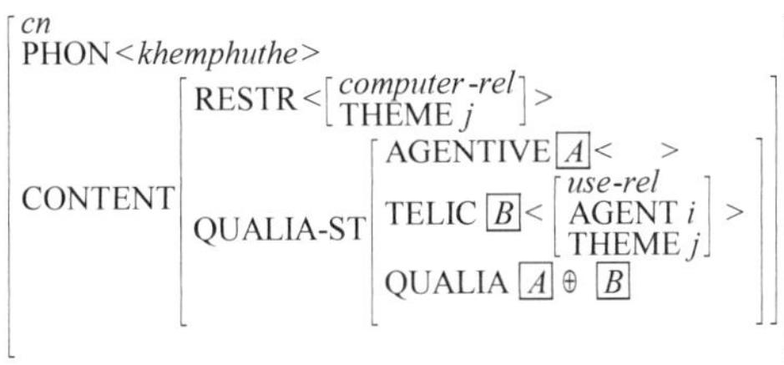

d. Lexical entry for *mwul* 'water'

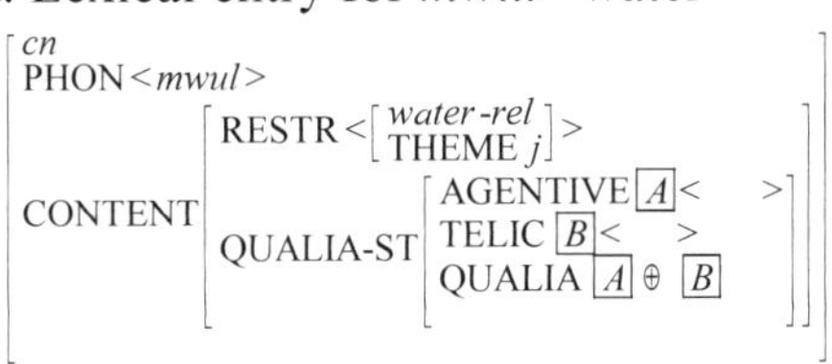

In (15a), *pap* 'rice' has its associated predicate *cook* as the value of the AGENTIVE, but it has no value for the TELIC. Then, the QUALIA list must have only one value *cook*. In (15b), *khephi* 'coffee' has *brew* and *drink* in the AGENTIVE and TELIC, respectively. Then its QUALIA list includes *brew* as its first value, and *drink* as its second value. In (15c), the associated predicate of *khemphuthe* 'computer' is *use* (a telic role), which is then the sole value for the QUALIA. In (15d), *mwul* 'water' is declared not to have any value for the AGENTIVE or TELIC. Thus, it does not have a value for the QUALIA, either.

Now as for the relevant verbs of the LVCs, I divide the type *tr*(*ansitive*)-*v*(*erb*) in the following type hierarchy further into *tr*(*ansitive*)-*light*-*v*(*erb*) and *tr*(*ansitive*)-*nonlight*-*v*(*erb*):

(16) Type hierarchy of non-stative verbs:

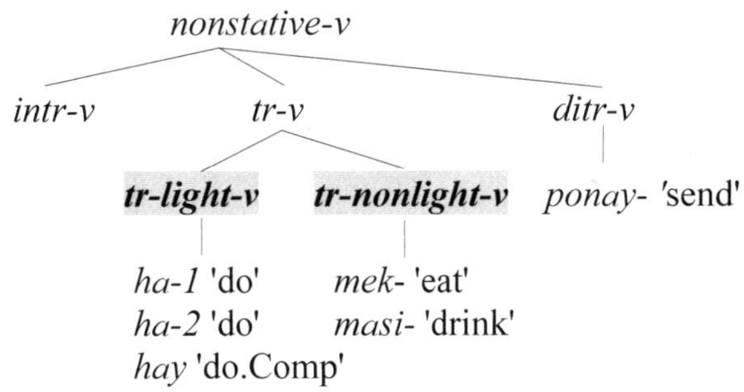

Three lexical entries of the light verbs are under the type *tr-light-v*. They have different properties that can be captured by the following constraints:

(17)a. Constraints on the type, *nonstative-v*:

nonstative - v : [LITE /-]

b. Constraints on the type, *tr-light-v*:

tr- light- v: [LITE +]

c. Constraints on *ha-1*:

d. Constraints on *ha-2*:

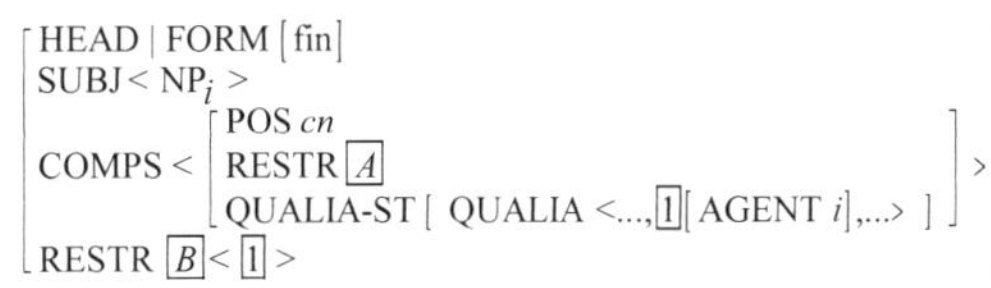

e. Constraints on *hay*:

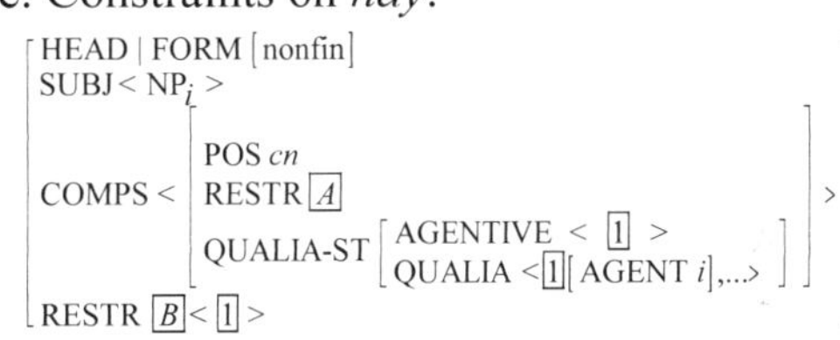

In (17a), the defeasible feature [LITE /–] is posited on *nonstative-v*. So, all the subtypes inherit [LITE /–], except for *tr-light-v* since in (17b), the defeasible feature [LITE /–] is overridden by the specification of the feature value. Only two types *tr-nonlight-v* and *ditr-v* can appear as V2 in SV-LVCs, and now they can be referred to as verbs that take at least one complement and have the feature [LITE /–]. In (17c), the RESTR of *ha-1* is claimed to be empty list since the light verb that combines with a verbal noun phrase does not seem to contribute a core meaning to the VP as shown in (1). However, in (17d), the meaning of *ha-2* is linked to a value of the QUALIA of the common noun object. This constraint of *ha-2* will guarantee that in CN-LVCs, any value in the QUALIA (e.g., *drink* or *brew* of *coffee*) can be chosen for the specific meaning of the light verb. Another effect of the constraint is preventing the common nouns like *mwul* 'water' from appearing in a CN-LVC since such common nouns are declared to not have a value for the QUALIA as in (15d). Finally, in (17e), a separate lexical entry for the V1 light verb *hay* is posited due to the different properties from *ha-2*: e.g., *ha-2* can get a tense, so is *finite* but *hay* cannot receive a tense, so is *nonfinite*. In addition, the meaning of the V1 light verb *hay* is identical only with the Agentive value of the common noun object.

5.2 Head-Complement Combinations

Along with the lexical entries, syntactic rules are needed. In the type hierarchy of (14), the relevant subtypes of *syn-st* are represented below (cf. Kim, 2004; Kim et al., 2004; Kim, 2010). I added the new type *hd-sv-lv-ex* as a subtype of *hd-lex-ex*:

(18)

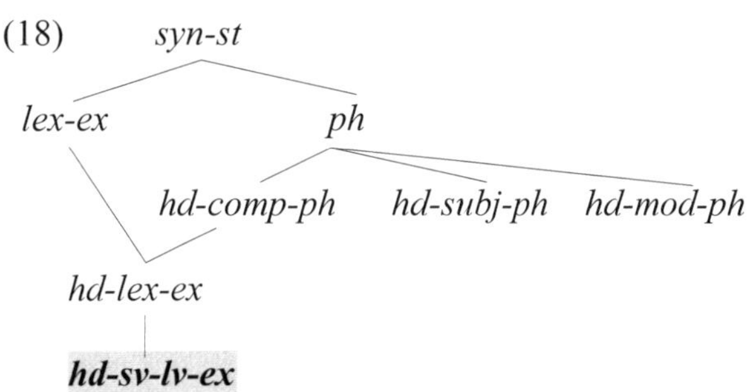

The following general head-complement rule (see Sag et al., 2003; Kim 2004) generates a phrase of the type *hd-comp-ph*:

(19) Head-Complement Rule:

$$\text{XP}[\textit{hd-comp-ph}] \rightarrow \boxed{1}, \mathbf{H}\left[\text{COMPS} <\ldots,\boxed{1},\ldots>\right]$$

In addition to the syntactic head-complement phrase rule, the following semantic constraints on the structures are defined (Sag et al., 2003):

(20)Semantic Compositionality Principle:

In any well-formed phrase structure, the mother's RESTR value is the sum of the RESTR values of the daughters.

Equipped with the Head-Complement Rule and the Semantic Compositionality Principle, VPs in CN- and VN-LVCs can be generated:

(21)a. Head-Complement Phrase of CN-LVC:

$$\begin{bmatrix} \textit{hd-comp-ph} \\ \text{COMPS} < \ > \\ \text{RESTR } \boxed{A} \oplus \boxed{B} \end{bmatrix} \rightarrow \boxed{1}, \mathbf{H} \begin{bmatrix} \textit{tr-light-v} \\ \text{HEAD} \mid \text{FORM [fin]} \\ \text{COMPS} < \boxed{1} \begin{bmatrix} \text{POS } \textit{cn} \\ \text{RESTR } \boxed{A} \\ \text{QUALIA-ST} \left[\text{QUALIA} <\ldots,\boxed{2},\ldots> \right] \end{bmatrix} > \\ \text{RESTR } \boxed{B} < \boxed{2} > \end{bmatrix}$$

b. Head-Complement Phrase of VN-LVC:

$$\begin{bmatrix} \textit{hd-comp-ph} \\ \text{COMPS} < \ > \\ \text{RESTR } \boxed{A} \end{bmatrix} \rightarrow \boxed{1}, \mathbf{H} \begin{bmatrix} \textit{tr-light-v} \\ \text{COMPS} < \boxed{1} \begin{bmatrix} \text{POS } \textit{vn} \\ \text{RESTR } \boxed{A} \end{bmatrix} > \\ \text{RESTR} < \ > \end{bmatrix}$$

In (21), according to the Semantic Compositionality Principle, the VP in the CN- or VN-LVC has the sum of the RESTR values of the object and the light verb.

In the type hierarchy (18), the type *hd-comp-ph* has the subtype which is constrained by the following Head-Lex Rule (cf. Kim et al., 2004):

(22) Head-Lex Rule:

$$\begin{bmatrix} \textit{hd-lex-ex} \\ \text{COMPS } \boxed{A} \oplus \boxed{B} \end{bmatrix} \rightarrow \boxed{1} \begin{bmatrix} \text{LEX} + \\ \text{COMPS } \boxed{A} \end{bmatrix}, \mathbf{H} \left[\text{COMPS} < \boxed{1} > \oplus \boxed{B} \right]$$

In (22), the head element combines with its complement, whose complements and some of head's complements are passed up to the resulting *hd-lex-ex*.

The constraints on *hd-lex-ex* are inherited to its subtype *hd-sv-lv-ex*. This phrase type is responsible for the combinations of the serial light verb expressions in SV-LVCs:

(23) Head-SV-LV-EX Rule:

$$\begin{bmatrix} \textit{hd-sv-lv-ex} \\ \text{SUBJ} < \boxed{1} > \\ \text{COMPS } \boxed{B} \oplus \boxed{D} \\ \text{RESTR } \boxed{C} \oplus \boxed{E} \end{bmatrix} \rightarrow \boxed{2} \begin{bmatrix} \textit{tr-light-v} \\ \text{HEAD} \mid \text{FORM [nonfin]} \\ \text{SUBJ} < \boxed{1} > \\ \text{COMPS } \boxed{B} < \boxed{4} \begin{bmatrix} \text{RESTR } \boxed{A} \\ \text{AGENTIVE} < \boxed{5} > \\ \text{QUALIA} < \boxed{5},\ldots> \end{bmatrix} > \\ \text{RESTR } \boxed{C} < \boxed{5} > \end{bmatrix},$$

$$\mathbf{H} \begin{bmatrix} \textit{nonstative-v} \\ \text{LITE } /- \\ \text{SUBJ} < \boxed{1} > \\ \text{COMPS} < \boxed{2} > \oplus \boxed{D} \\ \text{RESTR } \boxed{E} \end{bmatrix}$$

In (23), the nonstative verbs with [LITE /–] (which are not intransitive) like *eat*, *drink* and *send* require the V1 light verb *hay* as its complement.

Now, the serial light verb expressions (e.g., *hay mek-ess-ta* 'do.Pass eat-Pst-Dec') can be licensed with the Head-SV-LV-EX Rule and the Semantic Compositionality Principle. Furthermore, (23) can rule out the ill-formed SV-LVCs like (8) **ku-ka khemphwuthe-lul* [*hay ponay-ess-ta*] 'he-Nom computer-Acc do send-Pst-Dec' because *hd-sv-lv-ex* requires a common noun object that has an AGENTIVE value, but *khemphwuthe* 'computer' has no value for it. The implausible interpretation '#He *drank* the coffee and sent it (to me)' for (7b) [*ku-ka khephi-lul* [*hay ponay-ess-ta*]] is also blocked since the meaning of the light verb *hay* is linked only to the AGENTIVE value of the object.

The following feature structures show the analyses of the VP [*pap-ul ha-yess-ta*] 'rice-Acc do-Pst-Dec' in the CN-LVC (2a) and the VP [*pap-ul* [*hay mek-ess-ta*]] 'rice-Acc do eat-Pst-Dec' in the SV-LVC (3a):

(24) [*pap-ul ha-yess-ta*]:

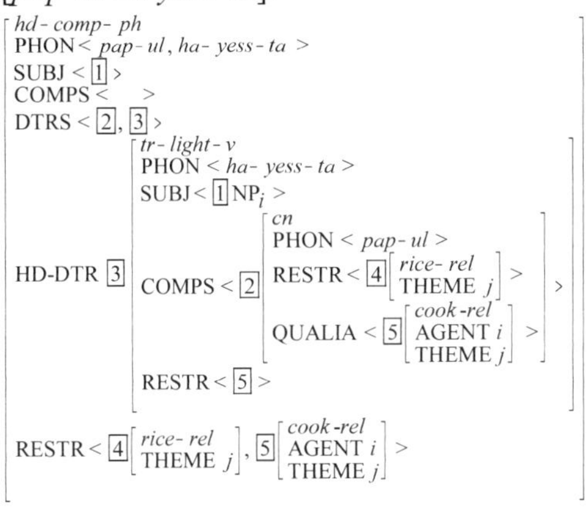

(25) [*pap-ul* [*hay mek-ess-ta*]]:

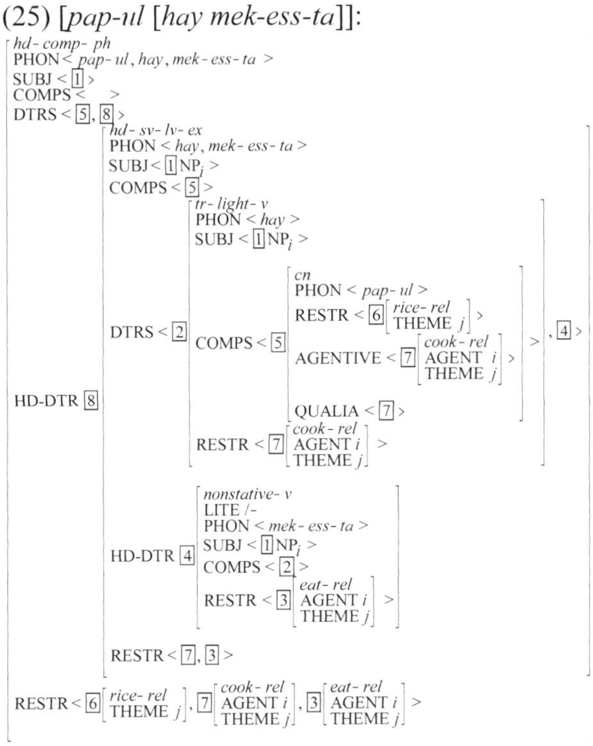

6 Conclusion and Future Work

The light verb *ha-2* 'do' is used for CN-LVCs and *hay* is used for SV-LVCs. I also proposed that certain Korean common nouns have their associated predicate meanings in the QUALIA-ST. These lexical constrains on individual common nouns and the light verbs, and the relevant phrase structure rules account for the regular and idiosyncratic properties of the two LVC constructions in a systematic manner.

I believe that the current analysis can possibly extend to the corresponding LVCs in other languages (especially Japanese since it has similar LVCs with the light verb *suru* 'do' and allows serial verbs). The VPs with the verbs *start* or *finish* (see Pustejovsky, 1991) can also be accounted for using the qualia structure: e.g., *pap-ul sicakhata/ kkuthnayta* 'start/ finish (**cooking**/*eating) the rice', *khephi-lul sicakhata/ kkuthnayta* 'start/ finish (**brewing**/*drinking) the coffee', *khemphuthe-lul sicakhata/ kkuthnayta* 'start/ finish (*building/**using**) the computer' and **mwul-ul sicakhata/ kkuthnayta*. My temporary hypothesis for such the VPs is that there is the ranking (that is, agentive role > telic role), so the agentive role of a common noun object is used first with *start* or *finish*, but if agentive role is not available, then telic role is used, and if even telic role is not available, then it is ungrammatical.

More comprehensive research with corpus data and the actual implementation of the analysis in the *Linguistic Knowledge Building* (LKB) system (Copestake, 2002) are left for future work.

Acknowledgment

I would like to thank Katrin Erk for her helpful comments. John Beavers and Stephen Wechsler have also greatly helped me to improve the paper. The insightful comments of the anonymous reviewers are gratefully acknowledged as well.

References

Anne Abeille. 1988. Light verb constructions and extraction out of NP in a tree adjoining grammar. In *Papers of the 24th Regional Meeting of the Chicago Linguistics Society*.

Ann Copestake. 1993. Defaults in Lexical Representation. In *Inheritance, Defaults, and the Lexicon*, 223-245. Cambridge: Cambridge University

Press.

Ann Copestake. 2002. *Implementing Typed Feature Structure Grammars*. Stanford, CA: CSLI Publications.

Briscoe Ted, Ann Copestake and Bran Boguraev. 1990. Enjoy the paper: Lexical semantics via lexicology. In *Proceedings of the 13th International Conference on Computational Linguistics*, 42-47.

Carl J. Pollard and Ivan A. Sag. 1994. *Head-Driven Phrase Structure Grammar*. Stanford, CA: CSLI Publications.

Christoper D. Manning. 1993. Analyzing the Verbal Noun: Internal and External Constraints. *Japanese/Korean Linguistics* 3, 236-253.

Hee-Rahk Chae. 1996. Light Verb Constructions and Structural Ambiguity. In *Proceedings of PACLIC 11: Language, Information and Computation,* 99-107.

Hee-Rahk Chae. 2002. Predicate Nominals and Light-er Verbs in Korean: An Indexed PSG Approach. In *Proceedings of the 2002 LSK International Summer Conference* I, 115-125.

Incheol Choi and Stephen Wechsler. 2001. Mixed Categories and Argument Transfer in the Korean Light Verb Construction. In *Proceedings of the 8th International Conference on Head-Driven Phrase Structure Grammar,* 103-120.

Ivan A. Sag, Timothy Baldwin, Francis Bond, Ann A. Copestake, and Dan Flickenger. 2002. Multiword expressions: A pain in the neck for nlp. In *Proceedings of the 3rd International Conference on Computational Linguistics and Intelligent Text Processing*, 1-15.

Ivan A. Sag, Thomas Washow, and Emily M. Bender. 2003. *Syntactic Theory: A Formal Introduction*, 2nd edition. Stanford, CA: CSLI Publications.

James Pustejovsky and Peter G. Aniek. 1988. On the Semantic Interpretation of Nominals. In *Proceedings of COLING-1988*, 518-523.

James Pustejovsky. 1989. Current Issues in Computational Lexical Semantics. In *Proceedings of 4th European ACL,* xvii-xxv.

James Pustejovsky. 1991. The Generative Lexicon. *Computational Linguistics* 17(4), 409-441.

Jane Grimshaw and Armin Mester. 1988. Light Verbs and Theta-Marking. *Linguistic Inquiry* 19, 205-232.

Jong-Bok Kim. 2004. *Korean Phrase Structure Grammar*. Seoul: Hankook Munhwasa.

Jong-Bok Kim, Jaehyung Yang, and Incheol Choi. 2004. Capturing and Parsing the Mixed Properties of Light Verb Constructions in a Typed Structure Grammar. In *Proceedings of PACLIC* 18, 81-92.

Jong-Bok Kim, Kyung-Sup Kim, and Jaehyung Yang. 2007. Structural Ambiguities in the Light Verb Constructions: Lexical Relatedness and Divergence. *The Linguistic Association of Korea Journal* 15(2), 207-231.

Jong-Bok Kim. 2010. Argument Composition in Korean Serial Verb Constructions. *Studies in Modern Grammar* 61, 1-24.

Kenji Yokota. 2005. The structure and meaning of Japanese light verbs. *Language Sciences* 27, 247-280.

Maria Lapata. 2001. A Corpus-based Account of Regular Polysemy: The Case of Context-sensitive Adjectives. In P*roceedings of the 2nd Meeting of the North American Chapter of the Association for Computational Linguistics*, 63-70.

Robert Malouf. 1998. *Mixed Categories in the Hierarchical Lexicon*, Linguistics Department, Stanford University, Ph.D. Dissertation.

Robert Malouf. 2000. *Mixed Categories in the Hierarchical Lexicon: Studies in constraint-based lexicalism*. Stanford, CA: CSLI Publications.

Shigeru Miyagawa. 1989. Light Verbs and the Ergative Hypothesis. *Linguistic Inquiry* 20, 659-88.

Yo Matsumoto. 1996. A Syntactic Account of Light Verb Phenomena in Japanese. *Journal of East Asian Linguistics* 5(2), 107-149.

Young-Mee Yu Cho and Peter Sells. 1991. A lexical account of phrasal suffixes in Korean. ms. Stanford University.

MWU-aware Part-of-Speech Tagging with a CRF model and lexical resources

Matthieu Constant
Université Paris-Est, LIGM
5, bd Descartes - Champs/Marne
77454 Marne-la-Vallée cedex 2, France
mconstan@univ-mlv.fr

Anthony Sigogne
Université Paris-Est, LIGM
5, bd Descartes - Champs/Marne
77454 Marne-la-Vallée cedex 2, France
sigogne@univ-mlv.fr

Abstract

This paper describes a new part-of-speech tagger including multiword unit (MWU) identification. It is based on a Conditional Random Field model integrating language-independent features, as well as features computed from external lexical resources. It was implemented in a finite-state framework composed of a preliminary finite-state lexical analysis and a CRF decoding using weighted finite-state transducer composition. We showed that our tagger reaches state-of-the-art results for French in the standard evaluation conditions (i.e. each multiword unit is already merged in a single token). The evaluation of the tagger integrating MWU recognition clearly shows the interest of incorporating features based on MWU resources.

1 Introduction

Part-of-speech (POS) tagging reaches excellent results thanks to powerful discriminative multi-feature models such as Conditional Random Fields (Lafferty et al., 2001), Support Vector Machine (Giménez and Márquez, 2004), Maximum Entropy (Ratnaparkhi, 1996). Some studies like (Denis and Sagot, 2009) have shown that featuring these models by means of external morphosyntactic resources still improves accuracy. Nevertheless, current taggers rarely take multiword units such as compound words into account, whereas they form very frequent lexical units with strong syntactic and semantic particularities (Sag et al., 2001; Copestake et al., 2002) and their identification is crucial for applications requiring semantic processing. Indeed, taggers are generally evaluated on perfectly tokenized texts where multiword units (MWU) have already been identified.

Our paper presents a MWU-aware POS tagger (i.e. a POS tagger including MWU recognition[1]). It is based on a Conditional Random Field (CRF) model that integrates features computed from large-coverage morphosyntactic lexicons and fine-grained MWU resources. We implemented it in a finite-state framework composed of a finite-state lexical analyzer and a CRF-decoder using weighted transducer composition.

In section 2, we will first describe statistical tagging based on CRF. Then, in section 3, we will show how to adapt the tagging models in order to also identify multiword unit. Next, section 4 will present the finite-state framework used to implement the tagger. Section 5 will focus on the description of our working corpus and the set of lexical resources used. In section 6, we then evaluate our tagger on French.

2 Statistical POS tagging with Linear Chain Conditional Random Fields

Linear chain Conditional Ramdom Fields (CRF) are discriminative probabilistic models introduced by (Lafferty et al., 2001) for sequential labelling. Given an input sequence $x = (x_1, x_2, ..., x_N)$ and an out-

[1] This strategy somewhat resembles the popular approach of joint word segmentation and part-of-speech tagging for Chinese, e.g. (Zhang and Clark, 2008). Moreover, other similar experiments on the same task for French are reported in (Constant et al., 2011).

put sequence of labels $y = (y_1, y_2, ..., y_N)$, the model is defined as follows:

$$P_\lambda(y|x) = \frac{1}{Z(x)} \cdot \sum_t^N \sum_k^K \lambda_k . f_k(t, y_t, y_{t-1}, x)$$

where $Z(x)$ is a normalization factor depending on x. It is based on K features each of them being defined by a binary function f_k depending on the current position t in x, the current label y_t, the preceding one y_{t-1} and the whole input sequence x. The feature is activated if a given configuration between t, y_t, y_{t-1} and x is satisfied (i.e. $f_k(t, y_t, y_{t-1}, x) = 1$). Each feature f_k is associated with a weight λ_k. The weights are the parameters of the model. They are estimated during the training process by maximizing the conditional loglikelihood on a set of examples already labeled (training data). The decoding procedure consists in labelling a new input sequence with respect to the model, by maximizing $P(y|x)$ (or minimizing $-logP(y|x)$). There exist dynamic programming procedures such as Viterbi algorithm in order to efficiently explore all labelling possibilities.

Features are defined by combining different properties of the tokens in the input sequence and the labels at the current position and the preceding one. Properties of tokens can be either binary or textual: e.g. token contains a digit, token is capitalized (binary property), form of the token, suffix of size 2 of the token (textual property). Most taggers exclusively use language-independent properties – e.g. (Ratnaparkhi, 1996; Toutanova et al., 2003; Giménez and Márquez, 2004; Tsuruoka et al., 2009). It is also possible to integrate language-dependant properties computed from an external broad-coverage morphosyntactic lexicon, that are POS tags found in the lexicon for the given token (e.g. (Denis and Sagot, 2009)). It is of great interest to deal with unknown words[2] as most of them are covered by the lexicon, and to somewhat filter the list of candidate tags for each token. We therefore added to our system a language-dependent property: a token is associated with the concatenation of its possible tags in an external lexicon, i.e. the ambibuity class of the token (AC).

[2]Unknown words are words that did not occur in the training data.

In practice, we can divide features f_k in two families: while *unigram features* (u_k) do not depend on the preceding tag, i.e. $f_k(t, y_t, y_{t-1}, x) = u_k(t, y_t, x)$, *bigram features* ($b_k$) depend on both current and preceding tags, i.e. $f_k(t, y_t, y_{t-1}, x) = b_k(t, y_t, y_{t-1}, x)$. In our practical case, bigrams exlusively depends on the two tags, i.e. they are independent from the input sequence and the current position like in the Hidden Markov Model (HMM)[3]. Unigram features can be sub-divided into internal and contextual ones. Internal features provide solely characteristics of the current token w_0: lexical form (i.e. its character sequence), lowercase form, suffice, prefix, ambiguity classes in the external lexicons, whether it contains a hyphen, a digit, whether it is capitalized, all capitalized, multiword. Contextual features indicate characteristics of the surroundings of the current token: token unigrams at relative positions -2,-1,+1 and +2 (w_{-2}, w_{-1}, w_{+1},w_{+2}); token bigrams $w_{-1}w_0$, w_0w_{+1} and $w_{-1}w_{+1}$; ambiguity classes at relative positions -2,-1,+1 and +2 (AC_{-2}, AC_{-1}, AC_{+1},AC_{+2}). The different feature templates used in our tagger are given in table 2.

Internal unigram features	
$w_0 = X$	$\&t_0 = T$
Lowercase form of $w_0 = L$	$\&t_0 = T$
Prefix of $w_0 = P$ with $\|P\| < 5$	$\&t_0 = T$
Suffix of $w_0 = S$ with $\|S\| < 5$	$\&t_0 = T$
w_0 contains a hyphen	$\&t_0 = T$
w_0 contains a digit	$\&t_0 = T$
w_0 is capitalized	$\&t_0 = T$
w_0 is all capital	$\&t_0 = T$
w_0 is capitalized and BOS[4]	$\&t_0 = T$
w_0 is multiword	$\&t_0 = T$
Lexicon tags AC_0 of $w_0 = A$ & w_0 is multiword	$\&t_0 = T$
Contextual unigram features	
$w_i = X, i \in \{-2, -1, 1, 2\}$	$\&t_0 = T$
$w_i w_j = XY, (j, k) \in \{(-1, 0), (0, 1), (-1, 1)\}$	$\&t_0 = T$
$AC_i = A$ & w_i is multiword, $i \in \{-2, -1, 1, 2\}$	$\&t_0 = T$
Bigram features	
$t_{-1} = T'$	$\&t_0 = T$

Table 1: Feature templates

3 MWU-aware POS tagging

MWU-aware POS tagging consists in identifying and labelling lexical units including multiword ones.

[3]Hidden Markov Models of order n use strong independance assumptions: a word only depends on its corresponding tag, and a tag only depends on its n previous tags. In our case, n=1.

It is somewhat similar to segmentation tasks like chunking or Named Entity Recognition, that identify the limits of chunk or Named Entity segments and classify these segments. By using an `IOB`[5] scheme (Ramshaw and Marcus, 1995), this task is then equivalent to labelling simple tokens. Each token is labeled by a tag in the form `X+B` or `X+I`, where `X` is the POS labelling the lexical unit the token belongs to. Suffix `B` indicates that the token is at the beginning of the lexical unit. Suffix `I` indicates an internal position. Suffix `O` is useless as the end of a lexical unit corresponds to the beginning of another one (suffix `B`) or the end of a sentence. Such procedure therefore determines lexical unit limits, as well as their POS.

A simple approach is to relabel the training data in the `IOB` scheme and to train a new model with the same feature templates. With such method, most of multiword units present in the training corpus will be recognized as such in a new text. The main issue resides in the identification of unknown multiword units. It is well known that statistically inferring new multiword units from a rather small training corpus is very hard. Most studies in the field prefer finding methods to automatically extract, from very large corpus, multiword lexicons, e.g. (Dias, 2003; Caseli et al., 2010), to be integrated in Natural Language Processing tools.

In order to improve the number of new multiword units detected, it is necessary to plug the tagger to multiword resources (either manually built or automatically extracted). We incorporate new features computed from such resources. The resources that we use (cf. section 5) include three exploitable features. Each MWU encoded is obligatory assigned a part-of-speech, and optionally an internal surface structure and a semantic feature. For instance, the organization name *Banque de Chine* (Bank of China) is a proper noun (NPP) with the semantic feature ORG; the compound noun *pouvoir d'achat* (purchasing power) has a syntactic form `NPN` because it is composed of a noun (`N`), a preposition (`P`) and a noun (`N`). By applying these resources to texts, it is therefore possible to add four new properties for each token that belongs to a lexical multiword unit: the part-of-speech of the lexical multiword unit (`POS`), its internal structure (`STRUCT`), its semantic feature (`SEM`) and its relative position in the `IOB` scheme (`POSITION`). Table 2 shows the encoding of these properties in an example. The property extraction is performed by a longest-match context-free lookup in the resources. From these properties, we use 3 new unigram feature templates shown in table 3: (1) one combining the MWU part-of-speech with the relative position; (2) another one depending on the internal structure and the relative position and (3) a last one composed of the semantic feature.

FORM	POS	STRUCT	POSITION	SEM	*Translation*
un	-	-	O	-	*a*
gain	-	-	O	-	*gain*
de	-	-	O	-	*of*
pouvoir	NC	NPN	B	-	*purchasing*
d'	NC	NPN	I	-	
achat	NC	NPN	I	-	*power*
de	-	-	O	-	*of*
celles	-	-	O	-	*the ones*
de	-	-	O	-	*of*
la	-	-	O	-	*the*
Banque	NPP	-	B	ORG	*Bank*
de	NPP	-	I	ORG	*of*
Chine	NPP	-	I	ORG	*China*

Table 2: New token properties depending on Multiword resources

New internal unigram features	
$POS_0/POSITION_0$	$\&t_0 = T$
$STRUCT_0/POSITION_0$	$\&t_0 = T$
SEM_0	$\&t_0 = T$

Table 3: New features based on the MW resources

4 A Finite-state Framework

In this section, we describe how we implemented a unified Finite-State Framework for our MWU-aware POS tagger. It is organized in two separate classical stages: a preliminary resource-based lexical analyzer followed by a CRF-based decoder. The lexical analyzer outputs an acyclic finite-state transducer (noted `TFST`) representing candidate tagging sequences for a given input. The decoder is in charge of selecting the most probable one (i.e. the path in the `TFST` which has the best probability).

[5] I: Inside (segment); O: Outside (segment); B: Beginning (of segment)

4.1 Weighted finite-state transducers

Finite-state technology is a very powerful machinery for Natural Language Processing (Mohri, 1997; Kornai, 1999; Karttunen, 2001), and in particular for POS tagging, e.g. (Roche and Schabes, 1995). It is indeed very convenient because it has simple factorized representations and interesting well-defined mathematical operations. For instance, weighted finite-state transducers (WFST) are often used to represent probabilistic models such as Hidden Markov Models. In that case, they map input sequences into output sequences associated with weights following a probability semiring ($\mathbb{R}_+$,+,×, 0, 1) or a log semiring ($\mathbb{R} \cup \{-\infty, +\infty\}$,$\oplus_{log}$,+, $+\infty$, 0) for numerical stability[6]. A WFST is a finite-state automaton which each transition is composed of an input symbol, an output symbol and a weight. A path in a WFST is therefore a sequence of consecutive transitions of the WFST going from an initial state to a final state, i.e. it puts a binary relation between an input sequence and an output sequence with a weight that is the product of the weights of the path transitions in a probability semiring (the sum in the log semiring). Note that a finite-state transducer is a WFST with no weights. A very nice operation on WFSTs is composition (Salomaa and Soittola, 1978). Let T_1 be a WFST mapping an input sequence x into an output sequence y with a weight $w_1(x, y)$, and T_2 be another WFST mapping a sequence y into a sequence z with a weight $w_2(y, z)$. The composition of T_1 with T_2 results in a WFST T mapping x into z with a weight $w_1(x, y).w_2(y, z)$ in the probability semiring ($w_1(x, y) + w_2(y, z)$ in the log semiring).

4.2 Lexical analysis and decoding

The lexical analyzer is driven by lexical resources represented by finite-state transducers like in (Silberztein, 2000) (cf. section 5) and generates a `TFST` containing candidate analyses. Transitions of the `TFST` are labeled by a simple token (as input) and a POS tag (as output). This stage allows for reducing the global ambiguity of the input sentence in two different ways: (1) tag filtering, i.e. each token is only assigned its possible tags in the lexical resources; (2) segment filtering, i.e. we only keep lexical multiword units present in the resources. This implies the use of large-coverage and fine-grained lexical resources.

The decoding stage selects the most probable path in the `TFST`. This involves that the `TFST` should be weighted by CRF-based probabilities in order to apply a shortest path algorithm. Our weighing procedure consists in composing a WFST encoding the sentence unigram probabilities (unigram WFST) and a WFST encoding the bigram probabilities (bigram WFST). The two WFSTs are defined over the log semiring. The unigram WFST is computed from the `TFST`. Each transition corresponds to a (x_t,y_t) pair at a given position t in the sentence x. So each transition is weighted by summing the weights of the unigram features activated at this position. In our practical case, bigram features are independent from the sentence x. The bigram WFST can therefore be constructed once and for all for the whole tagging process, in the same way as for order-1 HMM *transition* diagrams (Nasr and Volanschi, 2005).

5 Linguistic resources

5.1 French TreeBank

The French Treebank (FTB) is a syntactically annotated corpus[7] of 569,039 tokens (Abeillé et al., 2003). Each token can be either a punctuation marker, a number, a simple word or a multiword unit. At the POS level, it uses a tagset of 14 categories and 34 sub-categories. This tagset has been optimized to 29 tags for syntactic parsing (Crabbé and Candito, 2008) and reused as a standard in a POS tagging task (Denis and Sagot, 2009). Below is a sample of the FTB version annotated in POS.

,	PONCT	*,*
soit	CC	*i.e.*
une	DET	*a*
augmentation	NC	*raise*
de	P	*of*
1_,_2	DET	*1_,_2*
%	NC	*%*
par_rapport_au	P+D	*compared with the*
mois	NC	*preceding*
précédent	ADJ	*month*

[6]A semiring $\mathbb{K}$ is a 5-tuple ($\mathbb{K}, \oplus, \otimes, \bar{0}, \bar{1}$) where the set $\mathbb{K}$ is equipped with two operations $\oplus$ and $\otimes$; $\bar{0}$ and $\bar{1}$ are their respective neutral elements. The log semiring is an image of the probability semiring via the $-log$ function.

[7]It is made of journalistic texts from *Le Monde* newspaper.

Multiword tokens encode multiword units of different types: compound words and named entities. Compound words mainly include nominals such as *acquis sociaux* (social benefits), verbs such as *faire face à* (to face) adverbials like *dans l' immédiat* (right now), prepositions such as *en dehors de* (beside). Some Named Entities are also encoded: organization names like *Société suisse de microélectronique et d' horlogerie*, family names like *Strauss-Kahn*, location names like *Afrique du Sud* (South Africa) or *New York*. For the purpose of our study, this corpus was divided in three parts: 80% for training (TRAIN), 10% for development (DEV) and 10% for testing (TEST).

5.2 Lexical resources

The lexical resources are composed of both morphosyntactic dictionaries and strongly lexicalized local grammars. Firstly, there are two general-language dictionaries of simple and multiword forms: DELA (Courtois, 1990; Courtois et al., 1997) and Lefff (Sagot, 2010). DELA has been developped by a team of linguists. Lefff has been automatically acquired and then manually validated. It also resulted from the merge of different lexical sources. In addition, we applied specific manually built lexicons: Prolex (Piton at al., 1999) containing toponyms ; others including organization names and first names (Martineau et al., 2009). Figures on these dictionaries are detailed in table 4.

Name	# simple forms	#MW forms
DELA	690,619	272,226
Lefff	553,140	26,311
Prolex	25,190	97,925
Organizations	772	587
First names	22,074	2,220

Table 4: Morphosynctatic dictionaries

This set of dictionaries is completed by a library of strongly lexicalized local grammars (Gross, 1997; Silberztein, 2000) that recognize different types of multiword units such as Named Entities (organization names, person names, location names, dates), locative prepositions, numerical determiners. A local grammar is a graph representing a recursive finite-state transducer, which recognizes sequences belonging to an algebraic language. Practically, they describe regular grammars and, as a consequence, can be compiled into equivalent finite-state transducers. We used a library of 211 graphs. We manually constructed from those available in the online library GraalWeb (Constant and Watrin, 2007).

5.3 Lexical resources vs. French Treebank

In this section, we compare the content of the resources described above with the encodings in the FTB-DEV corpus. We observed that around 97,4% of lexical units encoded in the corpus (excluding numbers and punctuation markers) are present in our lexical resources (in particular, 97% are in the dictionaries). While 5% of the tokens are unknown (i.e. not present in the training corpus), 1.5% of tokens are unknown and not present in the lexical resources, which shows that 70% of unknown words are covered by our lexical resources.

The segmentation task is mainly driven by the multiword resources. Therefore, they should match as much as possible with the multiword units encoded in the FTB. Nevertheless, this is practically very hard to achieve because the definition of MWU can never be the same between different people as there exist a continuum between compositional and non-compositional sequences. In our case, we observed that 75.5% of the multiword units in the FTB-DEV corpus are in the lexical resources (87.5% including training lexicon). This means that 12.5% of the multiword tokens are totally unknown and, as a consequence, will be hardly recognized. Another significant issue is that many multiword units present in our resources are not encoded in the FTB. For instance, many Named Entities like dates, person names, mail addresses, complex numbers are absent. By applying our lexical resources[8] in a longest-match context-free manner with the platform Unitex (Paumier, 2011), we manually observed that 30% of the multiword units found were not considered as such in the FTB-DEV corpus.

6 Experiments and Evaluation

We firstly evaluated our system for standard tagging without MWU segmentation and compare it with other available statistical taggers that we all trained on the FTB-TRAIN corpus. We tested the

[8]We excluded local grammars recognizing dates, person names and complex numbers.

well-known TreeTagger (Schmid, 1994) based on probabilistic decision trees, as well as TnT (Brants, 2000) implementing second-order Hidden Markov. We also compared our system with two existing discriminative taggers: SVMTool (Giménez and Márquez, 2004) based on Support Vector Models with language-independent features; MElt (Denis and Sagot, 2009) based on a Maximum Entropy model also incorporating language-dependent feature computed from an external lexicon. The lexicon used to train and test MElt included all lexical resources[9] described in section 5. For our CRF-based system, we trained two models with `CRF++`[10]: (a) `STD` using language-independent template features (i.e. excluding AC-based features); (b) `LEX` using all feature templates described in table 2. We note `CRF-STD` and `CRF-LEX` the two related taggers when no preliminary lexical analysis is performed; `CRF-STD+` and `CRF-LEX+` when a lexical analysis is performed. The lexical analysis in our experiment consists in assigning for each token its possible tags found in the lexical resources[11]. Tokens not found in the resources are assigned all possible tags in the tagset in order to ensure the system robustness. If no lexical analysis is applied, our system constructs a `TFST` representing all possible analyzes over the tagset. The results obtained on the TEST corpus are summed up in table 5. Column `ACC` indicates the tagger accuracy in percentage. We can observe that our system (`CRF-LEX+`) outperforms the other existing taggers, especially MElt whose authors claimed state-of-the-art results for French. We can notice the great interest of a lexical analysis as `CRF-STD+` reaches similar results as a MaxEnt model based on features from an external lexicon.

We then evaluated our MWU-aware tagger trained on the TRAIN corpus whose complex tokens have been decomposed in a sequence of simple tokens and relabeled in the IOB representation. We used three different sets of feature templates leading to three CRF models: `CRF-STD`, `CRF-LEX` and `CRF-MWE`. The two first ones (STD and LEX) use the same feature templates as in the previous experiment. MWE includes all feature templates decribed in sections 2 and 3. `CRF-MWE+` indicates that a preliminary lexical analysis is performed before applying `CRF-MWE` decoding. The lexical analysis is achieved by assigning all possible tags of simple tokens found in our lexical resources, as well as adding, in the `TFST`, new transitions corresponding to MWU segments found in the lexical resources. We compared the three models with a baseline and SVMTool that have been learnt on the same training corpus. The baseline is a simple context-free lookup in the training MW lexicon, after a standard CRF-based tagging with no MW segmentation. We evaluated each MWU-aware tagger on the decomposed TEST corpus and computed the f-score, combining precision and recall[12]. The results are synthesized in table 6. The `SEG` column shows the segmentation f-score solely taking into account the segment limits of the identified lexical unit. The `TAG` column also accounts for the label assigned. The first observation is that there is a general drop in the performances for all taggers, which is not a surprise as regards with the complexity of MWU recognition (97.7% for the best standard tagger vs. 94.4% for the best MWU-aware tagger). Clearly, MWU-aware taggers which models incorporate features based on external MWU resources outperform the others. Nevertheless, the scores for the identification and the tagging of the MWUs are still rather low: 91%-precision and 71% recall. We can also see that a preliminary lexical analysis slightly lower the scores, which is due to

Tagger	Model	ACC
TnT	HMM	96.3
TreeTagger	Decision trees	96.4
SVMTool	SVM	97.2
CRF-STD	CRF	97.4
MElt	MaxEnt	97.6
CRF-STD+	CRF	97.6
CRF-LEX	CRF	**97.7**
CRF-LEX+	CRF	**97.7**

Table 5: Comparison of different taggers for French

[9] Dictionaries were all put together, as well as with the result of the application of the local grammars on the corpus.

[10] CRF++ is an open-source toolkit to train and test CRF models (http://crfpp.sourceforge.net/). For training, we set the cutoff threshold for features to 2 and the C value to 1. We also used the L2 regularization algorithm.

[11] Practically, as the tagsets of the lexical resources and the FTB were different, we had to first map tags used in the dictionaries into tags belonging to the FTB tagset.

[12] f-score $f = \frac{2pr}{p+r}$ where p is precision and r is recall.

missing MWUs in the resources and is a side effect of missing encodings in the corpus.

Tagger	Model	TAG	SEG
Baseline	CRF	91.2	93.6
SVMTool	SVM	92.1	94.7
CRF-STD	CRF	93.7	95.8
CRF-LEX	CRF	93.9	95.9
CRF-MWE	CRF	**94.4**	**96.4**
CRF-MWE+	CRF	94.3	96.3

Table 6: Evaluation of MWU-aware tagging

With respect to the statistics given in section 5.3, it appears clearly that the evaluation of MWU-aware taggers is somewhat biased by the fact that the definition of the multiword units encoded in the FTB and the ones listed in our lexical resources are not exactly the same. Nevertheless, this evaluation that is the first in this context, brings new evidences on the importance of multiword unit resources for MWU-aware tagging.

7 Conclusions and Future Work

This paper presented a new part-of-speech tagger including multiword unit identification. It is based on a CRF model integrating language-independent features, as well as features computed from external lexical resources. It was implemented in a finite-state framework composed of a preliminary finite-state lexical analysis and a CRF decoding using weighted finite-state transducer composition. The tagger is freely available under the LGPL license[13]. It allows users to incorporate their own lexicons in order to easily integrate it in their own applications.

We showed that the tagger reaches state-of-the-art results for French in the standard evaluation environment (i.e. each multiword unit is already merged in a single token). The evaluation of the tagger integrating MWU recognition clearly shows the interest of incorporating features based on MWU resources. Nevertheless, as there exist some differences in the MWU definitions between the lexical resources and the working corpus, this first experiment requires further investigations. First of all, we could test our tagger by incorporating lexicons of MWU automatically extracted from large raw corpora in order to deal with low recall. We could as well combine the lexical analyzer with a Named Entity Recognizer. Another step would be to modify the annotations of the working corpus in order to cover all MWU types and to make it more homogeneous with our definition of MWU. Another future work would be to test semi-CRF models that are well-suited for segmentation tasks.

[13]http://igm.univ-mlv.fr/~mconstan/research/software

References

A. Abeillé, L. Clément and F. Toussenel. 2003. Building a treebank for French. in A. Abeillé (ed), *Treebanks*, Kluwer, Dordrecht.

T. Brants. 2000. TnT - A Statistical Part-of-Speech Tagger. *In Proceedings of the Sixth Applied Natural Language Processing Conference (ANLP 2000)*, 224–231.

H. Caseli, C. Ramisch, M. das Graas Volpe Nunes, A. Villavicencio. 2010. Alignment-based extraction of multiword expressions. *Language Resources and Evaluation*, Springer, vol. 44(1), 59–77.

M. Constant, I. Tellier, D. Duchier, Y. Dupont, A. Sigogne, S. Billot. 2011. Intégrer des connaissances linguistiques dans un CRF : application à l'apprentissage d'un segmenteur-étiqueteur du français. *In Actes de la Conférence sur le traitement automatique des langues naturelles (TALN'11)*.

M. Constant and P. Watrin. 2007. Networking Multiword Units. *In Proceedings of the 6th International Conference on Natural Language Processing (GoTAL'08)*, Lecture Notes in Artificial Intelligence, Springer-Verlag, vol. 5221: 120 – 125.

A. Copestake, F. Lambeau, A. Villavicencio, F. Bond, T. Baldwin, I. A. Sag and D. Flickinger. 2002. Multiword expressions: linguistic precision and reusability. *In Proceedings of the Third conference on Language Resources and Evaluation (LREC' 02)*, 1941 – 1947.

B. Courtois. 1990. *Un système de dictionnaires électroniques pour les mots simples du français.* Langue Française, vol. 87: 1941 – 1947.

B. Courtois, M. Garrigues, G. Gross, M. Gross, R. Jung, M. Mathieu-Colas, A. Monceaux, A. Poncet-Montange, M. Silberztein, R. Vivés. 1990. *Dictionnaire électronique DELAC : les mots composés binaires.* Technical report, LADL, University Paris 7, vol. 56.

B. Crabbé and M. -H. Candito. 2008. Expériences d'analyse syntaxique statistique du franais. *In Proceedings of Traitement des Langues Naturelles (TALN 2008)*.

P. Denis et B. Sagot. 2009. Coupling an annotated corpus and a morphosyntactic lexicon for state-of-the-art

POS tagging with less human effort. *In Proceedings of the 23rd Pacific Asia Conference on Language, Information and Computation (PACLIC 2009).*

G. Dias. 2003. Multiword Unit Hybrid Extraction. *In proceedings of the Workshop on Multiword Expressions of the 41st Annual Meeting of the Association of Computational Linguistics (ACL 2003)*, 41–49.

J. Giménez and L. Márquez. 2004. SVMTool: A general POS tagger generator based on Support Vector Machines. *In Proceedings of the 4th International Conference on Language Resources and Evaluation (LREC'04).*

M. Gross. 2007. The construction of local grammars. In E. Roche and Y. Schabes (eds.). *Finite-State Language Processing*. The MIT Press, Cambridge, Mass. 329–352

L. Karttunen. 2001. Applications of Finite-State Transducers in Natural Language Processing. *In proceedings of the 5th International Conference on Implementation and Application of Automata (CIAA 2000)*. Lecture Notes in Computer Science. vol. 2088, Springer, 34–46

A. Kornai (Ed.). 1999. *Extended Finite State Models of Language*. Cambridge University Press

J. Lafferty, A. McCallum, and F. Pereira. 2001. Conditional random Fields: Probabilistic models for segmenting and labeling sequence data. *In Proceedings of the Eighteenth International Conference on Machine Learning (ICML 2001)*, 282–289.

C. Martineau, T. Nakamura, L. Varga and Stavroula Voyatzi. 2009. Annotation et normalisation des entités nommées. *Arena Romanistica*. vol. 4:234–243.

M. Mohri 1997. *Finite-state transducers in language and speech processing*. Computational Linguistics 23 (2):269–311.

A. Nasr, A. Volanschi. 2005. Integrating a POS Tagger and a Chunker Implemented as Weighted Finite State Machines. *Finite-State Methods and Natural Language Processing*, Lecture Notes in Computer Science, vol. 4002, Springer 167–178.

S. Paumier. 2011. *Unitex 2.1 user manual*. http://igm.univ-mlv.fr/~unitex.

O. Piton, D. Maurel, C. Belleil. 1999. The Prolex Data Base : Toponyms and gentiles for NLP. *In proceedings of the Third International Workshop on Applications of Natural Language to Data Bases (NLDB'99)*, 233–237.

L. A. Ramshaw and M. P. Marcus. 1995. Text chunking using transformation-based learning. *In Proceedings of the 3rd Workshop on Very Large Corpora*, 88 – 94.

A. Ratnaparkhi. 1996. A maximum entropy model for part-of-speech tagging. *In Proceedings of the Conference on Empirical Methods in Natural Language Processing (EMNLP 1996)*, 133 – 142.

E. Roche, Y. Schabes. 1995. Deterministic part-of-speech tagging with finite-state transducers. *Computational Linguistics*, MIT Press, vol. 21(2), 227–253

I. A. Sag, T. Baldwin, F. Bond, A. Copestake, D. Flickinger. 2001. Multiword Expressions: A Pain in the Neck for NLP. *In Proceedings of the 3rd International Conference on Intelligent Text Processing and Computational Linguistics (CICLing-2002)*, 1–15

B. Sagot. 2010. The Lefff, a freely available, accurate and large-coverage lexicon for French. *In Proceedings of the 7th International Conference on Language Resources and Evaluation (LREC'10).*

A. Salomaa, M. Soittola. 1978. *Automata-Theoretic Aspects of Formal Power Series*. Springer-Verlag.

H. Schmid. 1994. Probabilistic Part-of-Speech Tagging Using Decision Trees. *Proceedings of International Conference on New Methods in Language Processing*.

M. Silberztein. 2000. INTEX: an FST toolbox. *Theoretical Computer Science*, vol. 231 (1): 33–46.

K. Toutanova, D. Klein, C. D. Manning, Y. Yoram Singer. 2003. Feature-rich part-of-speech tagging with a cyclic dependency network. *Proceedings of HLT-NAACL 2003*, 252 – 259.

Y. Tsuruoka, J. Tsujii, S. Ananiadou. 2009. Fast Full Parsing by Linear-Chain Conditional Random Fields. *Proceedings of the 12th Conference of the European Chapter of the Association for Computational Linguistics (EACL 2009)*, 790–798.

Y. Zhang, S. Clark. 2008. Joint Word Segmentation and POS Tagging Using a Single Perceptron. *Proceedings of ACL 2008*, 888 – 896.

The Web is not a PERSON, Berners-Lee is not an ORGANIZATION, and African-Americans are not LOCATIONS: An Analysis of the Performance of Named-Entity Recognition

Robert Krovetz
Lexical Research
Hillsborough, NJ 08844
rkrovetz@lexicalresearch.com

Paul Deane **Nitin Madnani**
Educational Testing Service
Princeton, NJ 08541
{pdeane,nmadnani}@ets.org

Abstract

Most work on evaluation of named-entity recognition has been done in the context of competitions, as a part of Information Extraction. There has been little work on any form of extrinsic evaluation, and how one tagger compares with another on the major classes: PERSON, ORGANIZATION, and LOCATION. We report on a comparison of three state-of-the-art named entity taggers: Stanford, LBJ, and IdentiFinder. The taggers were compared with respect to: 1) Agreement rate on the classification of entities by class, and 2) Percentage of ambiguous entities (belonging to more than one class) co-occurring in a document. We found that the agreement between the taggers ranged from 34% to 58%, depending on the class and that more than 40% of the globally ambiguous entities co-occur within the same document. We also propose a unit test based on the problems we encountered.

1 Introduction

Named-Entity Recognition (NER) has been an important task in Computational Linguistics for more than 15 years. The aim is to recognize and classify different types of entities in text. These might be people's names, or organizations, or locations, as well as dates, times, and currencies. Performance assessment is usually made in the context of Information Extraction, of which NER is generally a component. Competitions have been held from the earliest days of MUC (Message Understanding Conference), to the more recent shared tasks in CoNLL. Recent research has focused on non-English languages such as Spanish, Dutch, and German (Meulder et al., 2002; Carreras et al., 2003; Rossler, 2004), and on improving the performance of unsupervised learning methods (Nadeau et al., 2006; Elsner et al., 2009).

There are no well-established standards for evaluation of NER. Since criteria for membership in the classes can change from one competition to another, it is often not possible to compare performance directly. Moreover, since some of the systems in the competition may use proprietary software, the results in a competition might not be replicable by others in the community; however, this applies to the state of the art for most NLP applications rather than just NER.

Our work is motivated by a vocabulary assessment project in which we needed to identify multi-word expressions and determine their association with other words and phrases. However, we found that state-of-the-art software for named-entity recognition was not reliable; false positives and tagging inconsistencies significantly hindered our work. These results led us to examine the state-of-the-art in more detail.

The field of Information Extraction (IE) has been heavily influenced by the Information Retrieval (IR) community when it comes to evaluation of system performance. The use of Recall and Precision metrics for evaluating IE comes from the IR community. However, while the IR community regularly conducts a set of competitions and shared tasks using standardized test collections, the IE community does not. Furthermore, NER is just one component of an IE pipeline and any proposed improvements to this component must be evaluated by determining whether the performance of the overall IE pipeline has improved. However, most, if not all, NER evaluations and shared tasks only focus on intrinsic NER performance and ignore any form of extrinsic evaluation. One of the contributions of this paper is a freely available unit test based on the systematic problems we found with existing taggers.

2 Evaluation Methodology

We compared three state-of-the-art NER taggers: one from Stanford University (henceforth, Stanford tagger), one from the University of Illinois (henceforth, the LBJ tagger) and BBN IdentiFinder (henceforth, IdentiFinder).

The Stanford Tagger is based on Conditional Random Fields (Finkel et al., 2005). It was trained on 100 million words from the English Gigawords corpus. The LBJ Tagger is based on a regularized average perceptron (Ratinov and Roth, 2009). It was trained on a subset of the Reuters 1996 news corpus, a subset of the North American News Corpus, and a set of 20 web pages. The features for both these taggers are based on local context for a target word, orthographic features, label sequences, and distributional similarity. Both taggers include non-local features to ensure consistency in the tagging of identical tokens that are in close proximity. IdentiFinder is a state-of-the-art commercial NER tagger that uses Hidden Markov Models (HMMs) (Bikel et al., 1999).

Since we did not have gold standard annotations for any of the real-world data we evaluated on, we instead compared the three taggers along two dimensions:

- **Agreement on classification**. How well do the taggers work on the three most difficult classes: PERSON, ORGANIZATION, and LOCATION and, more importantly, to what extent does one tagger agree with another? What types of mistakes do they make systematically?[1]

- **Ambiguity in discourse**. Although entities can potentially have more than one entity classification, such as *Clinton* (PERSON or LOCATION), it would be surprising if they co-occurred in a single discourse unit such as a document. How frequently does each tagger produce multiple classifications for the same entity in a single document?

We first compared the two freely available, academic taggers (Stanford and LBJ) on a corpus of 425 million words that is used internally at the Educational Testing Service. Note that we could not compare these two taggers to IdentiFinder on this corpus since IdentiFinder is not available for public use without a license.

Next, we compared all three taggers on the American National Corpus. The American National Corpus (ANC) has recently released a copy which is tagged by IdentiFinder.[2] Since the ANC is a publicly available corpus, we tagged it using both the Stanford and LBJ taggers and could then compare all three taggers along the two intended dimensions. We found that the public corpus had many of the same problems as the ones we found with our internally used corpus. Some of these problems have been discussed before (Marrero et al., 2009) but not in sufficient detail.

The following section describes our evaluation of the Stanford and LBJ taggers on the internal ETS corpus. Section 4 describes a comparison of all three taggers on the American National Corpus. Section 5 describes the unit test we propose. In Section 6, we propose and discuss the viability of the "one named-entity tag per discourse" hypothesis. In Section 7, we highlight the problems we find during our comparisons and propose a methodology for improved intrinsic evaluation for NER. Finally, we conclude in Section 8.

3 Comparing Stanford and LBJ

In this section, we compare the two academic taggers in terms of classification agreement by class and discourse ambiguity on the ETS SourceFinder corpus, a heterogeneous corpus containing approximately 425 million words, and more than $270,000$

[1] Although one could draw a distinction between named entity identification and classification, we focus on the final output of the taggers, i.e., classified named entities.

[2] `http://www.anc.org/annotations.html`

Person		Organization		Location	
Stanford	**LBJ**	**Stanford**	**LBJ**	**Stanford**	**LBJ**
Shiloh	A.sub.1	RNA	Santa Barbara	Hebrew	The New Republic
Yale	What	Arnold	FIGURE	ASCII	DNA
Motown	Jurassic Park	NaCl	Number:	Tina	Mom
Le Monde	Auschwitz	AARGH	OMITTED	Jr.	Ph.D
Drosophila	T. Rex	Drosophila	Middle Ages	Drosophila	Drosophila

Table 1: A sampling of false positives for each class as tagged by the Stanford and LBJ taggers

	Common Entities	Percentage
Person	548,864	58%
Organization	249,888	34%
Location	102,332	37%

Table 2: Agreement rate by class between the Stanford and LBJ taggers

articles. The articles were extracted from a set of 60 different journals, newspapers and magazines focused on both literary and scientific topics.

Although Named Entity Recognition is reported in the literature to have an accuracy rate of 85-95% (Finkel et al., 2005; Ratinov and Roth, 2009), it was clear by inspection that both the Stanford and the LBJ tagger made a number of mistakes. The ETS corpus begins with an article about Tim Berners-Lee, the man who created the World Wide Web. At the beginning of the article, "Tim" as well as "Berners-Lee" are correctly tagged by the Stanford tagger as belonging to the PERSON class. But later in the same article, "Berners-Lee" is incorrectly tagged as ORGANIZATION. The LBJ tagger makes many mistakes as well, but they are not necessarily the same mistakes as the mistakes made by the Stanford tagger. For example, the LBJ tagger sometimes classifies "The Web" as a PERSON, and the Stanford tagger classifies "Italian" as a LOCATION.[3] Table 1 provides an anecdotal list of the "entities" that were misclassified by the two taggers.[4]

Both taggers produced about the same number of entities overall: 1.95 million for Stanford, and 1.8 million for LBJ. The agreement rate between the taggers is shown in Table 2. We find that the highest rate of agreement is for PERSONS, with an agreement rate of 58%. The agreement rate on LOCATIONS is 37%, and the agreement rate on ORGANIZATIONS is 34%. Even on cases where the taggers agree, the classification can be incorrect. Both taggers classify "African Americans" as LOCATIONS.[5] Both treat "Jr." as being part of a person's name, as well as being a LOCATION (in fact, the tagging of "Jr." as a LOCATION is more frequent in both).

For our second evaluation criterion, i.e., within-discourse ambiguity, we determined the percentage of globally ambiguous entities (entities that had more than one classification across the entire corpus) that occurred with multiple taggings within a single document. This analysis showed that the problems described above are not anecdotal. Table 3 shows that at least 40% of the entities that have more than one classification co-occur within a document. This is true for both taggers and all of the named entity classes.[6]

[3]"Italian" is classified primarily as MISC by the LBJ tagger. These terms are sometimes called Gentilics or Demonyms.

[4]Both taggers can use a fourth class MISC in addition to the standard entity classes PERSON, ORGANIZATION, and LOCATION. We ran Stanford without the MISC class and LBJ with MISC. However, the problems highlighted in this paper remain equally prevalent even without this discrepancy.

[5]The LBJ tagger classifies the majority of instances of "African American" as MISC.

[6]The LBJ tagger also includes the class MISC. We looked at the co-occurrence rate between the different classes and MISC, and we found that the majority of each group co-occurred within a document there as well.

	Stanford		LBJ	
	Overlap	Co-occurrence	Overlap	Co-occurrence
Person-Organization	98,776	40%	58,574	68%
Person-Location	72,296	62%	55,376	69%
Organization-Location	80,337	45%	64,399	63%

Table 3: Co-occurrence rates between entities with more than one tag for Stanford and LBJ taggers

	Stanford-BBN		LBJ-BBN	
	Common Entities	Percentage	Common Entities	Percentage
Person	8034	28%	27,687	53%
Organization	12533	50%	21,777	51%
Location(GPE)	3289	28%	5475	47%

Table 4: Agreement rate by class between the Stanford (and LBJ) and BBN IdentiFinder taggers on the ANC Corpus

4 Comparing All 3 Taggers

A copy of the American National Corpus was recently released with a tagging by IdentiFinder. We tagged the corpus with the Stanford and LBJ tagger to see how the results compared.

We found many of the same problems with the American National Corpus as we found with the SourceFinder corpus used in the previous section. The taggers performed very well for entities that were common in each class, but we found misclassifications even for terms at the head of the Zipfian curve. Terms such as "Drosophila" and "RNA" were classified as a LOCATION. "Affymetrix" was classified as a PERSON, LOCATION, and ORGANIZATION.

Table 4 shows the agreement rate between the Stanford and IdentiFinder taggers as well as that between the LBJ and IdentiFinder taggers. A sample of terms that were classified as belonging to more than one class, across all 3 taggers, is given in Table 5.

All taggers differ in how the entities are tokenized. The Stanford tagger tags each component word of the multi-word expressions separately. For example, "John Smith" is tagged as John/PERSON and Smith/PERSON. But it would be tagged as [PER John Smith] by the LBJ tagger, and similarly by IdentiFinder. This results in a higher overlap between classes in general, and there is a greater agreement rate between LBJ and IdentiFinder than between Stanford and either one.

The taggers also differ in the number of entities that are recognized overall, and the percentage that are classified in each category. IdentiFinder recognizes significantly more ORGANIZATION entities than Stanford and LBJ. IdentiFinder also uses a GPE (Geo-Political Entity) category that is not found in the other two. This splits the LOCATION class. We found that many of the entities that were classified as LOCATION by the other two taggers were classified as GPE by IdentiFinder.

Although the taggers differ in tokenization as well as categories, the results on ambiguity in a discourse support our findings on the larger corpus. The results are shown in Table 6. For both the Stanford and LBJ tagger, between 42% and 58% of the entities with more than one classification co-occur within a document. For IdentiFinder, the co-occurrence rate was high for two of the groupings, but significantly less for PERSON and GPE.

5 Unit Test for NER

We created a unit test based on our experiences in comparing the different taggers. We were particular about choosing examples that test the following:

1. Capitalized, upper case, and lower case versions of entities that are true positives for PERSON, ORGANIZATION, and LOCATION (for a variety of frequency ranges).

2. Terms that are entirely in upper case that are not named entities (such as RNA and AAARGH).

Person/Organization	Person/Location	Organization/Location
Bacillus	Bacillus	Affymetrix
Michelob	Aristotle	Arp2/3
Phenylsepharose	ArrayOligoSelector	ANOVA
Synagogue	Auschwitz	Godzilla
Transactionalism	Btk:ER	Macbeth

Table 5: A sampling of terms that were tagged as belonging to more than one class in the American National Corpus

	Stanford		LBJ		IdentiFinder	
	Overlap	**Co-occurrence**	**Overlap**	**Co-occurrence**	**Overlap**	**Co-occurrence**
Person-Org	5738	53%	2311	58%	8379	57%
Person-Loc(GPE)	4126	58%	3283	43%	2412	22%
Org-Loc(GPE)	5109	57%	4592	50%	4093	60%

Table 6: Co-occurrence rates between entities with more than one tag for the American National Corpus

3. Terms that contain punctuation marks such as hyphens, and expressions (such as "A.sub.1") that are clearly not named entities.

4. Terms that contain an initial, such as "T. Rex", "M.I.T", and "L.B.J."

5. Acronym forms such as ETS and MIT, some with an expanded form and some without.

6. Last names that appear in close proximity to the full name (first and last). This is to check on the impact of discourse and consistency of tagging.

7. Terms that contain a preposition, such as "Massachusetts Institute of Technology". This is intended to test for correct extent in identifying the entity.

8. Terms that are a part of a location as well as an organization. For example, "Amherst, MA" vs. "Amherst College".

An excerpt from this unit test is shown in Table 7. We provide more information about the full unit test at the end of the paper.

6 One Named-Entity Tag per Discourse

Previous papers have noted that it would be unusual for multiple occurrences of a token in a document to be classified as a different type of entity (Mikheev et al., 1999; Curran and Clark, 2003). The Stanford and LBJ taggers have features for non-local dependencies for this reason. The observation is similar to a hypothesis proposed by Gale, Church, and Yarowsky with respect to word-sense disambiguation and discourse (Gale et al., 1992). They hypothesized that when an ambiguous word appears in a document, all subsequent instances of that word in the document will have the same sense. This hypothesis is incorrect for word senses that we find in a dictionary (Krovetz, 1998) but is likely to be correct for the subset of the senses that are homonymous (unrelated in meaning). Ambiguity between named entities is similar to homonymy, and for most entities it is unlikely that they would co-occur in a document.[7] However, there are cases that are exceptions. For example, Finkel et al. (2005) note that in the CoNLL dataset, the same term can be used for a location and for the name of a sports team. Ratinov and Roth (2009) note that "Australia" (LOCATION) can occur in the same document as "Bank of Australia" (ORGANIZATION).

Existing taggers treat the non-local dependencies as a way of dealing with the sparse data problem, and as a way to resolve tagging differences by looking at how often one token is classified as one type

[7] Krovetz (1998) provides some examples where different named entities co-occur in a discourse, such as "New York" (city) and "New York" (state). However, these are both in the same class (LOCATION) and are related to each other.

```
                  This is not a Unit Test
          (a tribute to Rene Magritte and RMS)

Although we created this test with humor, we intend it as a serious
test of the phenomena we encountered.  These problems include
ambiguity between entities (such as Bill Clinton and Clinton,
Michigan), uneven treatment of variant forms (MIT, M.I.T., and
Massachusetts Institute of Technology - these should all be
labeled the same in this text - are they?), and frequent false
positives such as RNA and T. Rex.

...
```

Table 7: Excerpt from a Unit test for Named-Entity Recognition

versus another. We propose that these dependencies can be used in two other aspects: (a) as a source of error in evaluation and, (b) as a way to identify semantically related entities that are systematic exceptions. There is a grammar to named entity types. "Bank of Australia" is a special case of *Bank of* [LOCATION]. The same thing is true for "China Daily" as a name for a newspaper. We propose that co-occurrences of different labels for particular instances can be used to create such a grammar; at the very least, particular types of co-occurrences should be treated as an exception to what is otherwise an indication of a tagging mistake.

7 Discussion

The Message Understanding Conference (MUC) has guidelines for named-entity recognition. But the guidelines are just that. We believe that there should be standards. Without such standards it is difficult to determine which tagger is correct, and how the accuracy varies between the classes.

We propose that the community focus on four classes: PERSON, ORGANIZATION, LOCATION, and MISC. This does not mean that the other classes are not important. Rather it is recognition of the following facts:

- These classes are more difficult than dates, times, and currencies.
- There is widespread disagreement between taggers on these classes, and evidence that they are misclassifying unique entities a significant percentage of the time.
- We need at least one class for handling terms that do not fit into the first three classes.
- The first three classes have important value in other areas of NLP.

Although we recognize that an extrinsic evaluation of named entity recognition would be ideal, we also realize that intrinsic evaluations are valuable in their own right. We propose that the existing methodology for intrinsically evaluating named entity taggers can be improved in the following manner:

1. Create test sets that are organized across a variety of domains. It is not enough to work with newswire and biomedical text.
2. Use standardized sets that are designed to test different types of linguistic phenomena, and make it a de facto norm to use more than one set as part of an evaluation.
3. Report accuracy rates separately for the three major classes. Accuracy rates should be further broken down according to the items in the unit test that are designed to assess mistakes: orthography, acronym processing, frequent false positives, and knowledge-based classification.
4. Establish a way for a tagging system to express uncertainty about a classification.

The approach taken by the American National Corpus is a good step in the right direction. Like the original Brown Corpus and the British National Corpus, it breaks text down according to informational/literary text types, and spoken versus written text. The corpus also includes text that is drawn from the literature of science and medicine. However, the relatively small number of files in the corpus makes it difficult to assess accuracy rates on the basis of repeated occurrences within a document, but with different tags. Because there are hundreds of thousands of files in the internal ETS corpus, there are many opportunities for observations. The tagged version of the American National Corpus has about 8800 files. This is one of the biggest differences between the evaluation on the corpus we used internally at ETS and the American National Corpus.

The use of a MISC class is needed for reasons that are independent of certainty. This is why we propose a goal of allowing systems to express this aspect of the classification. We suggest a meta-tag of a question-mark. The meta-tag can be applied to any class. Entities for which the system is uncertain can then be routed for active learning. This also allows a basic separation of entities into those for which the system is confident of its classification, and those for which it is not.

8 Conclusion

Although Named Entity Recognition has a reported accuracy rate of more than 90%, the results show they make a significant number of mistakes. The high accuracy rates are based on inadequate methods for testing performance. By considering only the entities where both taggers agree on the classification, it is likely that we can obtain improved accuracy. But even so, there are cases where both taggers agree yet the agreement is on an incorrect tagging.

The unit test for assessing NER performance is freely available to download.[8]

As with Information Retrieval test collections, we hope that this becomes one of many, and that they be adopted as a standard for evaluating performance.

[8] `http://bit.ly/nertest`

Acknowledgments

This work has been supported by the Institute for Education Sciences under grant IES PR/Award Number R305A080647. We are grateful to Michael Flor, Jill Burstein, and anonymous reviewers for their comments.

References

Daniel M. Bikel, Richard M. Schwartz, and Ralph M. Weischedel. 1999. An Algorithm that Learns What's in a Name. *Machine Learning*, 34:211–231.

Xavier Carreras, Llus Mrquez, and Llus Padr. 2003. Named entity recognition for Catalan using Spanish resources. In *Proceedings of EACL*.

James R. Curran and Stephen Clark. 2003. Language Independent NER using a Maximum Entropy Tagger. In *Proceeding of the 7th Conference on Computational Natural Language Learning (CoNLL)*, pages 164–167.

Micha Elsner, Eugene Charniak, and Mark Johnson. 2009. Structured Generative Models for Unsupervised Named-Entity Clustering. In *Proceedings of NAACL*, pages 164–172.

Jenny Rose Finkel, Trond Grenager, and Christopher D. Manning. 2005. Incorporating Non-local Information into Information Extraction Systems by Gibbs Sampling. In *Proceedings of ACL*, pages 363–370.

William A. Gale, Kenneth W. Church, and David Yarowsky. 1992. One Sense per Discourse. In *Proceedings of the ARPA Workshop on Speech and Natural Language Processing*, pages 233–237.

Robert Krovetz. 1998. More than One Sense Per Discourse. In *Proceedings of the ACL-SIGLEX Workshop: SENSEVAL-1*.

Monica Marrero, Sonia Sanchez-Cuadrado, Jorge Morato Lara, and George Andreadakis. 2009. Evaluation of Named Entity Extraction Systems. *Advances in Computational Linguistics, Research in Computing Science*, 41:47–58.

Fien De Meulder, V Eronique Hoste, and Walter Daelemans. 2002. A Named Entity Recognition System for Dutch. In *Computational Linguistics in the Netherlands*, pages 77–88.

Andrei Mikheev, Marc Moens, and Claire Grover. 1999. Named Entity Recognition Without Gazetteers. In *Proceedings of EACL*, pages 1–8.

David Nadeau, Peter D. Turney, and Stan Matwin. 2006. Unsupervised Named-Entity Recognition: Generating Gazetteers and Resolving Ambiguity. In *Proceedings of the Canadian Conference on Artificial Intelligence*, pages 266–277.

L. Ratinov and D. Roth. 2009. Design Challenges and Misconceptions in Named Entity Recognition. In *Proceedings of the Thirteenth Conference on Computational Natural Language Learning (CoNLL)*, pages 147–155.

Marc Rossler. 2004. Adapting an NER-System for German to the Biomedical Domain. In *Proceedings of the International Joint Workshop on Natural Language Processing in Biomedicine and its Applications*, pages 92–95.

A machine learning approach to relational noun mining in German

Berthold Crysmann
Arbeitsbereich Sprache und Kommunikation
Universität Bonn
crysmann@uni-bonn.de

Abstract

In this paper I argue in favour of a collocation extraction approach to the acquisition of relational nouns in German. We annotated frequency-based best lists of noun-preposition bigrams and subsequently trained different classifiers using (combinations of) association metrics, achieving a maximum F-measure of 69.7 on a support vector machine (Platt, 1998). Trading precision for recall, we could achieve over 90% recall for relational noun extraction, while still halving the annotation effort.

1 Mining relational nouns: almost a MWE extraction problem

A substantial minority of German nouns are characterised by having an internal argument structure that can be expressed as syntactic complements. A non-negligeable number of relational nouns are deverbal, inheriting the semantic argument structure of the verbs they derive from. In contrast to verbs, however, complements of nouns are almost exclusively optional.

The identification of relational nouns is of great importance for a variety of content-oriented applications: first, precise HPSG parsing for German cannot really be achieved, if a high number of noun complements is systematically analysed as modifiers. Second, recent extension of Semantic Role Labeling to the argument structure of nouns (Meyers et al., 2004) increases the interest in lexicographic methods for the extraction of noun subcategorisation information. Third, relational nouns are also a valuable resource for machine translation, separating the more semantic task of translating modifying prepositions from the more syntactic task of translating subcategorised for prepositions. Despite its relevance for accurate deep parsing, the German HPSG grammar developed at DFKI (Müller and Kasper, 2000; Crysmann, 2003; Crysmann, 2005) currently only includes 107 entries for proposition taking nouns, and lacks entries for PP-taking nouns entirely.

In terms of subcategorisation properties, relational nouns in German can be divided up into 3 classes:

- nouns taking genitival complements (e.g., *Beginn der Vorlesung* 'beginning of the lecture', *Zerstörung der Stadt* 'destruction of the city')
- nouns taking propositional complements, either a complementiser-introduced finite clause (*der Glaube, daß die Erde flach ist* 'the belief that earth is flat'), or an infinitival clause (*die Hoffnung, im Lotto zu gewinnen* 'the hope to win the lottery'), or both
- nouns taking PP complements

In this paper, I will be concerned with nouns taking prepositional complements, although the method described here can also be easily applied to the case of complementiser-introduced propositional complements.[1]

[1] In fact, I expect the task of mining relational nouns taking finite propositional complements to be far easier, owing to a reduced ambiguity of the still relatively local complementiser

The prepositions used with relational nouns all come from a small set of basic prepositions, mostly locative or directional.

A characteristic of these prepositions when used as a noun's complement, is that their choice becomes relatively fixed, a property shared with MWEs in general. Furthermore, choice of preposition is often arbitrary, sometimes differing between relational nouns and the verbs they derive from, e.g., *Interesse an* 'lit: interest at' vs. *interessieren für* 'lit: to interest for'. Owing to the lack of alternation, the preposition by itself does not compositionally contribute to sentence meaning, its only function being the encoding of a thematic property of the noun. Thus, in syntacto-semantic terms, we are again dealing with prototypical MWEs.

The fact that PP complements of nouns, like modifiers, are syntactically optional, together with the fact that their surface form is indistinguishable from adjunct PPs, makes the extraction task far from trivial. It is clear that grammar-based error mining techniques (van Noord, 2004; Cholakov et al., 2008) that have been highly successful in other areas of deep lexical acquisition (e.g., verb subcategorisation) cannot be applied here: first, given that an alternative analysis as a modifier is readily available in the grammar, missing entries for relational nouns will never incur any coverage problems. Furthermore, since PP modifiers are highly common we cannot expect a decrease in tree probability either.

Instead, I shall exploit the MWE-like properties of relational nouns, building on the expectation that the presence of a subcategorisation requirement towards a fixed, albeit optional, prepositional head should leave a trace in frequency distributions. Thus, building on previous work in MWE extraction, I shall pursue a data-driven approach that builds on a variety of association metrics combined in a probabilistic classifier. Despite the difference of the task, the approach suggested here shares some significant similarity to previous classifier-based approaches to MWE (Pecina, 2008).

daß. Although complement that-clauses in German can indeed can be extraposed, corpus studies on relative clause extraposition (Uszkoreit et al., 1998) have shown that the great majority of extrapositions operates at extremely short surface distance, typically crossing the verb or verb particle in the right sentence bracket. Since locality conditions on complement clause extraposition are more strict than those for relative clause extraposition (Kiss, 2005; Crysmann, to appear), I conjecture that the actual amount of non-locality found in corpora will be equally limited.

2 Data

2.1 Data preparation

As primary data for relational noun extraction, I used the deWaC corpus (Baroni and Kilgariff, 2006), a 1.6 billion token corpus of German crawled from the web. The corpus is automatically tagged and lemmatised by TreeTagger (Schmid, 1995). From this corpus, I extracted all noun (NN) and preposition (APPR) unigrams and noun–preposition bigrams. Noun unigrams occuring less than ten times in the entire corpus were subsequently removed. In addition to the removal of hapaxes, I also filtered out any abbreviations.

Frequency counts were lemma-based, a decision that was motivated by the intended application, namely mining of relational noun entries for a lemma-based HPSG lexicon.

From the corpus, I extracted a best-list, based on bigram frequency, a well-established heuristical measure for collocational status (Krenn, 2000). Using a frequency based best list not only minimises initial annotation effort, but also ensures the quickest improvement of the target resource, the grammar's lexicon. Finally, the use of ranked best lists will also ensure that we will always have enough positive items in our training data.

2.2 Annotation

The ranked best list was subsequently annotated by two human annotators (A1,A2) with relatively little prior training in linguistics. In order to control for annotation errors, the same list was annotated a second time by a third year student of linguistics (A3).

In order to operationalise the argument/modifier annotators were asked to take related verbs into consideration, as well as to test (local and temporal) prepositions for paradigmatic interchangeability. Furthermore, since we are concerned with logical complements of nouns but not possessors, which can be added quite freely, annotators were advised to further distinguish whether a *von*-PP was only possible as a possessor or also as a noun complement.

An initial comparison of annotation decisions

showed an agreement of .82 between A1 and A3, and an agreement of .84 between A2 and A3. In a second round discrepancies between annotators were resolved, yielding a gold standard annotation of 4333 items, out of which 1179 (=27.2%) were classified as relational nouns.

3 Experiments

All experiments reported here were carried out using WEKA, a Java platform for data exploration and experimentation developed at the University of Waikato (Hall et al., 2009).

Since our task is to extract relational nouns and since we are dealing with a binary decision, performance measures given here report on relational nouns only. Thus, we do not provide figures for the classification of non-relational nouns or any uninformative (weighted) averages of the two.[2]

3.1 Learners

In a pre-study, we conducted experiments with a single feature set, but different classifiers in order to determine which ones performed best on our data set. Amongst the classifiers we tested were 2 Bayesian classifiers (Naive Bayes and Bayesian Nets), a Support Vector Machine, a Multilayer Perceptron classifier, as well as the entire set of decision tree classifiers offered by WEKA 3.6.4 (cf. the WEKA documentation for an exhaustive list of references). All test runs were performed with default settings. Unless otherwise indicated, all tests were carried out using 10-fold cross-validation.

Among these, decision tree classifiers perform quite well in general, with NBTree, a hybrid decision tree classifier using Naive Bayes classifiers at leave nodes producing optimal results. Performance of the Naive Bayes classifier was suboptimal, with respect to both precision and recall. Overall performance of the Bayesian Net classifier (with a K2 learner) was competitive to average decision tree classifiers, delivering particularly good recall, but fell short of the best classifiers in terms of precision and F-measure.

[2]A base-line classifier that consistently choses the majority class (non-relational) and therefore does not detect a single relational noun, already achieves an F-measure for non-relational nouns of 84.3, and a weighted F-measure of 61.3%.

Thus, for further experimentation, we concentrated on the two best-performing classifiers, i.e., NBTree (Kohavi, 1996), which achieved the highest F-score and the second best precision, and SMO (Platt, 1998), a support vector machine, which produced the best precision value.

After experimentation regarding optimal feature selection (see next section), we re-ran our experiments with the modified feature set, in order to confirm that the classifiers we chose were still optimal. The results of these runs are presented in table 1.

	Prec.	Rec.	F-meas.
ADTree	68.3	61.1	64.5
BFTree	75.0	51.7	61.2
DecisionStump	52.5	80.2	63.5
FT	73.8	59.1	65.7
J48	72.9	58.4	64.8
J48graft	72.6	58.4	64.7
LADTree	70.5	57.5	63.3
LMT	74.9	59.8	66.5
NBTree	74.9	62.8	**68.7**
RandomForest	67.4	63.4	65.3
RandomTree	61.8	61.1	61.4
REPTree	74.5	61.2	67.2
Naive Bayes	70.5	53.9	61.1
Bayes Net	60.6	71.4	65.6
SMO	**76.5**	57.7	65.8
MultilayerPerceptron	67.5	64.5	65.9
Bagging (RepTree)	75.9	62.4	68.5
Voting (maj)	72.7	66.3	69.4
Voting (av)	71.3	68.4	**69.8**

Table 1: Performance of different classifiers

Finally, we did some sporadic test using a voting scheme incorporating 3 classifiers with high precision values (SMO, NBTree, Bagging(REPTree) (Breiman, 1996)), as well as two classifiers with high recall (BayesNet, recall-oriented SMO, see below). Using averaging, we managed to bring the F-measure up to 69.8, the highest value we measured in all our experiments.

3.2 Features

For NBTree, our best-performing classifier, we subsequently carried out a number of experiments to assess the influence and predictive power of individual association measures and to study their interactions.

Essentially, we make use of two basic types of features: string features, like the form of the preposition or the prefixes and suffixes of the noun, and association measures. As for the latter, we drew on the set of measures successfully used in previous studies on collocation extraction:

Mutual information (MI) An information theoretic measure proposed by (Church and Hanks, 1990) which measures the joint probability of the bigram in relation to the product of the marginal probabilities, i.e., the expected probability.

$$MI = \frac{p(noun, prep)}{p(noun) * p(prep)}$$

MI^2 A squared variant of mutal information, previously suggested by (Daille, 1994). Essentially, the idea behind squaring the joint probability is to counter the negative effect of extremely low marginal probabilities yielding high MI scores.

$$MI^2 = \frac{(p(noun, prep))^2}{p(noun) * p(prep)}$$

Likelihood ratios A measure suggested by (Dunning, 1993) that indicates how much more likely the cooccurence is than mere coincidence.

$$\begin{aligned} LR = \log L(p_i, k_1, n_1) + \log L(p_2, k_2, n_2) \\ - \log L(p, k_1, n_1) - \log L(p, k_2, n_2) \\ \text{where} \\ \log L(p, n, k) = k \log p + (n - k) \log(1 - p) \\ \text{and} \\ p_1 = \frac{k_1}{n_1}, p_2 = \frac{k_2}{n_2}, p = \frac{k_1 + k_2}{n_1 + n_2} \end{aligned}$$

t-score The score of Fisher's t-test. Although the underlying assumption regarding normal distribution is incorrect (Church and Mercer, 1993), the score has nevertheless been used with repeated success in collocation extraction tasks (Krenn, 2000; Krenn and Evert, 2001; Evert and Krenn, 2001).

$$tscore = \frac{p(noun, prep) - (p(noun) * p(prep))}{\sqrt{\frac{\sigma^2}{N}}}$$

As suggested by (Manning and Schütze, 1999) we use p as an approximation of σ^2.

Association Strength (Smadja, 1993)

A factor indicating how many times the standard deviation a bigram frequency differs from the average.

$$Strength = \frac{freq_i - \bar{f}}{\sigma}$$

Best Indicates whether a bigram is the most frequent one for the given noun or not.

Best-Ratio A relative version of the previous feature indicating the frequency ratio between the current noun–preposition bigram and the best bigram for the given noun.

In addition to the for,m of the preposition, we included information about the noun's suffixes or prefixes:

Noun suffix We included common string suffixes that may be clues as to the relational nature of the noun, as, e.g., the common derviational suffixes *-ion, -schaft, -heit, -keit* as well as the endings *-en*, which are found inter alia with nominalised infinitives, and *-er*, which are found, inter alia with agentive nominals. All other suffixes were mapped to the NONE class.

Noun prefix Included were prefixes that commonly appear as verb prefixes. Again, this was used as a shortcut for true lexical relatedness.

As illustrated by the diagrams in Figure 1, the aforementioned association measures align differently with the class of relational nouns (in black):

The visually discernible difference in alignment between association metrics and relational nouns was also confirmed by testing single-feature classifiers: as detailed in Table 2, *MI*, *MI^2*, and *t-score* all capable to successfully identify relational nouns by themselves, whereas *best*, *best-ratio* and *strength*

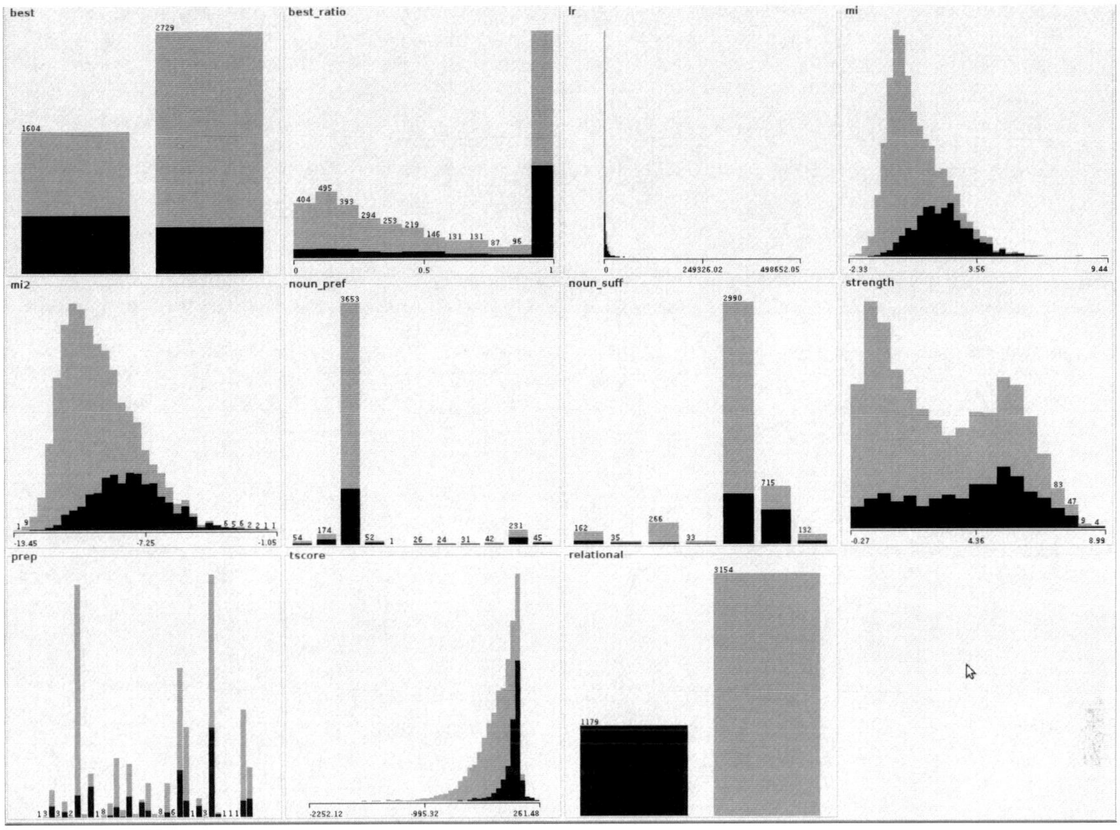

Figure 1: Distribution of relational and non-relational nouns across features (created with WEKA 3.6.4)

are entirely unable to partition the data appropriately. *LR* assumes an intermediate position, suffering mainly from recall problems.

	Prec.	Rec.	F-meas.
MI	65.2	45.2	53.4
MI2	62.2	50.7	55.9
LR	60	23.5	33.8
T-score	66.4	42	51.5
Strength	0	0	0
Best	0	0	0
Best-Ratio	0	0	0

Table 2: Classification by a single association metric

The second experiment regarding features differs from the first by the addition of form features:

Two things are worth noting here: first, the values achieved by *MI* and *T-score* now come very close to the values obtained with much more elaborate feature sets, confirming previous results on the usefulness of these metrics. Second, all association measures now display reasonable performance. Both

	Prec.	Rec.	F-meas.
MI	74.2	61.2	67.1
MI2	72.5	56.4	63.5
LR	73.1	54.4	62.4
T-score	74.9	60.6	67
Strength	72.5	52.4	60.9
Best	69.7	48.7	57.3
Best-Ratio	72.1	53.4	61.3

Table 3: Classification by a single association metric + form features (*preposition, noun prefix, noun suffix*)

these effects can be traced to a by-category sampling introduced by the form features. The most clear-cut case is probably the *best* feature: as shown in Figure 1, there is a clear increase in relational nouns in the TRUE category of the Boolean *best* feature, yet, they still do not represent a majority. Thus, a classifier with a balanced cost function will always prefer the majority vote. However, for particular noun classes (and prepositions for that matter) majorities can be tipped.

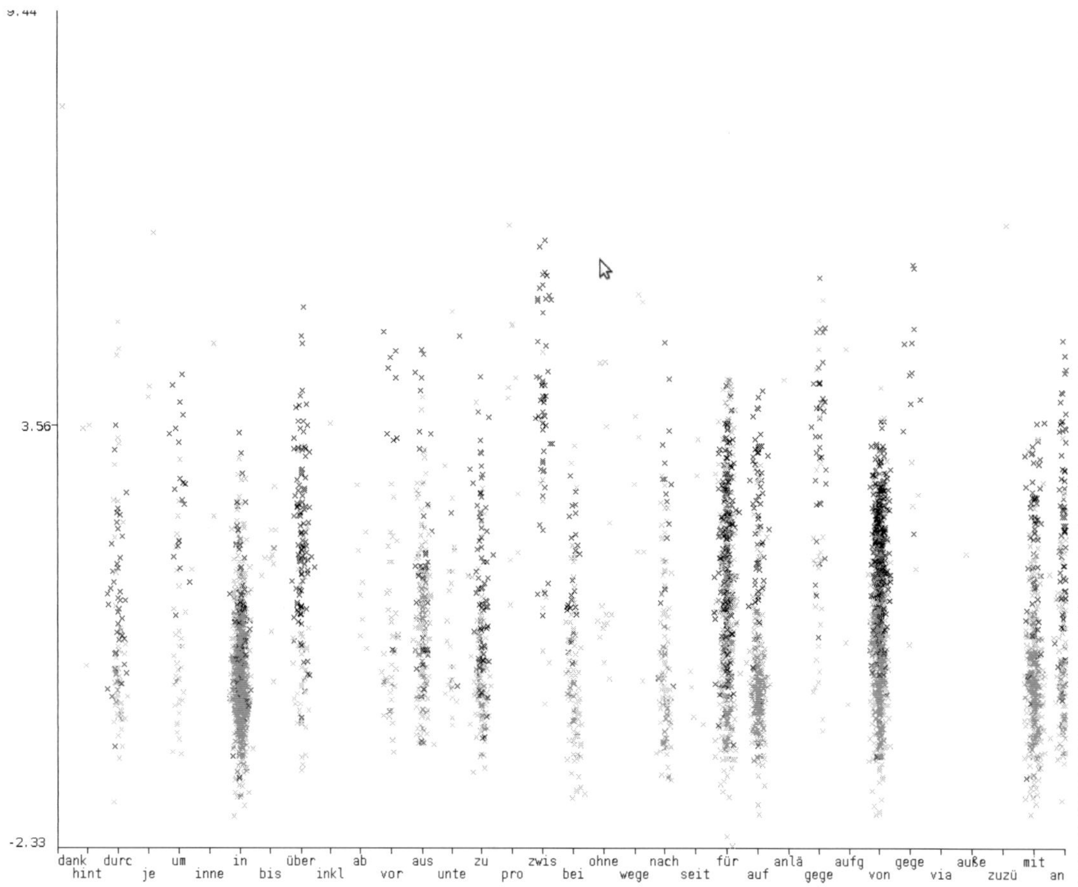

Figure 2: MI-values of relational nouns relative to preposition

As depicted by the preposition-specific plot of MI values in Figure 2, some prepositions have a clear bias for their use with relational nouns (e.g., *von* 'of') or against it (e.g., *ab* 'from'), while others appear non-commital (e.g., *für* 'for'). Similar observations can be made for noun suffixes and prefixes.

The next set of experiments were targetted at optimisation. Assuming that the candidate sets selected by different metrics will not stand in a subset relation I explored which combination of metrics yielded the best results. To do this, I started out with a full set of features and compared this to the results obtained with one feature left out. In a second and third step of iteration, I tested whether simultaneously leaving out some features for which we observed some gain would produce an even more optimised classifier.

Table 4 presents the result of the first step. Here, two outcomes are of particular interest: deleting information about the noun suffix is detrimental, whereas ignoring the t-score value appears to be beneficial to overall performance.

	Prec.	Rec.	F-meas.
All	74.4	61.2	67.2
−T-score	**75.3**	**62.4**	**68.3**
−MI	72.8	62.3	67.1
−MI^2	75.1	61.6	67.7
−LR	74.1	60.1	66.3
−Strength	73.4	62	67.2
−Best	73.7	60.7	66.6
−Best-Ratio	74.2	61.8	67.4
−Prep	74.7	61.1	67.2
−Noun-Prefix	74.7	61.1	67.2
−Noun-Suffix	71.3	55.3	62.3

Table 4: Effects of leaving one feature out

In a second (and third) iteration, I tested whether any additional feature deletion apart from *t-score* would give rise to any further improvements.

−t-score	Prec.	Rec.	F-meas.
	75.3	62.4	68.3
−MI	74.4	57.6	64.9
−LR	74.8	61.3	67.4
−MI2	74.1	61.7	67.4
−Strength	75.1	62.8	**68.4**
−Best	74.1	61.5	67.2
−Best-Ratio	75.4	62.6	**68.4**
−Best-Ratio −Strength	74.9	63.4	**68.7**

Table 5: Effects of leaving two or more features out

In fact, removal of the *Strength* feature provided good results, whether taken out individually or in combination, which may be due to this feature's inherently poor statistical properties (cf. Figure 1). Ignoring *best-ratio* was also beneficial, probably due to the fact that most of its benefical properties are already covered by the *best* feature and that non-best noun-preposition combinations hardly ever give rise to positive hits.

As a matter of fact, simultaneous removal of *best-ratio* and *strength*, in addition to the removal of *t-score* of course, yielded best overall results. As a consequence, all remaining test runs were based on this feature set. In separate test runs with the SMO classifier, I finally confirmed that the optimality of this feature set was not just an artifact of the classifier, but that it generalises to SVMs as well.

3.3 Trade-offs

Since our main aim in relational noun mining is the improvement of the accuracy of our grammar's lexicon, and since the quickest improvement are expected for highly frequent noun-preposition bigrams, I tested whether I could bring the recall of our classifiers up, at the expense of moderate losses in precision. For this evaluation, I used again our best-performing classifier (NBTree), as well as SMO, which had the highest head-room in terms of precision, while already providing satisfactory recall. To this end, I manipulated the classifier's cost matrix during training and testing, gradually increasing the costs for false negatives compared to false positives.

The results of this evaluation are given in Figure 3. First, we obtained a new optimal f-measure for the SMO classifier: at a cost factor of 2.1 for false negatives, the f-measure peaks at 69.7, with a recall of 75.1% and precision still acceptable (65.1%). At this level, we still save more than two thirds of the annotation effort.

By way of penalising false negatives 6 times more than false positives, the suppport vector machine was able to detect over 90% of all relational nouns, at a precision of 50%. At these levels, we can still save more than half of the entire annotation effort.

Going further down the Zipf distribution, we expect the savings in terms of annotation effort to go further up, since our bigram frequency ranking ensures that relational nouns are overrepresented at the top of the list, a rate that will gradually go down.

Finally, including false positives in the data to be annotated will also ensure that we always have enough positive and negative training data for learning a classifier on an extended data set.

3.4 Outlook

Although results are already useful at this point, I hope to further improve precision and recall rates by means of additional features. Evaluating the NBTree classifier on the training data, we observe an F-measure of only 74.7%, which suggests that the current set of features models the training data still quite imperfectly. Thus, one needs to incorporate further independent evidence in order to predict relation nouns more reliably. Owing to the semantic nature of the relational vs. non-relational distinction one type of additional evidence could come from multilingual resources: as a first step, I envisage incorporating the classification of nouns in the English Resource Grammar (ERG; (Copestake and Flickinger, 2000)) as prior information regarding relational status. In a second step I shall explore whether one can exploit information from parallel corpora, using in particular item-specific divergence of preposition choice to detect whether we are dealing with a contentful or rather a functional preposition.[3] The intuition behind using cross-linguistic evidence to try and boost the performance of the learner is based on the observation that predicate argument structure in closely related languages such as English and German tends to be highly similar, with differences mostly located in syntactic proper-

[3] I expect that arbitrary divergence in the choice of preposition provides an indicator of grammaticalisation.

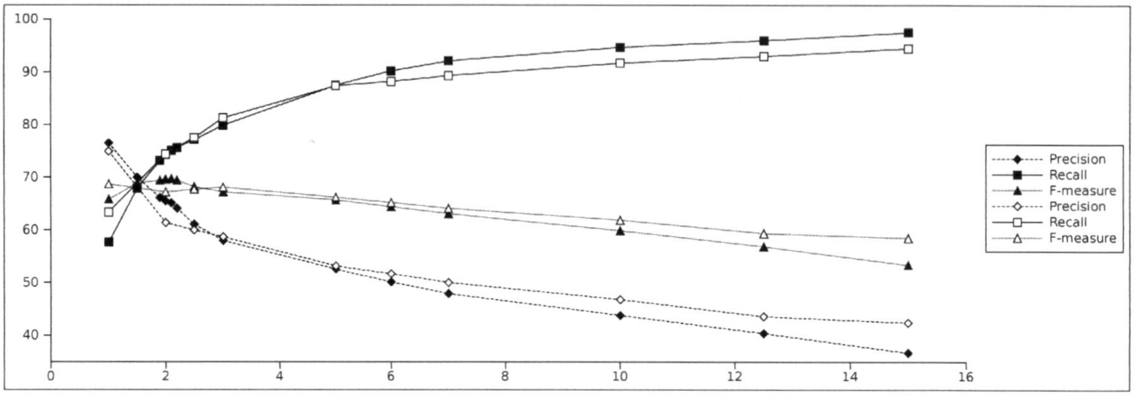

Figure 3: Effect of trading precision for recall (NBTree: white; SMO: black)

ties such as selection for case or choice of preposition. As a consequence, I do not expect to be able to predict the actual form of the German preposition, but rather gain additional evidence as to whether a given noun has some relational use at all or not.

The second type of information that I plan to use more systematically in the future is morphological and lexical relatedness which is only approximated at present by the noun sufix and noun prefix features which hint at the derived (deverbal) nature of the noun under discussion. In addition to these brute-force features, I plan to incorporate the HPSG grammar's verb subcategorisation lexicon, pairing nouns and verbs by means of minimum edit distance.[4] In essence, we hope to provide a more general approach to lexical relatedness between relational nouns and the non-unary verbal predicates they derive from: in the current feature set, this was only suboptimally approximated by the use of noun suffix and prefix features, resulting in most nouns being mapped to the unpredictive class NONE.[5]

Finally, I plan to apply the current approach to the extraction of nouns taking propositional complements. Given the comparative ease of that task compared to the extraction of PP-taking nouns, I shall investigate whether we can exploit the fact that many relational nouns taking propositional complements (e.g., *der Glaube, daß ...* 'the belief that') also take PP-complements (*der Glaube an* 'the belief in') in order to further improve our present classifier. In a similar vein, I shall experiment whether it is possible to extrapolate from relational nouns taking *von*-PPs to genitive complements.

4 Conclusion

In this paper I have suggested to treat the task of mining relational nouns in German as a MWE extraction problem. Based on the first 4333 hand-annotated items of a best-list ranked by bigram frequencies, several classifiers have been trained in order to determine which learner and which (combination of) association measures performed best for the task.

Testing different classifiers and different metrics, we found that optimal results were obtained using a support vector machine (Platt, 1998), including Mutual Information (MI), its squared variant (MI^2), and Likelihood Ratios (LR) as association measures, together with information about the identity of the preposition and the noun's prefix and suffix. The second best classifier, a hybrid decision tree with Naive Bayes classifiers at the leaves produced highly competitive results. T-scores, while being a good predictor on its own, however, led to a slight decrease in performance, when a full feature set was used. Likewise, performance suffered when Association Strength (Smadja, 1993) was included. Overall performance of the best individual classifier figured at an F-score of 69.7.

[4]Being aware of the fact that lexical derivation may give rise to arbitrary changes in syntactic subcategorisation, I minimally expect to gather evidence regarding the arity of the derived noun predicate. To what extent actual selectional properties as to the shape of the functional preposition are maintained by derivational processes remains a matter of empirical research.

[5]The inclusion of noun prefixes, which are actually verb prefixes, is inherently limited to mimick lexical relatedness to prefix verbs.

References

Marco Baroni and Adam Kilgariff. 2006. Large linguistically-processed web corpora for multiple languages. In *Proceedings of EACL 2006*.

Leo Breiman. 1996. Bagging predictors. *Machine Learning*, 24(2):123–140.

Kostadin Cholakov, Valia Kordoni, and Yi Zhang. 2008. Towards domain-independent deep linguistic processing: Ensuring portability and re-usability of lexicalised grammars. In *Coling 2008: Proceedings of the workshop on Grammar Engineering Across Frameworks*, pages 57–64, Manchester, England, August. Coling 2008 Organizing Committee.

Kenneth Church and Patrick Hanks. 1990. Word association norms, mutual information, and lexicography. *Computational Linguistics*, 16(1):22–29.

Kenneth Church and Robert Mercer. 1993. Introduction to the special issue on computational linguistics using large corpora. *Computational Linguistics*, 19:1–24.

Ann Copestake and Dan Flickinger. 2000. An open-source grammar development environment and broad-coverage English grammar using HPSG. In *Proceedings of the Second conference on Language Resources and Evaluation (LREC-2000)*, Athens.

Berthold Crysmann. 2003. On the efficient implementation of German verb placement in HPSG. In *Proceedings of RANLP 2003*, pages 112–116, Borovets, Bulgaria.

Berthold Crysmann. 2005. Relative clause extraposition in German: An efficient and portable implementation. *Research on Language and Computation*, 3(1):61–82.

Berthold Crysmann. to appear. On the locality of complement clause and relative clause extraposition. In Gert Webelhuth, Manfred Sailer, and Heike Walker, editors, *Rightward Movement in a Comparative Perspective*. John Benjamins, Amsterdam.

Béatrice Daille. 1994. *Approche mixte pour l'extraction automatique de terminologie : statistique lexicale et filtres linguistiques*. Ph.D. thesis, Université Paris 7.

Ted Dunning. 1993. Accurate methods for the statistics of surprise and coincidence. *Computational Linguistics*, 19:61–74.

Stefan Evert and Brigitte Krenn. 2001. Methods for the qualitative evaluation of lexical association measures. In *Proceedings of the 39th Annual Meeting of the Association for Computational Linguistics, Toulouse, France*, pages 188–195.

Mark Hall, Eibe Frank, Geoffrey Holmes, Bernhard Pfahringer, Peter Reutemann, and Ian H. Witten. 2009. The WEKA data mining software: an update. *SIGKDD Explorations*, 11(1):10–18.

Tibor Kiss. 2005. Semantic constraints on relative clause extraposition. *Natural Language and Linguistic Theory*, 23:281–334.

Ron Kohavi. 1996. Scaling up the accuracy of naive-bayes classifiers: A decision-tree hybrid. In *Second International Conference on Knowledge Discovery and Data Mining*, pages 202–207.

Brigitte Krenn and Stefan Evert. 2001. Can we do better than frequency? a case study on extracting PP-verb collocations. In *Proceedings of the ACL Workshop on Collocations, Toulouse, France*, pages 39–46.

Brigitte Krenn. 2000. *The Usual Suspects: Data-oriented Models for the Identification and Representation of Lexical Collocations*. Ph.D. thesis, Universität des Saarlandes.

Christopher Manning and Hinrich Schütze. 1999. *Foundations of Statistical Natural Language Processing*. MIT Press.

A. Meyers, R. Reeves, C. Macleod, R. Szekely, V. Zielinska, B. Young, and R. Grishman. 2004. The nombank project: An interim report. In A. Meyers, editor, *HLT-NAACL 2004 Workshop: Frontiers in Corpus Annotation*, pages 24–31, Boston, Massachusetts, USA, May 2 - May 7. Association for Computational Linguistics.

Stefan Müller and Walter Kasper. 2000. HPSG analysis of German. In Wolfgang Wahlster, editor, *Verbmobil: Foundations of Speech-to-Speech Translation*, pages 238–253. Springer, Berlin.

Pavel Pecina. 2008. A machine learning approach to multiword expression extraction. In *Proceedings of the LREC Workshop Towards a Shared Task for Multiword Expressions (MWE 2008)*, pages 54–61.

J. Platt. 1998. Fast training of support vector machines using sequential minimal optimization. In B. Schoelkopf, C. Burges, and A. Smola, editors, *Advances in Kernel Methods - Support Vector Learning*. MIT Press.

Helmut Schmid. 1995. Improvements in part-of-speech tagging with an application to German. In *Proceedings of the ACL SIGDAT-Workshop*, March.

Frank Smadja. 1993. Retrieving collocations from text: Xtract. *Computational Linguistics*, 19(1):143–177.

Hans Uszkoreit, Thorsten Brants, Denys Duchier, Brigitte Krenn, Lars Konieczny, Stephan Oepen, and Wojciech Skut. 1998. Studien zur performanzorientierten Linguistik. Aspekte der Relativsatzextraposition im Deutschen. *Kognitionswissenschaft*, 7:129–133.

Gertjan van Noord. 2004. Error mining for wide coverage grammar engineering. In *Proceedings of the 42nd Meeting of the Association for Computational Linguistics (ACL'04), Barcelona, Spain*, pages 446–453.

Identifying and Analyzing Brazilian Portuguese Complex Predicates

Magali Sanches Duran[♡] Carlos Ramisch[♠ ◇] Sandra Maria Aluísio[♡] Aline Villavicencio[♠]

♡ Center of Computational Linguistics (NILC), ICMC, University of São Paulo, Brazil

♠ Institute of Informatics, Federal University of Rio Grande do Sul, Brazil

◇ GETALP – LIG, University of Grenoble, France

magali.duran@uol.com.br ceramisch@inf.ufrgs.br

sandra@icmc.usp.br avillavicencio@inf.ufrgs.br

Abstract

Semantic Role Labeling annotation task depends on the correct identification of predicates, before identifying arguments and assigning them role labels. However, most predicates are not constituted only by a verb: they constitute Complex Predicates (CPs) not yet available in a computational lexicon. In order to create a dictionary of CPs, this study employs a corpus-based methodology. Searches are guided by POS tags instead of a limited list of verbs or nouns, in contrast to similar studies. Results include (but are not limited to) light and support verb constructions. These CPs are classified into idiomatic and less idiomatic. This paper presents an in-depth analysis of this phenomenon, as well as an original resource containing a set of 773 annotated expressions. Both constitute an original and rich contribution for NLP tools in Brazilian Portuguese that perform tasks involving semantics.

1 Introduction

Semantic Role Labeling (SRL), independently of the approach adopted, comprehends two steps before the assignment of role labels: (a) the delimitation of argument takers and (b) the delimitation of arguments. If the argument taker is not correctly identified, the argument identification will propagate the error and SRL will fail. Argument takers are predicates, frequently represented only by a verb and occasionally by Complex Predicates (CPs), that is, "predicates which are multi-headed: they are composed of more than one grammatical element" (Alsina et al., 1997, p. 1), like *give a try, take care, take a shower*. In SRL, the verbal phrases (VPs) identified by a parser are usually used to automatically identify argument takers, but do no suffice. A lexicon of CPs, as well as the knowledge about verbal chains composition, would complete a fully automatic identification of argument takers. Consequently, the possibility of disagreement between SRL annotators would rely only on the assignment of role labels to arguments. This paper reports the investigation of such multi-word units, in order to meet the needs arisen from an SRL annotation task in a corpus of Brazilian Portuguese[1].

To stress the importance of these CPs for SRL, consider the sentence *John takes care of his business* in three alternatives of annotation:

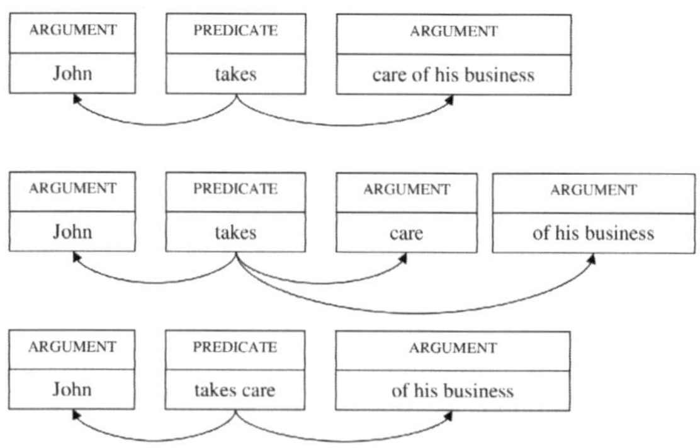

The first annotation shows *care of his business* as a unique argument, masking the fact that this segment is constituted of a predicative noun, *care*, and its internal argument, *of his business*. The second annotation shows *care* and *of his business* as arguments of *take*, which is incorrect because *of his business* is clearly an argument of *care*. The third annotation is the best for SRL purposes: as a unique predicate — *take care, take* shares its external argu-

[1] CPs constituted by verbal chains (e.g. *have been working*) are not focused here.

ment with *care* and *care* shares its internal argument with *take*.

The goal of this paper is twofold: first, we briefly describe our computer-aided corpus-based method used to build a comprehensive machine-readable dictionary of such expressions. Second and most important, we analyze these expressions and their behavior in order to shed some light on the most adequate lexical representation for further integration of our resource into an SRL annotation task. The result is a database of 773 annotated CPs, that can be used to inform SRL and other NLP applications.

In this study we classify CPs into two groups: idiomatic CPs and less idiomatic CPs. Idiomatic CPs are those whose sense may not be inferred from their parts. Examples in Portuguese are *fazer questão (make a point), ir embora (go away), dar o fora (get out), tomar conta (take care), dar para trás (give up), dar de ombros (shrug), passar mal (get sick)*. On the other hand, we use "less idiomatic CPs" to refer to those CPs that vary in a continuum of different levels of compositionality, from fully compositional to semi-compositional sense, that is, at least one of their lexical components may be litterally understood and/or translated. Examples of less idiomatic CPs in Portuguese are: *dar instrução (give instructions), fazer menção (make mention), tomar banho (take a shower), tirar foto (take a photo), entrar em depressão (get depressed), ficar triste (become sad)*.

Less idiomatic CPs headed by a predicative noun have been called in the literature "light verb constructions" (LVC) or "support verb constructions" (SVC). Although both terms have been employed as synonyms, "light verb" is, in fact, a semantic concept and "support verb" is a syntactic concept. The term "light verb" is attributed to Jespersen (1965) and the term "support verb" was already used by Gross in 1981. A light verb is the use of a polysemous verb in a non prototypical sense or "with a subset of their [its] full semantic features", North (2005). On the other hand, a support verb is the verb that combines with a noun to enable it to fully predicate, given that some nouns and adjectives may evoke internal arguments, but need to be associated with a verb to evoke the external argument, that is, the subject. As the function of support verb is almost always performed by a light verb, attributes of LVCs and SVCs have been merged, making them near synonyms. Against this tendency, this study will show cases of SVCs without light verbs (*trazer prejuízo = damage*, lit. *bring damage*) and cases of LVCs without support verbs (*dar certo = work well*, lit. *give correct*).

To the best of our knowledge, to date, there is no similar study regarding these complex predicates in Brazilian Portuguese, focusing on the development of a lexical resource for NLP tasks, such as SRL. The remainder of this paper is organized as follows: in §2 we discuss related work, in §3 we present the corpus and the details about our methodology, in §4 we present and discuss the resulting lists of candidates, in §5 we envisage further work and draw our conclusions.

2 Related Work

Part of the CPs focused on here are represented by LVCs and SVCs. These CPs have been studied in several languages from different points of view: diacronic (Ranchhod, 1999; Marchello-Nizia, 1996), language contrastive (Danlos and Samvelian, 1992; Athayde, 2001), descriptive (Butt, 2003; Langer, 2004; Langer, 2005) and for NLP purposes (Salkoff, 1990; Stevenson et al., 2004; Barreiro and Cabral, 2009; Hwang et al., 2010). Closer to our study, Hendrickx et al. (2010) annotated a Treebank of 1M tokens of European Portuguese with almost 2,000 CPs, which include LVCs and verbal chains. This lexicon is relevant for many NLP applications, notably for automatic translation, since in any task involving language generation they confer fluency and naturalness to the output of the system.

Work focusing on the automatic extraction of LVCs or SVCs often take as starting point a list of recurrent light verbs (Hendrickx et al., 2010) or a list of nominalizations (Teufel and Grefenstette, 1995; Dras, 1995; Hwang et al., 2010). These approaches are not adopted here because our goal is precisely to identify which are the verbs, the nouns and other lexical elements that take part in CPs.

Similar motivation to study LVCs/SVCs (for SRL) is found within the scope of Framenet (Atkins et al., 2003) and Propbank (Hwang et al., 2010). These projects have taken different decisions on how to annotate such constructions. Framenet annotates the head of the construction (noun or adjective) as argument taker (or frame evoker) and the light verb separately; Propbank, on its turn, first annotates separately light verbs and the predicative nouns (as ARG-PRX) and then merges them, annotating the whole construction as an argument taker.

We found studies regarding Portuguese LVCs/SVCs in both European (Athayde, 2001; Rio-Torto, 2006; Barreiro and Cabral, 2009; Duarte et al., 2010) and Brazilian Portuguese (Neves, 1996; Conejo, 2008; Silva, 2009; Abreu, 2011). In addition to the variations due to dialectal aspects, a brief comparison between these papers enabled us to verify differences in combination patterns of both variants. In addition, Brazilian Portuguese studies do not aim at providing data for NLP applications, whereas in European Portuguese there are at least two studies focusing on NLP applications: Barreiro and Cabral (2009), for automatic translation and Hendrickx et al. (2010) for corpus annotation.

3 Corpus, Extraction Tool and Methods

We employ a corpus-based methodology in order to create a dictionary of CPs. After a first step in which we use a computer software to automatically extract candidate n-grams from a corpus, the candidate lists have been analyzed by a linguist to distinguish CPs from fully compositional word sequences.

For the automatic extraction, the PLN-BR-FULL[2] corpus was used, consisting of news texts from *Folha de São Paulo* from 1994 to 2005, with 29,014,089 tokens. The corpus was first preprocessed for sentence splitting, case homogenization, lemmatization and POS tagging using the PALAVRAS parser (Bick, 2000).

Differently from the studies referred to in Section 2, we did not presume any closed list of light verbs or nouns as starting point to our searches. The search criteria we used contain seven POS patterns observed in examples collected during previous corpus annotation tasks[3]:

1. V + N + PRP: *abrir mão de* (*give up*, lit. *open hand of*);
2. V + PRP + N: *deixar de lado* (*ignore*, lit. *leave at side*);
3. V + DET + N + PRP: *virar as costas para* (*ignore*, lit. *turn the back to*);
4. V + DET + ADV: *dar o fora* (*get out*, lit. *give the out*);
5. V + ADV: *ir atrás* (*follow*, lit. *go behind*);
6. V + PRP + ADV: *dar para trás* (*give up*, lit. *give to back*);
7. V + ADJ: *dar duro* (*work hard*, lit. *give hard*).

This strategy is suitable to extract occurrences from active sentences, both affirmative and negative. Cases which present intervening material between the verb and the other element of the CP are not captured, but this is not a serious problem considering the size of our corpus, although it influences the frequencies used in candidate selection. In order to facilitate human analysis of candidate lists, we used the `mwetoolkit`[4]: a tool that has been developed specifically to extract MWEs from corpora, which encompasses candidate extraction through pattern matching, candidate filtering (e.g. through association measures) and evaluation tools (Ramisch et al., 2010). After generating separate lists of candidates for each pattern, we filtered out all those occurring less than 10 times in the corpus. The entries resulting of automatic identification were classified by their frequency and their annotation is discussed in the following section.

4 Discussion

Each pattern of POS tags returned a large number of candidates. Our expectation was to identify CPs among the most frequent candidates. First we annotated "interesting" candidates and then, in a deep analysis, we judged their idiomaticity. In the Table 1, we show the total number of candidates extracted before applying any threshold, the number of analyzed candidates using a threshold of 10 and the number of CPs by pattern divided into two columns: idiomatic and less idiomatic CPs. Additionally, each CP was annotated with one or more single-verb

[2] `www.nilc.icmc.usp.br/plnbr`

[3] V = VERB, N = NOUN, PRP = PREPOSITION, DET = DETERMINER, ADV = ADVERB, ADJ = ADJECTIVE.

[4] `www.sf.net/projects/mwetoolkit`

Pattern	Extracted	Analyzed	Less idiomatic	Idiomatic
V + N + PRP	69,264	2,140	327	8
V + PRP + N	74,086	1,238	77	8
V + DET + N + PRP	178,956	3,187	131	4
V + DET + ADV	1,537	32	0	0
V + ADV	51,552	3,626	19	41
V + PREP + ADV	5,916	182	0	2
V + ADJ	25,703	2,140	145	11
Total	407,014	12,545	699	74

Table 1: Statistics for the Patterns.

paraphrases. Sometimes it is not a simple task to decide whether a candidate constitutes a CP, specially when the verb is a very polysemous one and is often used as support verb. For example, *fazer exame em/de alguém/alguma coisa* (lit. *make exam in/of something/somebody*) is a CP corresponding to *examinar* (*exam*). But *fazer exame* in another use is not a CP and means to submit oneself to someone else's exam or to perform a test to pass examinations (take an exam). In the following sections, we comment the results of our analysis of each of the patterns.

4.1 VERB + NOUN + PREPOSITION

The pattern V + N is very productive, as every complement of a transitive verb not introduced by preposition takes this form. For this reason, we restricted the pattern, adding a preposition after the noun with the aim of capturing only nouns that have their own complements.

We identified 335 complex predicates, including both idiomatic and less idiomatic ones. For example, *bater papo* (*shoot the breeze*, lit. *hit chat*) or *bater boca* (*have an argument*, lit. *hit mouth*) are idiomatic, as their sense is not compositional. On the other side, *tomar consciência* (*become aware*, lit. *take conscience*) and *tirar proveito* (*take advantage*) are less idiomatic, because their sense is more compositional. The candidates selected with the pattern V + N + PRP presented 29 different verbs, as shown in Figure 1[5].

Sometimes, causative verbs, like *causar* (*cause*) and *provocar* (*provoke*) give origin to constructions paraphrasable by a single verb. In spite of taking them into consideration, we cannot call them LVCs, as they are used in their full sense. Examples:

- *provocar alteração* (*provoke alteration*)= *alterar* (*alter*);
- *causar tumulto* (*cause riot*) = *tumultuar* (*riot*).

Some of the candidates returned by this pattern take a deverbal noun, that is, a noun created from the verb, as stated by most works on LVCs and SVCs; but the opposite may also occur: some constructions present denominal verbs as paraphrases, like *ter simpatia por* (*have sympathy for*) = *simpatizar com* (*sympathize with*) and *fazer visita* (lit. *make visit*) = *visitar* (*visit*). These results oppose the idea about LVCs resulting only from the combination of a deverbal noun and a light verb. In addition, we have identified idiomatic LVCs that are not paraphrasable by verbs of the same word root, like *fazer jus a* (lit. *make right to*) = *merecer* (*deserve*).

Moreover, we have found some constructions that have no correspondent paraphrases, like *fazer sucesso* (lit. *make success*) and *abrir exceção* (lit. *open exception*). These findings evidence that, the most used test to identify LVCs and SVC — the existence of a paraphrase formed by a single verb, has several exceptions.

We have also observed that, when the CP has a paraphrase by a single verb, the prepositions that introduce the arguments may change or even be suppressed, like in:

- *Dar apoio* **a** *alguém* = *apoiar alguém* (*give support* **to** *somebody* = *support somebody*);

[5]We provide one possible (most frequent sense) English translation for each Portuguese verb.

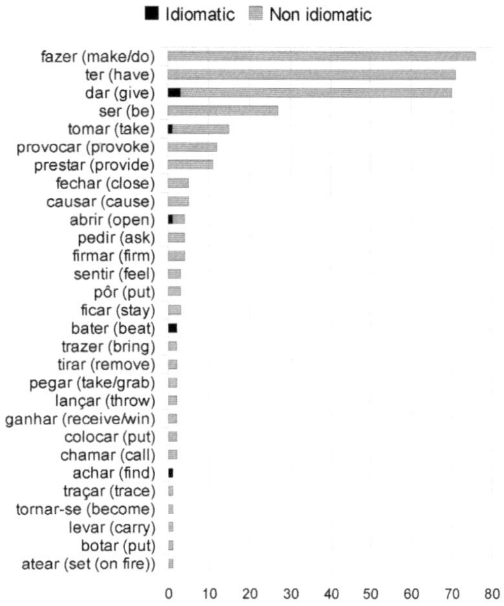

Figure 1: Distribution of verbs involved in CPs, considering the pattern V + N + PRP.

- *Dar cabo* **de** *alguém ou* **de** *alguma coisa* = *acabar* **com** *alguém ou* **com** *alguma coisa* (*give end* **of** *somebody or* **of** *something* = *end* **with** *somebody or* **with** *something*).

Finally, some constructions are polysemic, like:

- *Dar satisfação a alguém* (lit. *give satisfaction to somebody*) = make somebody happy or provide explanations to somebody;

- *Chamar atenção de alguém* (lit. *call the attention of somebody*) = attract the attention of somebody or reprehend somebody.

4.2 Verb + Preposition + Noun

The results of this pattern have too much noise, as many transitive verbs share with this CP class the same POS tags sequence. We found constructions with 12 verbs, as shown in Figure 2. We classified seven of these constructions as idiomatic CPs: *dar de ombro* (*shrug*), *deixar de lado* (*ignore*), *pôr de lado* (*put aside*), *estar de olho* (*be alert*), *ficar de olho* (*stay alert*), *sair de férias* (*go out on vacation*). The later example is very interesting, as *sair de férias* is synonym of *entrar em férias* (*enter on vacation*), that is, two antonym verbs are used to express the same idea, with the same syntactic frame. In the remaining constructions, the more frequent

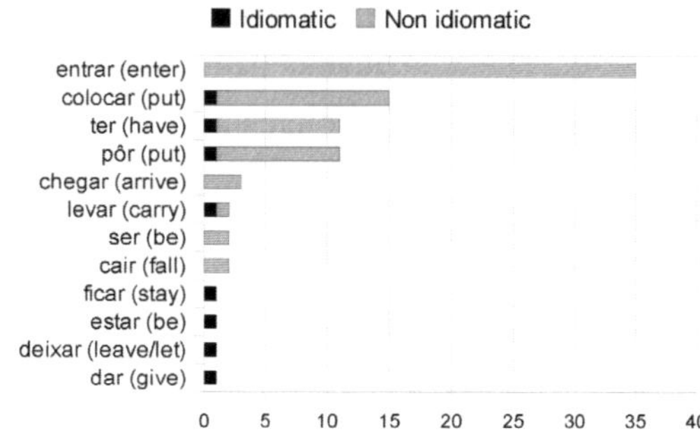

Figure 2: Distribution of verbs involved in CPs, considering the pattern V + PRP + N.

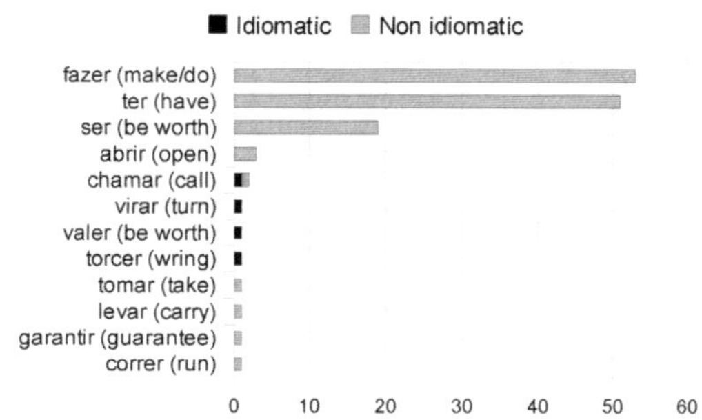

Figure 3: Distribution of verbs involved in CPs, considering the pattern V + DET + N + PRP.

verbs are used to give an aspectual meaning to the noun: *cair em*, *entrar em*, *colocar em*, *pôr em* (*fall in*, *enter in*, *put in*) have inchoative meaning, that is, indicate an action starting, while *chegar a* (*arrive at*) has a resultative meaning.

4.3 Verb + Determiner + Noun + Preposition

This pattern gave us results very similar to the pattern V + N + PRP, evidencing that it is possible to have determiners as intervening material between the verb and the noun in less idiomatic CPs. The verbs involved in the candidates validated for this pattern are presented in Figure 3.

The verbs *ser* (*be*) and *ter* (*have*) are special cases. Some *ter* expressions are paraphrasable by an expression with *ser* + ADJ, for example:

- *Ter a responsabilidade por* = *ser responsável por* (*have the responsibility for* = *be responsible for*);

- *Ter a fama de* = *ser famoso por* (*have the fame of* = *be famous for*);

- *Ter a garantia de* = *ser garantido por* (*have the guarantee of* = *be guaranteed for*).

Some *ter* expressions may be paraphrased by a single verb:

- *Ter a esperança de* = *esperar* (*have the hope of* = *hope*);
- *Ter a intenção de* = *tencionar* (*have the intention of* = *intend*);
- *Ter a duração de* = *durar* (*have the duration of* = *last*).

Most of the *ser* expressions may be paraphrased by a single verb, as in *ser uma homenagem para* = *homenagear* (*be a homage to* = *pay homage to*). The verb *ser*, in these cases, seems to mean "to constitute". These remarks indicate that the patterns *ser* + DET + N and *ter* + DET + N deserve further analysis, given that they are less compositional than they are usually assumed in Portuguese.

4.4 Verb + Determiner + Adverb

We have not identified any CP following this pattern. It was inspired by the complex predicate *dar o fora* (*escape*, lit. *give the out*). Probably this is typical in spoken language and has no similar occurrences in our newspaper corpus.

4.5 Verb + Adverb

This pattern is the only one that returned more idiomatic than less idiomatic CPs, for instance:

- *Vir abaixo* = *desmoronar* (lit. *come down* = *crumble*);
- *Cair bem* = *ser adequado* (lit. *fall well* = *be suitable*);
- *Pegar mal* = *não ser socialmente adequado* (lit. *pick up bad* = *be inadequate*);
- *Estar de pé*[6] = *estar em vigor* (lit. *be on foot* = *be in effect*);
- *Ir atrás (de alguém)* = *perseguir* (lit. *go behind (somebody)* = *pursue*);
- *Partir para cima (de alguém)* = *agredir* (lit. *leave upwards* = *attack*);
- *Dar-se bem* = *ter sucesso* (lit. *give oneself well* = *succeed*);
- *Dar-se mal* = *fracassar* (lit. *give oneself bad* = *fail*).

In addition, some CPs identified through this pattern present a pragmatic meaning: *olhar lá* (*look there*), *ver lá* (*see there*), *saber lá* (*know there*), *ver só* (*see only*), *olhar só* (*look only*), provided they are employed in restricted situations. The adverbials in these expressions are expletives, not contributing to the meaning, exception made for *saber lá*, (lit. *know there*) which is only used in present tense and in first and third persons. When somebody says "Eu sei lá" the meaning is "I don't know".

4.6 Verb + Preposition + Adverb

This is not a productive pattern, but revealed two verbal expressions: *deixar para lá (put aside)* and *achar por bem (decide)*.

4.7 Verb + Adjective

Here we identified three interesting clusters:

1. **Verbs of double object**, that is, an object and an attribute assigned to the object. These verbs are: *achar* (*find*), *considerar* (*consider*), *deixar* (*let/leave*), *julgar* (*judge*), *manter* (*keep*), *tornar* (*make*) as in: *Ele acha você inteligente* (lit. *He finds you intelligent* = *He considers you intelligent*). For SRL annotation, we will consider them as full verbs with two internal arguments. The adjective, in these cases, will be labeled as an argument. However, constructions with the verbs *fazer* and *tornar* followed by adjectives may give origin to some deadjectival verbs, like *possibilitar* = *tornar possível* (*possibilitate* = *make possible*). Other examples of the same type are: *celebrizar* (*make famous*), *esclarecer* (*make clear*), *evidenciar* (*make evident*), *inviabilizar* (*make unfeasible*), *popularizar* (*make popular*), *responsabilizar* (*hold responsible*), *viabilizar* (*make feasible*).

[6] The POS tagger classifies *de pé* as ADV.

2. **Expressions involving predicative adjectives**, in which the verb performs a functional role, in the same way as support verbs do in relation to nouns. In contrast to predicative nouns, predicative adjectives do not select their "support" verbs: they combine with any verb of a restrict set of verbs called copula. Examples of copula verbs are: *acabar* (*finish*), *andar* (*walk*), *continuar* (*continue*), *estar* (*be*), *ficar* (*stay*), *parecer* (*seem*), *permanecer* (*remain*), *sair* (*go out*), *ser* (*be*), *tornar-se* (*become*), *viver* (*live*). Some of these verbs add an aspect to the predicative adjective: durative (*andar*, *continuar*, *estar*, *permanecer*, *viver*) and resultative (*acabar*, *ficar*, *tornar-se*, *sair*).

    - The resultative aspect may be expressed by an infix, substituting the combination of V + ADJ by a full verb: *ficar triste* = *entristecer* (*become sad*) or by the verbalization of the adjective in reflexive form: *ficar tranquilo* = *tranquilizar-se* (*calm down*); *estar incluído* = *incluir-se* (*be included*).
    - In most cases, adjectives preceded by copula verbs are formed by past participles and inherit the argument structure of the verb: *estar arrependido de* = *arrepender-se de* (lit. *be regretful of* = *regret*).

3. **Idiomatic CPs**, like *dar duro* (lit. *give hard* = *make an effort*), *dar errado* (lit. *give wrong* = *go wrong*), *fazer bonito* (lit. *make beautiful* = *do well*), *fazer feio* (*make ugly* = *fail*), *pegar leve* (lit. *pick up light* = *go easy*), *sair errado* (lit. *go out wrong* = *go wrong*), *dar certo* (lit. *give correct* = *work well*).

4.8 Summary

We identified a total of 699 less idiomatic CPs and observed the following recurrent pairs of paraphrases:

- V = V + DEVERBAL N, e.g. *tratar* = *dar tratamento* (*treat* = *give treatment*);
- DENOMINAL V = V + N, e.g. *amedrontar* = *dar medo* (*frighten* = *give fear*);

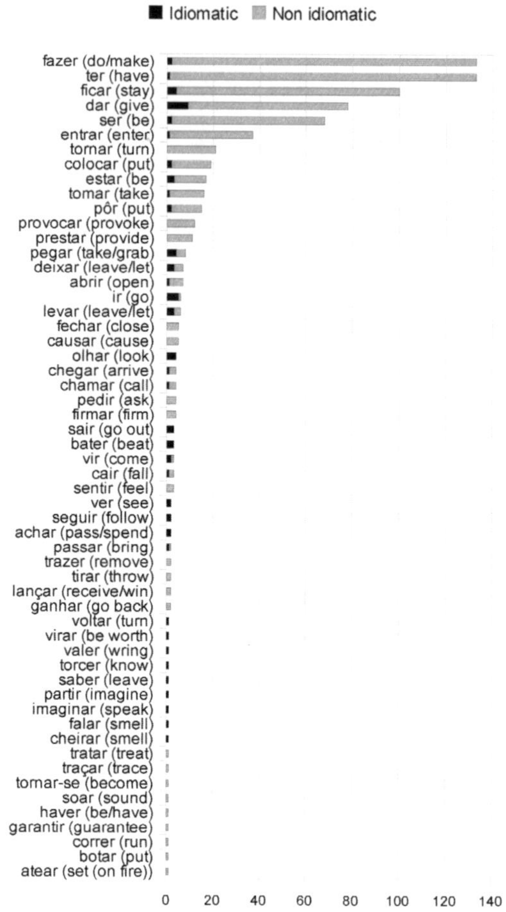

Figure 4: Distribution of verbs involved in CPs, considering the total number of CPs (i.e. all patterns).

- DEADJECTIVAL V = V + ADJ, e.g. *responsabilizar* = *tornar responsável* (lit. *responsibilize* = *hold responsible*).

This will help our further surveys, as we may search for denominal and deadjectival verbs (which may be automatically recognized through infix and suffix rules) to manually identify corresponding CPs. Moreover, the large set of verbs involved in the analyzed CPs, summarized in Figure 4, shows that any study based on a closed set of light verbs will be limited, as it cannot capture common exceptions and non-prototypical constructions.

5 Conclusions and Future Work

This study revealed a large number of CPs and provided us insights into how to capture them with more precision. Our approach proved to be very useful to identify verbal MWEs, notably with POS tag patterns that have not been explored by other studies (patterns not used to identify LVCs/SVCs). However, due to the onus of manual annotation, we assume an arbitrary threshold of 10 occurrences that removes potentially interesting candidates. Our hypothesis is that, in a machine-readable dictionary, as well as in traditional lexicography, rare entries are more useful than common ones, and we would like to explore two alternatives to address this issue. First, it would be straightforward to apply more sophisticated filtering techniques like lexical association measures to our candidates. Second, we strongly believe that our patterns are sensitive to corpus genre, because the CPs identified are typical of colloquial register. Therefore, the same patterns should be applied on a corpus of spoken Brazilian Portuguese, as well as other written genres like web-crawled corpora. Due to its size and availability, the latter would also allow us to obtain better frequency estimators.

We underline, however, that we should not underestimate the value of our original corpus, as it contains a large amount of unexplored material. We observed that only the context can tell us whether a given verb is being used as a full verb or as a light and/or support verb[7]. As a consequence, it is not possible to build a comprehensive lexicon of light and support verbs, because there are full verbs that function as light and/or support verbs in specific constructions, like *correr* (*run*) in *correr risco* (*run risk*). As we discarded a considerable number of infrequent lexical items, it is possible that other unusual verbs participate in similar CPs which have not been identified by our study.

For the moment, it is difficult to assess a quantitative measure for the quality and usefulness of our resource, as no similar work exists for Portuguese. Moreover, the lexical resource presented here is not complete. Productive patterns, the ones involving nouns, must be further explored to enlarge the aimed lexicon. A standard resource for English like DANTE[8], for example, contains 497 support verb constructions involving a fixed set of 5 support verbs, and was evaluated extrinsically with regard to its contribution in complementing the FrameNet data (Atkins, 2010). Likewise, we intend to evaluate our resource in the context of SRL annotation, to measure its contribution in automatic argument taker identification. The selected CPs will be employed in an SRL project and, as soon as we receive feedback from this experience, we will be able to report how many CPs have been annotated as argument takers, which will represent an improvement in relation to the present heuristic based only on parsed VPs.

Our final goal is to build a broad-coverage lexicon of CPs in Brazilian Portuguese that may contribute to different NLP applications, in addition to SRL. We believe that computer-assisted language learning systems and other Portuguese as second language learning material may take great profit from it. Analysis systems like automatic textual entailment may use the relationship between CPs and paraphrases to infer equivalences between propositions. Computational language generation systems may also want to choose the most natural verbal construction to use when generating texts in Portuguese. Finally, we believe that, in the future, it will be possible to enhance our resource by adding more languages and by linking the entries in each language, thus developing a valuable resource for automatic machine translation.

Acknowledgements

We thank the Brazilian research foundation FAPESP for financial support.

References

Débora Taís Batista Abreu. 2011. A semântica de construções com verbos-suporte e o paradigma Framenet. Master's thesis, São Leopoldo, RS, Brazil.

1997. *Complex Predicates*. CSLI Publications, Stanford, CA, USA.

Maria Francisca Athayde. 2001. *Construções com verbo-suporte (funktionsverbgefüge) do português e do alemão*. Number 1 in Cadernos do CIEG Centro Interuniversitário de Estudos Germanísticos. Universidade de Coimbra, Coimbra, Portugal.

Sue Atkins, Charles Fillmore, and Christopher R. Johnson. 2003. Lexicographic relevance: Selecting information from corpus evidence. *International Journal of Lexicography*, 16(3):251–280.

Sue Atkins, 2010. *The DANTE Database: Its Contribution to English Lexical Research, and in Particular to Complementing the FrameNet Data*. Menha Publishers, Kampala, Uganda.

[7] A verb is not light or support in the lexicon, it is light and/or support depending on the combinations in which it participates.

[8] www.webdante.com

Anabela Barreiro and Luís Miguel Cabral. 2009. ReEscreve: a translator-friendly multi-purpose paraphrasing software tool. In *Proceedings of the Workshop Beyond Translation Memories: New Tools for Translators, The Twelfth Machine Translation Summit*, pages 1–8, Ottawa, Canada, Aug.

Eckhard Bick. 2000. *The parsing system Palavras*. Aarhus University Press.

Miriam Butt. 2003. The light verb jungle. In *Proceedings of the Workshop on Multi-Verb Constructions*, pages 243–246, Trondheim, Norway.

Cássia Rita Conejo. 2008. O verbo-suporte fazer na língua portuguesa: um exercício de análise de base funcionalista. Master's thesis, Maringá, PR, Brazil.

Laurence Danlos and Pollet Samvelian. 1992. Translation of the predicative element of a sentence: category switching, aspect and diathesis. In *Proceedings of the Fourth International Conference on Theoretical and Methodological Issues in Machine Translation (TMI)*, pages 21–34, Montréal, Canada.

Mark Dras. 1995. Automatic identification of support verbs: A step towards a definition of semantic weight. In *Proceedings of the Eighth Australian Joint Conference on Artificial Intelligence*, pages 451–458, Canberra, Australia. World Scientific Press.

Inês Duarte, Anabela Gonçalves, Matilde Miguel, Amália Mendes, Iris Hendrickx, Fátima Oliveira, Luís Filipe Cunha, Fátima Silva, and Purificação Silvano. 2010. Light verbs features in European Portuguese. In *Proceedings of the Interdisciplinary Workshop on Verbs: The Identification and Representation of Verb Features (Verb 2010)*, Pisa, Italy, Nov.

Iris Hendrickx, Amália Mendes, Sílvia Pereira, Anabela Gonçalves, and Inês Duarte. 2010. Complex predicates annotation in a corpus of Portuguese. In *Proceedings of the ACL 2010 Fourth Linguistic Annotation Workshop*, pages 100–108, Uppsala, Sweden.

Jena D. Hwang, Archna Bhatia, Claire Bonial, Aous Mansouri, Ashwini Vaidya, Yuping Zhou, Nianwen Xue, and Martha Palmer. 2010. Propbank annotation of multilingual light verb constructions. In *Proceedings of the ACL 2010 Fourth Linguistic Annotation Workshop*, pages 82–90, Uppsala, Sweden.

Otto Jespersen. 1965. *A Modern English Grammar on Historical Principles*. George Allen and Unwin Ltd., London, UK.

Stefan Langer. 2004. A linguistic test battery for support verb constructions. *Special issue of Linguisticae Investigationes*, 27(2):171–184.

Stefan Langer, 2005. *Semantik im Lexikon*, chapter A formal specification of support verb constructions, pages 179–202. Gunter Naar Verlag, Tübingen, Germany.

Christiane Marchello-Nizia. 1996. A diachronic survey of support verbs: the case of old French. *Langages*, 30(121):91–98.

Maria Helena Moura Neves, 1996. *Gramática do português falado VI: Desenvolvimentos*, chapter Estudo das construções com verbos-suporte em português, pages 201–231. Unicamp FAPESP, Campinas, SP, Brazil.

Ryan North. 2005. Computational measures of the acceptability of light verb constructions. Master's thesis, Toronto, Canada.

Carlos Ramisch, Aline Villavicencio, and Christian Boitet. 2010. Multiword expressions in the wild? the mwetoolkit comes in handy. In *Proc. of the 23rd COLING (COLING 2010) — Demonstrations*, pages 57–60, Beijing, China, Aug. The Coling 2010 Organizing Committee.

Elisabete Ranchhod, 1999. *Lindley Cintra. Homenagem ao Homem, ao Mestre e ao Cidadão*, chapter Construções com Nomes Predicativos na Crónica Geral de Espanha de 1344, pages 667–682. Cosmos, Lisbon, Portugal.

Graça Rio-Torto. 2006. O Léxico: semântica e gramática das unidades lexicais. In *Estudos sobre léxico e gramática*, pages 11–34, Coimbra, Portugal. CIEG/FLUL.

Morris Salkoff. 1990. Automatic translation of support verb constructions. In *Proc. of the 13th COLING (COLING 1990)*, pages 243–246, Helsinki, Finland, Aug. ACL.

Hilda Monetto Flores Silva. 2009. Verbos-suporte ou expressões cristalizadas? *Soletras*, 9(17):175–182.

Suzanne Stevenson, Afsaneh Fazly, and Ryan North. 2004. Statistical measures of the semi-productivity of light verb constructions. In , *Proc. of the ACL Workshop on MWEs: Integrating Processing (MWE 2004)*, pages 1–8, Barcelona, Spain, Jul. ACL.

Simone Teufel and Gregory Grefenstette. 1995. Corpus-based method for automatic identification of support verbs for nominalizations. In *Proc. of the 7th Conf. of the EACL (EACL 1995)*, pages 98–103, Dublin, Ireland, Mar.

An N-gram frequency database reference to handle MWE extraction in NLP applications

Patrick Watrin
Centre for Natural Language Processing
Institut Langage et Communication
UCLouvain
patrick.watrin@uclouvain.be

Thomas François
Aspirant F.N.R.S.
Centre for Natural Language Processing
Institut Langage et Communication
UCLouvain
thomas.francois@uclouvain.be

Abstract

The identification and extraction of Multiword Expressions (MWEs) currently deliver satisfactory results. However, the integration of these results into a wider application remains an issue. This is mainly due to the fact that the association measures (AMs) used to detect MWEs require a critical amount of data and that the MWE dictionaries cannot account for all the lexical and syntactic variations inherent in MWEs. In this study, we use an alternative technique to overcome these limitations. It consists in defining an n-gram frequency database that can be used to compute AMs on-the-fly, allowing the extraction procedure to efficiently process all the MWEs in a text, even if they have not been previously observed.

1 Introduction

Multiword Expressions (MWEs) are commonly defined as "recurrent combinations of words that co-occur more often than expected by chance and that correspond to arbitrary word usages" (Smadja, 1993, 143). Their importance in the field of natural language processing (NLP) is undeniable. Although composed of several words, these sequences are nonetheless considered as simple units with regard to part-of-speech at the lexical as well as syntactic levels. Their identification is therefore essential to the efficiency of applications such as parsing (Nivre and Nilsson, 2004), machine translation (Ren et al., 2009), information extraction, or information retrieval (Vechtomova, 2005). In these systems, the principle of syntactic or semantic/informational unit is particularly important.

Although the identification and extraction of MWEs now deliver satisfactory results (Evert and Krenn, 2001; Pearce, 2002), their integration into a broader applicative context remains problematic (Sag et al., 2001). The explanations for this situation are twofold.

1. The most effective extraction methods resort to statistical association measures based on the frequency of lexical structures. They, therefore, require a critical amount of data and cannot function properly from a simple phrase or even from a short text.
2. Since the syntactic and lexical variability of MWEs may be high, lexical resources learned from a corpus cannot take it into account. The coverage of these resources is indeed too limited when applied to a new text.

To address these two limitations, this article describes how an n-gram frequency database can be used to compute association measures (AMs) efficiently, even for small texts. The specificity of this new technique is that AMs are computed on-the-fly, freeing it from the coverage limitation that afflicts more simple techniques based on a dictionary.

We start off focussing on our extraction method, and more particularly on the process via which a candidate structure is statistically validated (Section 2). This presentation principally aims to identify the precise needs of a frequency database reference, both in terms of the interrogation process and in the type of information to be kept in the database. Then, we will address various issues of storage and query performance raised by the design of the frequency database (Section 3). Finally, Section 4 reports the results of our experiments and Section 5 concludes and open up future perspectives.

2 Extraction process

Our extraction procedure is comparable to those developed by Smadja (1993) and Daille (1995). They use a linguistic filter upstream of the statistical estimation. Unlike purely statistical techniques, this solution provides less coverage but greater accuracy. It also allows us to assign a unique morpho-syntactic category to each extracted unit (as well as a description of its internal structure), which facilitates its integration into a more complex procedure.

Concretely, we first tagged the texts to clear any lexical ambiguities [1]. We then identified all MWE candidates in the tagged text with the help of a library of transducers [2] (or syntactic patterns). Finally, the list of candidates was submitted to the statistical validation module which assigns an AM to each of these.

2.1 Linguistic filters

In this study, we consider four basic types of nominal structures [3] : adjective-noun (*AN*), noun-adjective (*NA*), noun-preposition-noun (*NprepN*), and noun-noun (*NN*), which are likely to undergo three types of variations : modification (mainly adverbial insertion and / or adjectival), coordination, and juxtaposition (*e.g. NprepNprepN*, *NprepNN*, etc). This enables us to identify a wide variety of sequences that are labelled by XML tags which specify :

- the lexical heads of the various components ;
- the adjectival and prepositional dependencies ;
- any possible coordination.

This information can be exploited later to carry out the syntactic decomposition of the extracted structures and also to limit the statistical validation to the content words of each structure.

1. The tagging is done with the *TreeTagger* (Schmid, 1994).

2. To apply our transducers to the tagged text, we use *Unitex* (Paumier, 2003). The output of the process is a file containing only the recognized sequences.

3. As we work in the field of indexation, we limit our extraction to nominal terms.

2.2 Statistical validation

Association measures are conventionally used to automatically determine whether an extracted phrase is an MWE or not. They are mathematical functions that aim to capture the degree of cohesion or association between the constituents. The most frequently used measures are the *log-likelihood ratio* (Dunning, 1993), the *mutual information* (Church and Hanks, 1990) or the ϕ^2 (Church and Gale, 1991), although up to 82 measures have been considered by Pecina and Schlesinger (2006). In this paper, we did not aim to compare AMs, but simply to select some effective ones in order to evaluate the relevance of a reference for MWE extraction.

However, association measures present two main shortcomings that were troublesome for us : they are designed for bigrams, although longer MWEs are quite frequent in any corpus [4], and they require the definition of a threshold above which an extracted phrase is considered as an MWE. The first aspect is very limiting when dealing with real data where longer units are common. The second may be dealt with some experimental process to obtain the optimal value for a given dataset, but is prone to generalization problems. In the next two sections, we present the strategies we have used to overcome these two limitations.

2.2.1 Beyond bigrams

A common way to go beyond the bigram limitation is to compute the AMs at the bigram level and then use the results as input for the computation of higher order AMs (Seretan et al., 2003). However, our preliminary experimentations have yielded unsatisfactory results for this technique when it is applied to all words and not to heads only. This is probably a side effect of high frequency bigrams such as preposition-determiner (*prep det*) in French.

Another strategy explored by Silva and Lopes (1999) is the fair dispersion point normalization. For a given n-gram, which has $n-1$ dispersion points that define $n-1$ "pseudo-bigrams", they compute the arithmetic mean of the probabilities of the various combinations rather than attempting to pick up the right point. This technique enables the

4. In our test corpus (see Section 4), 2044 MWEs out of 3714 are longer than the bigrams.

authors to generalize various conventional measures beyond the bigram level. Among these, we selected the *fair log-likelihood ratio* as the second AM for our experiments (see Equation 1), given that the classic *log-likelihood ratio* has been found to be one of the best measures (Dunning, 1993; Evert and Krenn, 2001).

$$\begin{aligned} LogLik_f(w_1 \cdots w_n) &= 2 * \log L(pf1, kf1, nf1) \\ &+ \log L(pf2, kf2, nf2) \\ &- \log L(pf, kf1, nf1) \\ &- \log L(pf, kf2, nf2) \quad (1) \end{aligned}$$

where

$$kf1 = f(w_1 \cdots w_n) \quad nf1 = Avy$$
$$kf2 = Avx - kf1 \quad nf2 = N - nf1$$

$$Avx = \frac{1}{n-1} \sum_{i=1}^{i=n-1} f(w_1 \cdots w_i)$$

$$Avy = \frac{1}{n-1} \sum_{i=2}^{i=n} f(w_i \cdots w_n)$$

$$pf = \frac{kf1+kf2}{N} \quad pf1 = \frac{kf1}{nf1} \quad pf2 = \frac{kf2}{nf2}$$

and N is the number of n-grams in the corpus.

Silva and Lopes (1999) also suggested an AM of their own : the *Symmetrical Conditional Probability*, which corresponds to $P(w_1|w_2)P(w_2|w_1)$ for a bigram. They defined the fair dispersion point normalization to extend it to larger n-grams, as shown in Equation 2.

$$SCP_f([w_1 \cdots w_n]) = \frac{p(w_1 \cdots w_n)^2}{Avp} \quad (2)$$

where $w_1 \cdots w_n$ is the n-gram considered and Avp is defined as follows :

$$Avp = \frac{1}{n-1} \sum_{i=1}^{i=n-1} p(w_1 \cdots w_i) * p(w_{i+1} \cdots w_n) \quad (3)$$

Finally, we considered a last AM : the Mutual Expectation (Dias et al., 1999) (see Equation 4). Its specificity lies in its ability to take into account non-contiguous MWEs such as "to take __ decision" or "a __ number of", which can also be realized using the heads (see above).

$$ME(w_1 \cdots w_n) = \frac{f(w_1 \cdots w_n) * p(w_1 \cdots w_n)}{FPE} \quad (4)$$

where FPE is defined as follows :

$$FPE = \frac{1}{n}[p(w_2 \cdots w_n) + \sum_{i=2}^{n} p(w_1 \cdots \widehat{w_i} \cdots w_n)] \quad (5)$$

It should be noted that the expression $w_1 \cdots \widehat{w_i} \cdots w_n$, where the $\widehat{}$ indicates an omitted term, represents all the n (n-1)-grams the candidate MWE comprises. FPE is then able to estimate the "glue" between all the constituents separated by a gap, but this nevertheless requires a more complex string matching process.

To summarize, we have selected the three following association measures for n-grams : the fair log-likelihood ratio, SCP_f, and ME. Their efficiency is further discussed in Section 4.

2.2.2 Selection of MWEs

The second problem that arises when one wants to locate all the MWEs in a given text is the classification criterion. For the *log-likelihood ratio*, which follows a chi-square distribution once it is transformed as $-2 * log\lambda$, a first solution is to base the decision on the p-value. However, significance tests become highly unreliable for large corpora, since the high frequencies produce high scores for the chi-square and all phenomena then appear significant (Kilgarriff, 2005).

A second technique commonly used in the MWE literature is to select a threshold for the AM above which an analyzed phrase is considered as an MWE. Again, this threshold depends on the size of the corpus used and cannot be fixed once and for all for a specific AM. It must be obtained empirically for each application of an MWE extractor to a new text or to a new domain. In order not to resort to a threshold, (Silva et al., 1999) suggested the *LocalMax* algorithm that selects MWEs whose AMs are higher than those of their neighborhood. In other words, a given unit is classified as an MWE if $g(w_1 \cdots w_n)$, the associative function, is a local maximum.

In our case, since the notion of reference implies a large corpus and high frequencies, we rejected the first of these three approaches. We experimented with the second and third and show in Section 5 how the use of a reference could partially solve the threshold issues.

3 Reference Building

The integration of MWEs in an NLP system is usually done via a dictionary. MWEs are then regarded as a sequence of simple words separated by spaces (Sag et al., 2001). As a result, their lexical and syntactic structure is fixed and cannot be used to take into account variation at this level.

Several methods have been proposed to overcome this limitation. Nerima et al. (2006) and Sag et al. (2001) associate each MWE with a feature structure specifying the nature of units and the type of fixedness. This approach requires a manual validation of the features when inserting them into the dictionary. Watrin (2007) considers a simpler technique that consists in identifying, for each type of structure, all the possible insertion points and specifying the lexical and syntactic nature of possible modifiers. In this case, each MWE takes the form of a regular expression formalizing all possible variations from the canonical form.

Both solutions enable to consider more MWEs but fail to express all possible variations. For instance, phenomena such as coordination or juxtaposition do not seem to be taken into account by the authors mentioned above including Nerima et al. (2006). Moreover, they limit lexical variations to a finite set of canonical structures that have been encountered and are therefore unable to recognize new candidates.

The notion of reference which we define in this article aims to overcome these two limitations. Rather than providing a list of MWEs that are precomputed on a corpus, we suggest storing the information needed to calculate various AMs within a database. Hence, we no longer restrict MWEs to a finite set of lexical entries but allow the on-the-fly computation of AMs for any MWE candidate, whatever the size of the input text.

3.1 Implementation details

From a computational point of view, this idea involves the compression of a large number of lexical structures of order N as well as their absolute frequency. Moreover, the calculation of the various AMs considered in this study also requires the frequencies of all structures of order n, strictly lower than N ($0 < n < N$). The second type of information can however be inferred from the frequency of the structures of order N, provided the storage and questioning system is efficient enough for real-time applications. The need for efficiency also applies to queries related to the ME measure or the LocalMax algorithm that partly involve the use of wildcards.

This type of search tool can be efficiently implemented with a PATRICIA tree (Morrison, 1968). This data structure enables the compression of n-grams that share a common prefix and of the nodes that have only one child. The latter compression is even more effective as most of the n-grams have a unique suffix (Sekine, 2008). Beyond the compression that this structure allows, it also guarantees a very fast access to data insofar as a query is a simple tree traversal that can be done in constant time.

In order to further optimize the final data structure, we store the vocabulary in a table and associate an integer as a unique identifier for every word. In this way, we avoid the word repetition (whose size in memory far exceeds that of an integer) in the tree. Moreover, this technique also enables to speed up the query mechanism, since the keys are smaller.

We derived two different implementations of this structure. The first stores the data directly in memory. While it enables easy access to data, the number of n-grams that can be stored is limited by the capacity of the RAM. Therefore, in order to take a huge number of n-grams into account, we also implemented a "disk" version of the tree.

Finally, in order to treat wildcard queries needed by the ME and the LocalMax, we enhanced our structure with a set of indexes to improve access to each word, whatever its depth within the tree. Obviously, this mechanism might not be robust enough for a system multiplying the number of wildcards, but it is perfectly suited to the needs of an MWEs extraction process.

3.2 References used

Once the computational aspects of reference building have been dealt with, a corpus from which to populate the database needs to be selected. This aspect raises two issues : the size and the nature of the corpus used. Dunning (1993) has demonstrated that the size of the corpus from which MWEs are extracted matters. On the other hand, common characteristics of a corpus, such as its register, the contempora-

Reference	# 5-Grams	# Nodes
500 K	500,648	600,536
1000 K	1,001,080	1,183,346
5000 K	5,004,987	5,588,793
Google	1,117,140,444	62,159,203

TABLE 1: Number of 5-grams and nodes in the references used

neity of its language or the nature of the topics covered, may impact the performances of a reference when used on a text with different characteristics.

Given these issues, four corpora were selected (*cf.* Table 1). The first three are made up of articles published in the Belgian daily newspaper *Le Soir* in 2009, with 500K, 1000K and 5000K words respectively. They share many characteristics with our test corpus. The last corpus is made up of the largest amount of n-grams publicly available for French : the Google 5-grams [5] (Michel et al., 2011). Its size reaches 1T words [6], and its coverage in terms of topic and register is supposedly wider than corpora of newspaper articles only. In a sense, the Google reference may be viewed as an attempt to a universal reference.

4 Evaluation

Most evaluations of MWE extraction systems are based on human judgments and restrict the validation process to the n-best candidates. Inevitably partial, this method is unable to estimate performance in terms of recall. To overcome these limitations, we use the evaluation method described by Evert and Krenn (2001). They propose an automatic method that consists in computing both recall and precision using various n-best samples. It involves the formation of a golden standard (i.e. a list of MWEs manually identified in a corpus) and a sorted list of MWEs extracted automatically by applying AM on the same corpus. The recall and precision rates are therefore calculated by comparing the n-best (where n increases from 0 till n in steps of x) to the golden standard list [7].

4.1 The test corpus

In this study, we use the corpus described in Laporte et al. (2006). It is a French corpus in which all MWEs have been manually annotated. It consists of two sub-corpora :

- the transcription, in a written style, of the October 3rd and 4th, 2006 meetings of the French National Assembly (FNA), and
- the complete text of Jules Verne's novel "Around the World in 80 Days", published in 1873 (JV).

These two sub-corpora respectively contain 98,969 and 69,877 words for a total of 3,951 and 1,103 MWEs [8]. We limit our evaluation to the FNA corpus in order to keep data consistent both in terms of register and time. We assume that these two variables have a direct impact on the use of MWEs, a hypothesis that seems to be confirmed by the rate of MWEs in both sub-corpora.

4.2 Extractor Parameters

Before evaluating the performance of each of the above mentioned references, we first assessed the influence of the various parameters involved in the extraction process and which affect the performance of the AMs. These parameters are the LocalMax, the smoothing technique, the lemmatization of the MWE constituents (LEMMA) [9] and the head-driven validation (HDV) [10]. To select the optimal parameters for our extractor, we established an additional reference (1000K words from *Le Soir*).

5. For the purposes of comparison, we also limited the size of the n-grams indexed in *Le Soir* to 5 words.

6. In order to model a contemporary language, we only kept the frequencies observed in texts written between 2000 and 2008.

7. We build these lists from MWE types to avoid introducing a bias in the evaluation process. Well-recognised high frequency MWEs might indeed gloss over poorly recognised low-frequency MWEs.

8. These occurrences correspond to 1,384 MWE types for the FNA corpus and 521 for the JV corpus.

9. The lemmatization of the MWE constituents is based on the assumption that the inflexion of the lemmas implies a dispersal of the frequency mass (the overall frequency of a lemma is split between its inflected forms) that may affect the behavior of the AMs.

10. The HDV aims to focus on the lexical heads of the MWE candidates. Therefore, function words (prepositions, conjunctions, etc.) are ignored and replaced by wildcards in the queries sent to the reference in order to keep the distance information. For instance, from the sequence *ministre de l'agriculture* (Minister for Agriculture), we derive the form *ministre * * agriculture*.

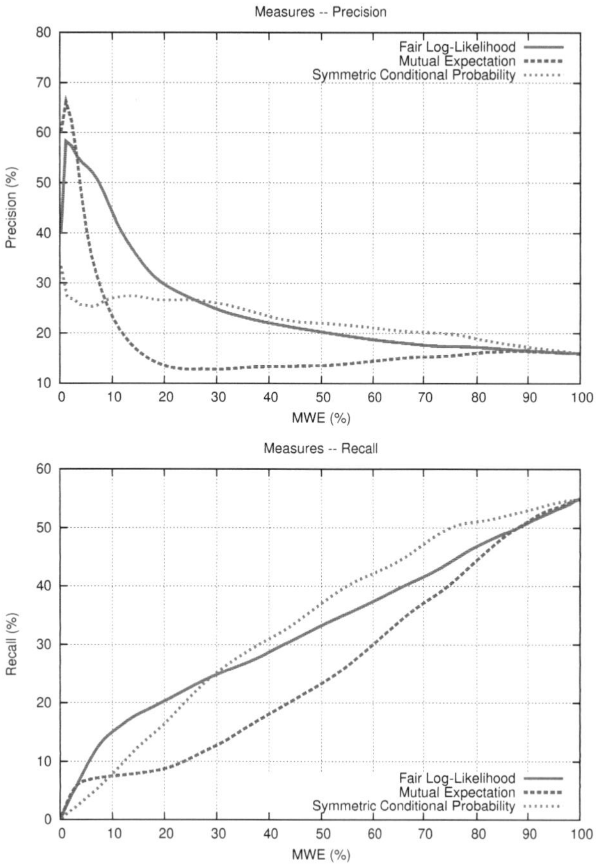

FIGURE 1: Evaluation of AMs

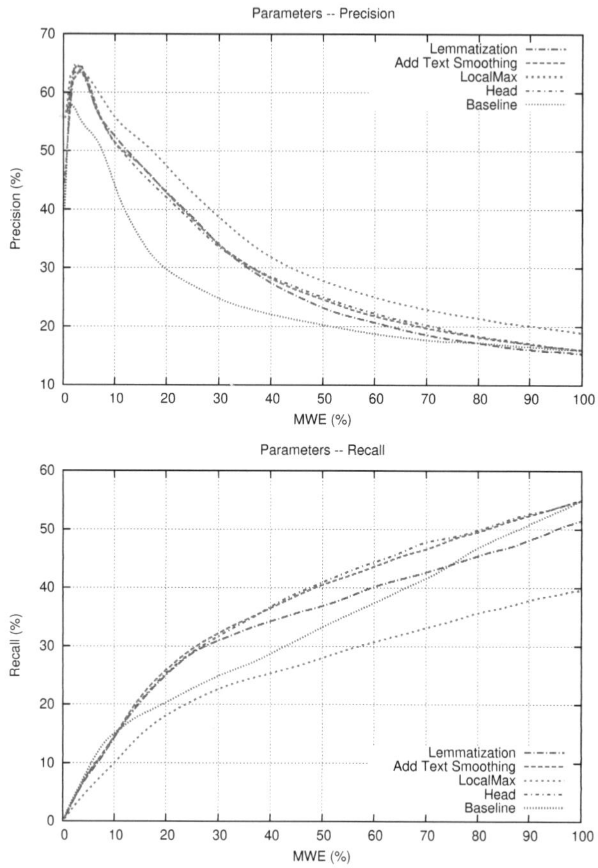

FIGURE 2: Evaluation of the parameters

The first step of this selection procedure was to define a baseline. For this purpose, we compared the precision and recall rates of our three AMs (see Figure 1) and kept only the best, namely the *log-likelihood ratio*, for the rest of our experiments. While the ME provides better precision for the top five percent of the extracted units, the *log-likelihood ratio* appears more reliable in that it maintains its efficiency over time (for recall as well as precision). The SCP, for its part, displays more stable results but does not reach sufficient precision.

On the basis of this baseline, we then separately compared the contribution of each of the four parameters. Results are reported in Figure 2 and detailed in the following subsections.

4.2.1 The LocalMax

Figure 2 shows that the LocalMax significantly improves the precision of the extraction. It emerges as the most relevant parameter at this level. However, unlike other parameters, its application directly affects the recall that falls below our baseline. This may not be a problem for certain applications. In our case, we aim to index and classify documents. Therefore, while we can accommodate a lower precision, we cannot entirely neglect the recall. We thus abandoned this parameter which, moreover, indubitably increases the processing time in that it requires the use of approximate matching (see Section 3.1).

4.2.2 The *Add-text smoothing*

Smoothing is another aspect worthy of consideration. No matter how large the reference used is, it will never constitute more than a subset of the language. Therefore, it is necessary to find a solution to estimate the frequency of unobserved n-grams. For the baseline, we used a simple "add-one" (or Laplace) smoothing (Manning and Schütze, 1999) which presents a severe flaw when the size of the n-grams to smooth increases : the normalization process discounts too much probability mass from observed events.

We therefore compare this simple method with another one we consider more "natural" : the "add-text" smoothing that adds the text to process to the reference. We view this method as more natural to the extent that it simulates a standard MWE extraction process. In this case, the reference complements the frequency universe of the input corpus as if it formed a homogeneous whole. Figure 2 demonstrates a clear superiority of the second smoothing procedure over the first one which was therefore discarded.

4.2.3 Lemmatization and HDV

The lemmatization and HDV follow a similar curve with regard to precision, although HDV is better for recall. Nonetheless, this difference only appears when precision falls below 35%. This does not seem sufficient to reject the lemmatization process whose computation time is significantly lower than for the HDV. We therefore limit the use of this last parameter to the reference built from Google whose n-grams cannot be lemmatized due to lack of context. [11]

4.3 Evaluation of the references

The estimation of the parameters allowed us to establish a specific evaluation framework. Two sets of parameters were defined depending on whether they apply to Google (ATS + HDV) or to the references built from *Le Soir* (ATS + LEMMA). From a practical standpoint, we limited the MWE extraction to nominal units of size inferior to five in order to meet the characteristics of our test corpus (the annotations of which are limited to nominal sequences), on the one hand, and to allow comparability of results on the other hand (the n-grams from Google do not exceed the order 5).

Initially, we considered the extraction of MWEs in the whole evaluation corpus. Results displayed in Figure 3 provide an advantage over the use of a reference with respect to the extraction carried out on the test corpus only. In addition, we see a clear improvement in performance with respect to that obtainable with a dictionary of MWEs. [12]

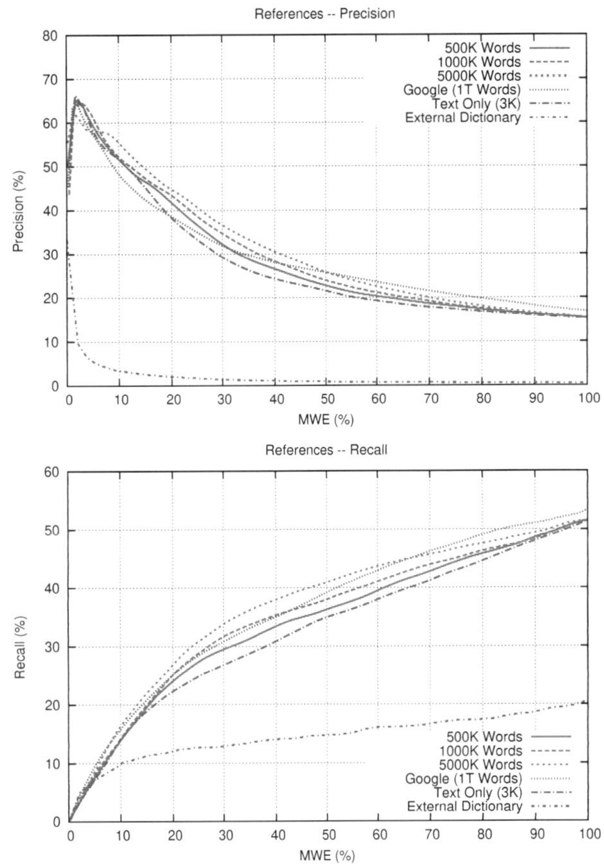

FIGURE 3: Evaluation on the 100K Corpus

In a second step, we wanted to test the efficiency of our references in the more adverse context of a short text. We randomly selected 3K words of our test corpus to simulate a short text while maintaining a sufficient number of MWEs (i.e. 151 nominal MWEs). Results shown in Figure 4 further confirm our first experience and validate our concept of a reference in a real application context.

Beyond validating the use of a frequency base, these results also confirm the general idea that the size of the corpus used for the reference matters. The differences between the references of 500K, 1000K and 5000K words showed a continuous improvement both in precision and recall. The results obtained with the Google reference are more surprising, since they do not meet that growing trend. However, given the number of errors that those n-grams contain (mainly due to the OCR-ization and tokeni-

11. References constructed on the basis of the newspaper *Le Soir* have been reindexed from a lemmatized text.

12. The MWE dictionary used in this experiment was initially derived from the corpus of 5000K words used to build the corresponding reference.

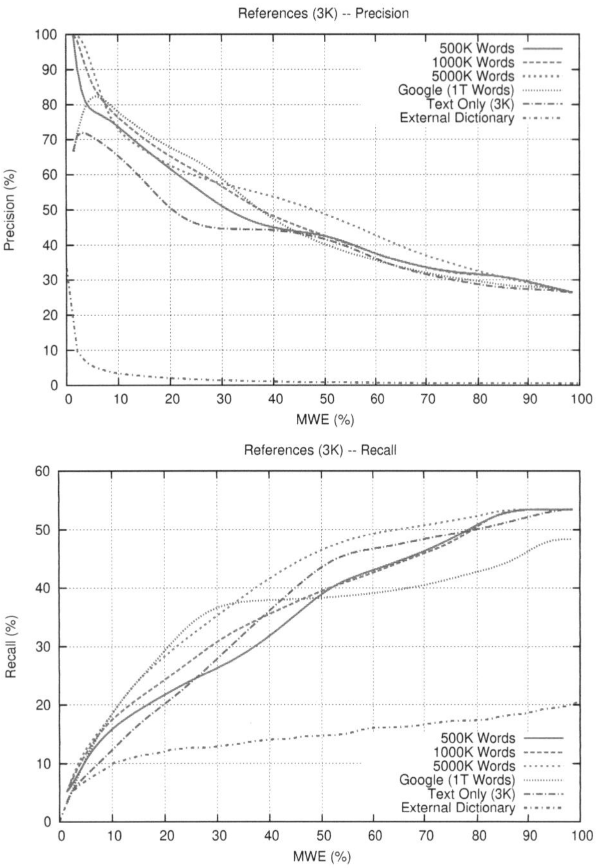

FIGURE 4: Evaluation on the 3K Corpus

zation processes), the result remains satisfactory. It even confirms to some extent the importance of size in the sense that preprocessing errors are being mitigated by the global mass of the frequencies.

5 Conclusion and perspectives

In this paper, we presented an MWE extraction system based on the use of frequency references. We have shown that its use enables MWE extraction on short texts with performances that are at least comparable to those achieved by standard solutions and far superior to solutions based on the use of MWE dictionaries.

Moreover, as this system has been integrated within an indexing engine, various issues were raised, some of which constitute avenues for future research. First, since our indexer aims at the identification of entities and terms specific to a given specialty area, the question of data representativeness is of particular importance. It is not clear to what

MWE	500 K	1000 K	5000 K	Google
même groupe	0.73	1.44	3.85	1,746.03
nouveaux instruments	3.81	3.3	49.83	2,793.65
lettres de noblesse	33.99	52.43	232.51	27,202.17

TABLE 2: Examples of MWEs candidates whose *log-likelihood ratio* is not significant on a small corpus and becomes extremely significant on a large corpus. They are compared to the score of an actual MWE.

extent a given reference can be applied to various types of texts. We only noticed that the Google reference, whose features were less similar to the test corpus, nevertheless yielded satisfactory results in comparison with our other references that better fitted the test corpus features.

In addition, our results show that the threshold issue remains relevant. Although the LocalMax seems to allow better discrimination of the MWE candidates, it is not selective enough to keep only the actual MWEs. On the other hand, as the size of the references increases, some results of the AMs based on the *log-likelihood ratio* reach high values that can no longer be interpreted by a chi-square significance test (see Table 2).

We believe that our references offer an interesting perspective to face this problem. The stability of their frequencies makes it possible to define a threshold corresponding to a specific percentage of precision and recall (set according to the needs of a given application). Therefore, as long as the size of the analyzed texts remains limited – which can be controlled –, the efficiency of this threshold should remain constant. Further experimentations on this aspect are however required to determine to what extent this assumption stands true as the size of the analyzed texts grows.

References

K.W. Church and W.A. Gale. 1991. Concordances for parallel text. In *Proceedings of the Seventh Annual Conference of the UW Centre for the New OED and Text Research*, pages 40–62.

K.W. Church and P. Hanks. 1990. Word association norms, mutual information, and lexicography. *Computational linguistics*, 16(1) :22–29.

J. da Silva and G.P. Lopes. 1999. A local maxima method and a fair dispersion normalization for extracting multi-word units from corpora. In *Sixth Meeting on Mathematics of Language*.

B. Daille. 1995. Combined approach for terminology extraction : lexical statistics and linguistic filtering. Technical report, Lancaster University.

G. Dias, S. Guilloré, and J.G.P. Lopes. 1999. Language independent automatic acquisition of rigid multiword units from unrestricted text corpora. *Proceedings of the 6th Conference on the Traitement Automatique des Langues Naturelles (TALN1999)*, pages 333–339.

T. Dunning. 1993. Accurate methods for the statistics of surprise and coincidence. *Computational linguistics*, 19(1) :61–74.

S. Evert and B. Krenn. 2001. Methods for the qualitative evaluation of lexical association measures. In *Proceedings of the 39th Annual Meeting on Association for Computational Linguistics*, pages 188–195.

A. Kilgarriff. 2005. Language is never ever ever random. *Corpus linguistics and linguistic theory*, 1(2) :263–276.

E. Laporte, T. Nakamura, and S. Voyatzi. 2006. A french corpus annotated for multiword expressions with adverbial function. In *Proceedings of the Language Resources and Evaluation Conference (LREC) : Linguistic Annotation Workshop*, pages 48–51.

C.D. Manning and H. Schütze, editors. 1999. *Foundations of Statistical Natural Language Processing*. MIT Press.

J.B. Michel, Y.K. Shen, A.P. Aiden, A. Veres, M.K. Gray, The Google Books Team, J.P. Pickett, D. Hoiberg, D. Clancy, P. Norvig, J. Orwant, S. Pinker, M.A. Nowak, and E.L. Aiden. 2011. Quantitative analysis of culture using millions of digitized books. *Science*, 331(6014) :176–182.

D.R. Morrison. 1968. PATRICIA—practical algorithm to retrieve information coded in alphanumeric. *Journal of the ACM*, 15(4) :514–534.

L. Nerima, V. Seretan, and E. Wehrli. 2006. Le problème des collocations en TAL. *Nouveaux cahiers de linguistique française*, 27 :95–115.

J. Nivre and J. Nilsson. 2004. Multiword units in syntactic parsing. In *Proceedings of LREC-04 Workshop on Methodologies & Evaluation of Multiword Units in Real-world Applications*, pages 37–46.

S. Paumier. 2003. *De la reconnaissance de formes linguistiques à l'analyse syntaxique*. Ph.D. thesis, Université de Marne-la-Vallée.

D. Pearce. 2002. A comparative evaluation of collocation extraction techniques. In *Proc. of the 3rd International Conference on Language Resources and Evaluation (LREC 2002)*, pages 1530–1536.

P. Pecina and P. Schlesinger. 2006. Combining association measures for collocation extraction. In *Proceedings of the 21th International Conference on Computational Linguistics and 44th Annual Meeting of the Association for Computational Linguistics (COLING/ACL 2006)*, pages 651–658.

Z. Ren, Y. L, J. Cao, Q. Liu, and Y. Huang. 2009. Improving statistical machine translation using domain bilingual multiword expressions. In *Proceedings of the Workshop on Multiword Expressions : Identification, Interpretation, Disambiguation and Applications*, pages 47–54.

I. Sag, T. Baldwin, F. Bond, A. Copestake, and D. Flickinger. 2001. Multiword expressions : A pain in the neck for NLP. In *In Proc. of the 3rd International Conference on Intelligent Text Processing and Computational Linguistics (CICLing-2002)*, pages 1–15.

H. Schmid. 1994. Probabilistic part-of-speech tagging using decision trees. In *Proceedings of International Conference on New Methods in Language Processing*, volume 12. Manchester, UK.

S. Sekine. 2008. A linguistic knowledge discovery tool : Very large ngram database search with arbitrary wildcards. In *COLING : Companion volume : Demonstrations*, pages 181–184.

V. Seretan, L. Nerima, and E. Wehrli. 2003. Extraction of Multi-Word Collocations Using Syntactic Bigram Composition. In *Proceedings of the 4th International Conference on Recent Advances in NLP (RANLP2003)*, pages 424–431.

J. da Silva, G. Dias, S. Guilloré, and J. Pereira Lopes. 1999. Using localmaxs algorithm for the extraction of contiguous and non-contiguous multiword lexical units. *Progress in Artificial Intelligence*, pages 849–849.

F. Smadja. 1993. Retrieving collocations from text : Xtract. *Computational Linguistics*, 19 :143–177.

O. Vechtomova. 2005. The role of multi-word units in interactive information retrieval. In D.E. Losada and J.M. Fernández-Luna, editors, *ECIR 2005, LNCS 3408*, pages 403–420. Springer-Verlag, Berlin.

P. Watrin. 2007. Collocations et traitement automatique des langues. In *Actes du 26e Colloque international sur le lexique et la grammaire*, pages 1530–1536.

Extracting Transfer Rules for Multiword Expressions from Parallel Corpora

Petter Haugereid and Francis Bond
Division of Linguistics and Multilingual Studies,
Nanyang Technological University, Singapore
petterha@ntu.edu.sg, bond@ieee.org

Abstract

This paper presents a procedure for extracting transfer rules for multiword expressions from parallel corpora for use in a rule based Japanese-English MT system. We show that adding the multi-word rules improves translation quality and sketch ideas for learning more such rules.

1 Introduction

Because of the great ambiguity of natural language, it is hard to translate from one language to another. To deal with this ambiguity it is common to try to add more context to a word, either in the form of multi-word translation patterns (Ikehara et al., 1991) or by adding more context to the translations in statistical MT systems (Callison-Burch et al., 2005).

In this paper, we present a way to learn large numbers of multi-word translation rules from either dictionaries or parallel text, and show their effectiveness in a semantic–transfer-based Japanese-to-English machine translation system. This research is similar to work such as Nichols et al. (2007). The novelty lies in (i) the fact that we are learning rules from parallel text and (ii) that we are learning much more complex rules.

In Section 2, we outline the semantic transfer machinery and we introduce the DELPH-IN machine translation initiative that provided the resources used in its construction. We describe in more detail how we learn new rules in Section 3, and show their effect in Section 4. We briefly discuss the results and outline future work in Section 5 and, finally, we conclude this paper in Section 6.

2 Semantic transfer

All experiments are carried out using Jaen, a semantic transfer based machine translation system (Bond et al., 2011). The system uses Minimal Recursion Semantics (MRS) as its semantic representation (Copestake et al., 2005). The transfer process takes place in three steps. First, a Japanese string is parsed with the Japanese HPSG grammar, JACY. The grammar produces an MRS with Japanese predicates. Second, the Japanese MRS is transferred into an English MRS. And finally, the English HPSG grammar ERG generates an English string from the English MRS.

At each step of the translation process, stochastic models are used to rank the output. There is a cutoff at 5, so the maximal amount of generated sentences is 125 (5x5x5). The final results are reranked using a combined model (Oepen et al., 2007).

While JACY and the ERG have been developed over many years, less effort has been put into the transfer grammar, and this component is currently the bottleneck of the system. In general, transfer rules are the bottleneck for any system, and there is a long history of trying to expand the number of transfer rules types (Matsuo et al., 1997) and tokens (Yamada et al., 2002).

In order to increase the coverage of the system (the number of words that we can translate) we build rules automatically. We look at strings that have a high probability of being a translation (identified from parallel corpora), and see if they fit a pattern defined in the transfer grammar. A very simple pattern would be that of a noun predicate being transferred as another noun predicate. The transfer rule type for this pattern is given in (1). The type makes sure that the LBL and the ARG0 values are kept when the relation is transferred, while the PRED value is left underspecified.[1]

(1) *noun-mtr*
IN|RELS ⟨[LBL *h1*, ARG0 *x1*]⟩
OUT|RELS ⟨[LBL *h1*, ARG0 *x1*]⟩

The rule for 本 (hon) → *book*, which is a subtype of *noun-mtr*, is given in (2).

(2) *hon_book*
IN|RELS ⟨[PRED _hon_n_rel]⟩
OUT|RELS ⟨[PRED _book_n_of_rel]⟩

A linguistically more interesting transfer rule is that for *PP* → *Adjective* transfer (see (3)), which takes as input 3 relations (the first for the noun, the second for the postposition, and the third for the quantifier of the noun, all properly linked), and outputs one relation (for the adjective), for example *of an angle* → *angular*, to give an English-to-English example. The output adjective relation is given the same handle, index and external argument as the input postposition, so that the semantic linking with the rest of the MRS is preserved. In this way, modifiers of the PP will modify the Adjective, and so on. The use of this transfer rule is demonstrated in Section 3.1.[2]

[1]the LBL (label) of the relation is a tag, which can be used to refer to the relation (conventionally written with an *h* for handle). The ARG0 is the index of the relation. Nouns and determiners have referential indices (conventionally written with an *x*), while adjectives and verbs have event indices (written with an *e*).

[2]The HCONS feature has as value a list of *qeq* constraints (equality modulo quantifiers), which function is to express that the label of a relation is equal to a handle in an argument position (without unifying them).

(3) *pp-adj_mtr*
IN [
RELS ⟨[LBL *h1*, ARG0 *x1*], [LBL *h0*, ARG0 *e0*, ARG1 *ext*, ARG2 *x1*], [ARG0 *x1*, RSTR *hr*]⟩
HCONS ⟨[HARG *hr*, LARG *h1*]⟩
]
OUT|RELS ⟨[LBL *h0*, ARG0 *e0*, ARG1 *ext*]⟩

3 Procedure

We are using GIZA++ (Och and Ney, 2003) and Anymalign (Lardilleux and Lepage, 2009) to generate phrase tables from a collection of four Japanese English parallel corpora and one bilingual dictionary. The corpora are the Tanaka Corpus (2,930,132 words: Tanaka (2001)), the Japanese Wordnet Corpus (3,355,984 words: Bond et al. (2010)), the Japanese Wikipedia corpus (7,949,605),[3] and the Kyoto University Text Corpus with NICT translations (1,976,071 words: Uchimoto et al. (2004)). The dictionary is Edict, a Japanese English dictionary (3,822,642 words: Breen (2004)). The word totals include both English and Japanese words.

We divided the corpora into development, test, and training data, and extracted the transfer rules from the training data. The training data of the four corpora together with the Edict dictionary form a parallel corpus of 20 million words (9.6 million English words and 10.4 million Japanese words). The Japanese text is tokenized and lemmatized with the MeCab morphological analyzer (Kudo et al., 2004), and the English text is tokenized and lemmatized with the Freeling analyzer (Padró et al., 2010), with MWE, quantities, dates and sentence segmentation turned off.

When applying GIZA++ and Anymalign to the lemmatized parallel corpus they produced phrase tables with 10,812,423 and 5,765,262 entries, respectively, running GIZA++ with the default MOSES settings and Anymalign for approximately 16 hours.

[3]The Japanese-English Bilingual Corpus of Wikipedia's Kyoto Articles: `http://alaginrc.nict.go.jp/WikiCorpus/index_E.html`

We filtered out the entries with an absolute frequency of 1,[4] and which had more than 4 words on the Japanese side or more than 3 words on the English side. This left us with 6,040,771 Moses entries and 3,435,176 Anymalign entries. We then checked against the Jacy lexicon on the Japanese side and the ERG lexicon on the English side to ensure that the source and the target could be parsed/generated by the MT system. Finally, we filtered out entries with a translation probability, P(English|Japanese), of less than 0.1. This gave us 1,376,456 Moses entries and 234,123 Anymalign entries. These were all phrase table entries with a relatively high probability, containing lexical items known both to the parser and the generator.

For each of these phrase table entries, we looked up the lexemes on either side in the Jacy/ERG lexicons, and represented them with the semantic predicate (and their syntactic category).[5] Ambiguous lexemes were represented with a list of predicates. We represented each possible surface rule with a list of all possible semantic predicate rules. So a possible surface rule with two (two times) ambiguous lexical items would give four possible semantic rules, a possible surface rule with three (two times) ambiguous lexical items would give eight possible semantic rules, and so on. A total of 53,960,547 possible semantic rules were created. After filtering out semantic transfer rules containing English predicates of probability less than 0.2 compared to the most frequent predicate associated with the same surface form, this number was reduced to 26,875,672.[6] Each of these rules consists of two ordered lists of semantic predicates (one for Japanese and one for English).

From these possible semantic transfer rules, we extracted transfer rules that fitted nine different patterns. We extracted 81,690 rules from the Moses entries, and 52,344 rules from the Anymalign entries. The total number of rules extracted was 97,478. (36,556 rules overlapped.) Once the rule templates have been selected and the thresholds set, the entire process is automatic.

The distribution of the extracted rules over the nine patterns is shown in Table 1.

In the first three patterns, we would simply see if the predicates had the appropriate '_n_' and '_a_' infixes in them (for nouns and adjectives respectively). 82,651 rules fitted these patterns and were accepted as transfer rules. The last six patterns were slightly more complex, and are described below.

3.1 PP → adjective

Japanese PPs headed by the postposition の *no* "of" often correspond to an adjective in English as illustrated in (4).

(4) a. 小型 の
small.size of
small

b. 音楽 の
music of
musical

In order to extract transfer rules that fit this pattern, we checked for possible semantic rules having two predicates on the Japanese side and one on the English side. The first Japanese predicate would have the infix '_n_' (be a noun), and the second would be '_no_p_rel' (the predicate of the postposition の). The sole English predicate would have the infix '_a_' (be an adjective).

3.2 PP → PP

Japanese PPs headed by the postposition で *de* "with/by/in/on/at" are, given certain NP complements, translated into English PPs headed by the preposition 'by' (meaning 'by means of') where the prepositional object does not have a determiner, as illustrated in (5).

(5) タクシーで
taxi DE
by taxi

By checking for possible semantic transfer rules fitting the pattern *noun* + *de_p_rel* on the Japanese

[4] The absolute frequency number can, according to Adrien Lardilleux (p.c.), be thought of as a confidence score. The larger, the more accurate and reliable the translation probabilities. 1 is the lowest score.

[5] As shown in (2), predicates reflect the syntactic category of the lexical item by means of an infix, e.g. '_n_' for *noun*.

[6] We used a profile of the English training data from the Tanaka Corpus and the Japanese Wordnet Corpus, parsed with the ERG grammar, to find the probability of each English predicate, given its surface form. For example the word *sleep* is assigned the predicate "_sleep_n_1_rel" 103 times, the predicate "_sleep_v_1_rel" 89 times, and "_sleep_v_in_rel" 2 times. Hence, semantic transfer rules containing the first two are accepted, while rules conataining the last are filtered out.

Input		Output	Moses	Anymalign	Merged rules
noun + noun	→	noun + noun	34,691	23,333	38,529
noun + noun	→	adj + noun	21,129	13,198	23,720
noun + noun	→	noun	11,824	12,864	20,402
PP	→	adj	753	372	1,022
PP	→	PP	131	24	146
verb + NP	→	verb + NP	9,985	1,926	10,256
noun + adj	→	adj	544	243	566
postp + noun + verb	→	verb	1,821	173	1,921
PP + verb	→	verb	812	211	916
Total			81,690	52,344	97,478

Table 1: Transfer rule patterns.

side, and the pattern *by_p_rel* and *noun* on the English side, we created PP to PP transfer rules where, in addition to the predicates stemming from the lexical items, the English determiner was set to the empty determiner (*udef_q_rel*). The resulting transfer rule for (5) is illustrated in (6).

(6) [*pp_pp_mtr*
IN ⟨[PRED _de_p_rel], [PRED udef_q_rel], [PRED _takushii_n_rel]⟩
OUT ⟨[PRED _by_p_means_rel], [PRED udef_q_rel], [PRED _taxi_n_1_rel]⟩]

With this particular pattern we get transfer rules which prevent us from generating all possible translations of で ('with', 'by', 'on', 'in', or 'at'), and keeps the quantifier unexpressed.

There are many other possible PP→PP patterns, such as 始めに *start in/on/at/to* "in the beginning". We started with one well known idiomatic English type, but should learn many more.

3.3 Verb + NP → Verb + NP

Japanese MWEs fitting the pattern *noun* + *object marker* (を) + *verb* usually are translated into English MWEs fitting one out of three *verb* + *NP* patterns, illustrated in (7). In (7a), the NP has an unexpressed quantifier. The English pattern in these cases will be *verb* + *noun*. In (7b), the NP has an indefinite article. The English pattern will then be *verb* + *_a_q_rel* + *noun*. And in (7c), the NP has definite article. The English pattern will then be *verb* + *_the_q_rel* + *noun*.

(7) a. テニスを します
tenisu wo shi masu
tennis ACC do POLITE
play tennis

b. 生計 を 立てる
seikei wo tateru
living ACC stand up
make a living

c. 責め を 負う
seme wo ou
blame ACC bear
take the blame

By adding these rules to the transfer grammar, we avoid generating sentences such as *I play the tennis* and *He took a blame*. In addition, we are able to constrain the translations of the individual words, greatly reducing the transfer search space

3.4 Noun + Adjective → Adjective

Japanese has a multiword expression pattern that is not found in English. In this pattern, *noun* + が (ga) + *adjective* usually correspond to English adjectives, as shown in (8). The pattern is an example of a double subject construction. The Japanese adjective has its subject provided by a noun, but still takes an external subject. Our transfer rule takes this external subject and links it to the subject of the English adjective.

(8) X ga 背 が 高い
X ga se ga takai
X ga NOM height NOM high
X is tall

With the new rules, the transfer grammar now correctly translates (9) as *She is very intelligent.* and not *Her head is very good.*, which is the translation produced by the system without the new multiword rules. Notice the fact that the adverb modifying the adjective in Japanese is also modifying the adjective in English.

(9) 彼女 は 大変 頭 が いい 。
kanojo wa taihen atama ga yoi .
She TOPIC very head NOM good .
She is very intelligent.

Because of the flexibility of the rule based system, we can also parse, translate and generate many variants of this, including those where the adverb comes in the middle of the MWE, or where a different topic marker is used as in (10). We learn the translation equivalences from text n-grams, but then match them to complex patterns, thus taking advantage of the ease of processing of simple text, but still apply them flexibly, with the power of the deep grammar.

(10) 彼女 も 頭 が 大変 いい 。
kanojo mo atama ga taihen yoi .
She FOCUS head NOM very good .
She is also very intelligent.
She is very intelligent also.

3.5 Postp + Noun + Verb → Verb / PP + Verb → Verb

Japanese has two MWE patterns consisting of a postposition, a noun, and a verb, corresponding to a verb in English. The first is associated with the postposition の *no* "of" (see (11)), and the second is associated with the postposition に *ni* "in/on/at/to" (see (12)).

(11) 歴史 の 勉強 を する
rekishi no benkyou wo suru
history of study ACC make
study history

(12) 金魚 に えさ を やる
kingyo ni esa wo yaru
goldfish in/on/at/to feed ACC give
feed the goldfish

In (11), the postposition の *no* "of", the noun 勉強 *benkyou* "study", and the verb する *suru* "make" are translated as *study*, while in (12), the postposition に *ni* "in/on/at/to", the noun えさ *esa* "feed", and the verb やる *yaru* "give" are translated as *feed*. In both MWE patterns, the noun is marked with the object marker を *wo*. The two patterns have different analysis: In (11), which has the *no*-pattern, the postposition attaches to the noun, and the object of the postposition 歴史 *rekishi* "history" functions as a second subject of the verb. In (12), which has the *ni*-pattern, the postposition attaches to the verb, and the object of the postposition 金魚 *kingyo* "goldfish" is a part of a PP. Given the different semantic representations assigned to the two MWE patterns, we have created two transfer rule types. We will have a brief look at the transfer rule type for the *no* translation pattern, illustrated in (13).[7]

(13)
$$\left[\begin{array}{l} \textit{p+n+arg12\_arg12\_mtr} \\ \text{IN} \left[\begin{array}{l} \text{RELS} \left\langle \begin{array}{l} \left[\begin{array}{l}\text{LBL } \boxed{h2}, \text{ ARG0 } \textit{event}, \\ \text{ARG1 } \boxed{x3}, \text{ ARG2 } \boxed{\mathbf{x2}}\end{array}\right] \\ \left[\text{LBL } \boxed{h2}, \text{ ARG0 } \boxed{x3}\right] \\ \left[\text{ARG0 } \boxed{x3}, \text{ RSTR } \boxed{h3}\right] \\ \left[\begin{array}{l}\text{LBL } \boxed{h1}, \text{ ARG0 } \boxed{e1}, \\ \text{ARG1 } \boxed{\mathbf{x1}}, \text{ ARG2 } \boxed{x3}\end{array}\right] \end{array} \right\rangle \\ \text{HCONS} \left\langle \left[\text{HARG } \boxed{h3}, \text{ LARG } \boxed{h2}\right] \right\rangle \end{array}\right] \\ \text{OUT}|\text{RELS} \left\langle \left[\begin{array}{l}\text{LBL } \boxed{h1}, \text{ ARG0 } \boxed{e1}, \\ \text{ARG1 } \boxed{\mathbf{x1}}, \text{ ARG2 } \boxed{\mathbf{x2}}\end{array}\right] \right\rangle \end{array}\right]$$

The input of the *p+n+arg12_arg12_mtr* transfer rule type consists of (i) a postposition relation, (ii) a noun relation, (iii) a quantifier (of the the noun),

[7] The transfer rule type for the *ni* translation pattern (*pp+arg12_arg12_mtr*) is identical to the transfer rule type for the *no* translation pattern except from the linking of the postposition in the input.

and (iv) a verb relation (listed as they appear on the RELS list). The output relation is a verb relation. Notice that the ARG1 of the input verb relation is reentered as ARG1 of the output relation (x1), and the ARG2 of the input postposition relation is reentered as ARG2 of the output relation (x2). The output relation is also given the same LBL and ARG0 value as the input verb relation. In this way, the Japanese MWE is collapsed into one English relation while semantic links to the rest of the semantic representation are maintained.

3.6 Summary

Out of the 26,875,672 possible semantic predicate rules, we extracted 97,478 rules that fitted one of the nine patterns. These rules were then included in the transfer grammar of the MT system.

4 Results

The impact of the MWE transfer rules on the MT system is illustrated in Table 2.

We compare two versions of the system, one with automatically extracted MWE rules and one without. They both have hand-written MWE and single word rules as well as automatically extracted single word rules extracted from Edict by Nichols et al. (2007).

The additional rules in + MWE are those produced in Section 3. The system was tested on held out sections of the Tanaka Corpus (sections 003 to 005). As can be seen from the results, the overall system is still very much a research prototype, the coverage being only just over 20%.

Adding the new rules gave small but consistent increases in both end-to-end coverage (19.3% to 20.1%) and translation quality (17.80% to 18.18%) measured with NEVA (Forsbom, 2003).[8]

When we look only at the 105 sentences whose translations were changed by the new rules the NEVA increased from 17.1% to 21.36%. Investigating the effects on development data, we confirmed that when the new MWE rules hit, they almost always improved the translation. However, there is still a problem of data-sparseness, we are missing instances of rule-types as well as missing many potential rule types.

As an example of the former, we have a pattern for verb+NP → verb+NP, but were unable to learn 慈悲を願う *jihi wo negau* "beg for mercy: lit. ask for compassion". We had one example in the training data, and this was not enough to get over our threshold. As an example of the latter, we do not currently learn any rules for Adverb+Verb→Verb although this is a common pattern.

5 Discussion and Further Work

The transfer rules learned here are based on cooccurrence data from corpora and a Japanese-to-English dictionary. Many of the translations learned are in fact compositional, especially for the compound noun and verb-object patterns. For example, 穴 を 掘る *ana-wo horu* "dig hole" → *dig a whole* would have been translated using existing rules. In this case the advantage of the MWE rule is that it reduces the search space, so the system does not have to consider less likely translations such as *carve the shortages*. More interestingly, many of the rules find non-compositional translations, or those where the structure cannot be translated word for word. Some of these are also idiomatic in the source and target language. One of our long term goals is to move these expressions into the source and target grammars. Currently, both Jacy and the ERG have idiom processing (based on Copestake et al., 2002), but there are few idiomatic entries in their lexicons. Bilingual data can be a good source for identifying these monolingual idioms, as it makes the non-compositionality explicit. An example of a rule that uses the current idiom machinery is the (hand-built) rule *N-ga chie-wo shiboru* "N squeezes knowledge" → *N racks N's brains*, where the subject is co-indexed with a possessive pronoun modifying the object: *I/You rack my/your brains*. Adding such expressions to the monolingual grammars simplifies the transfer rules and makes the grammars more useful for other tasks.

In this paper we only presented results for nine major multi-word transfer rule types. These were those that appeared often in the training and development data. We can straightforwardly extend this in two ways: by extending the number of rule types

[8]NEVA is an alternative to BLEU that is designed to provide a more meaningful sentence-level score for short references. It is calculated identically to BLEU, but leaving out the log and exponent calculations. We find it correlates highly with BLEU.

Version	Parse coverage	Transfer coverage	Generation coverage	Total coverage	NEVA (%)	F1
− MWE (0 rules)	3614/4500 (80.3%)	1647/3614 (45.6%)	870/1647 (52.8%)	870/4500 (19.3%)	17.80	0.185
+ adj/n (83,217 rules)	3614/4500 (80.3%)	1704/3614 (47.1%)	900/1704 (52.8%)	900/4500 (20.0%)	17.99	0.189
+ PP (1,168 rules)	3614/4500 (80.3%)	1659/3614 (45.9%)	877/1659 (52.9%)	877/4500 (19.5%)	17.88	0.187
+ verb (13,093 rules)	3614/4500 (80.3%)	1688/3614 (46.7%)	885/1688 (52.4%)	885/4500 (19.7%)	17.89	0.186
+ MWE (97,478 rules)	3614/4500 (80.3%)	1729/3614 (47.8%)	906/1729 (52.4%)	906/4500 (20.1%)	18.18	0.190

Table 2: Coverage of the MT system before and after adding the MWE transfer rules.

and by extending the number of rule instances.

Shirai et al. (2001) looked at examples in a 65,500-entry English-Japanese lexicon and estimated that there were at least 80 multi-word Japanese patterns that translated to a single word in English. As we are also going from multi-word to multi-word we expect that there will be even more than this. Currently, adding another pattern is roughly an hour's work (half to make the rule-type in the transfer engine, half to make the rule matcher in the rule builder). To add another 100 patterns is thus 6 weeks work. Almost certainly this can be speeded up by sharing information between the templates. We therefore estimate that we can greatly reduce the sparseness of rule-types with four weeks work.

To improve the coverage of rule instances, we need to look at more data, such as that aligned by Utiyama and Takahashi (2003).

Neither absolute frequency nor estimated translation probability give reliable thresholds for determining whether rules are good or not. Currently we are investigating two solutions. One is feedback cleaning, where we investigate the impact of each new rule and discard those that degrade translation quality, following the general idea of Imamura et al. (2003). The second is the more traditional human-in-the loop: presenting each rule and a series of relevant translation pairs to a human and asking them to judge if it is good or not. Ultimately, we would like to extend this approach to crowd source the decisions. There are currently two very successful online collaborative Japanese-English projects (Edict and Tatoeba, producing lexical entries and multilingual examples respectively) which indicates that there is a large pool of interested knowledgeable people.

Finally, we are working in parallel to qualitatively improve the MWE rules in two ways. The first is to extend rules using semantic classes, not just words. This would mean we would need fewer rules, but each rule would be more powerful. Of course, many rules are very idiomatic and should trigger on actual lexemes, but there are many, such as 慈悲を願う *himei wo negau* "beg for mercy" which allow some variation — in this case there are at least three different verbs that are commonly used. At a lower level we need to improve our handling of orthographic variants so that a rule can match on different forms of the same word, rather than requiring several rules. We are working together with the Japanese WordNet to achieve these goals.

The second approach is to learn complex rules directly from the parallel text, in a similar way to (Jellinghaus, 2007) or (Way, 1999). This will be necessary to catch rules that our templates do not include, but it is very easy to over-fit the rules to the translation data. For this reason, we are still constraining rules with templates.

Resource Availability

The MWE expression rules made here and the machine translation system that uses them are available through an open source code repository. Installation details can be found at `http://wiki.delph-in.net/moin/LogonInstallation`. The code to make the rules is undergoing constant revision, when it settles down we intend to also add it to the repository.

6 Conclusion

This paper presented a procedure for extracting transfer rules for multiword expressions from parallel corpora for use in a rule based Japanese-English MT system. We showed that adding the multiword rules improves translation coverage (19.3% to 20.1%) and translation quality (17.8% to 18.2% NEVA). We show how we can further improve by learning even more rules.

Acknowledgments

We would like to thank the members of the LOGON, and DELPH-IN collaborations for their support and encouragement. In addition we would like to thank the developers and maintainers of the other resources we used in our project, especially JMDict, Tatoeba, Anymalign and Moses. This project was supported in part by Nanyang Technological University (through a start-up grant on "Automatically determining meaning by comparing a text to its translation").

References

Francis Bond, Hitoshi Isahara, Kiyotaka Uchimoto, Takayuki Kuribayashi, and Kyoko Kanzaki. 2010. Japanese WordNet 1.0. In *16th Annual Meeting of The Association for Natural Language Processing*, pages A5–3. Tokyo.

Francis Bond, Stephan Oepen, Eric Nichols, Dan Flickinger, Erik Velldal, and Petter Haugereid. 2011. Deep open source machine translation. *Machine Translation*. (Special Issue on Open source Machine Translation, to appear).

James W. Breen. 2004. JMDict: a Japanese-multilingual dictionary. In *Coling 2004 Workshop on Multilingual Linguistic Resources*, pages 71–78. Geneva.

Chris Callison-Burch, Colin Bannard, and Josh Schroeder. 2005. Scaling phrase-based statistical machine translation to larger corpora and longer phrases. In *43nd Annual Meeting of the Association for Computational Linguistics: ACL-2005*.

Ann Copestake, Dan Flickinger, Carl J. Pollard, and Ivan A. Sag. 2005. Minimal Recursion Semantics: an introduction. *Research on Language and Computation*, 3(4):281–332. URL `http://lingo.stanford.edu/sag/papers/copestake.pdf`.

Ann Copestake, Fabre Lambeau, Aline Villavicencio, Francis Bond, Timothy Baldwin, Ivan Sag, and Dan Flickinger. 2002. Multiword expressions: Linguistic precision and reusability. In *Proceedings of the Third International Conference on Language Resources and Evaluation (LREC 2002)*, pages 1941–7. Las Palmas, Canary Islands.

Eva Forsbom. 2003. Training a super model look-alike: Featuring edit distance, n-gram occurrence, and one reference translation. In *In Proceedings of the Workshop on Machine Translation Evaluation. Towards Systemizing MT Evaluation*.

Satoru Ikehara, Satoshi Shirai, Akio Yokoo, and Hiromi Nakaiwa. 1991. Toward an MT system without pre-editing — effects of new methods in **ALT-J/E** —. In *Third Machine Translation Summit: MT Summit III*, pages 101–106. Washington DC. URL `http://xxx.lanl.gov/abs/cmp-lg/9510008`.

Kenji Imamura, Eiichiro Sumita, and Yuji Matsumoto. 2003. Feedback cleaning of machine translation rules using automatic evaluation. In *Proceedings of the 41st Annual Meeting of the Association for Computational Linguistics*, pages 447–454. Association for Computational Linguistics, Sapporo, Japan. URL `http://www.aclweb.org/anthology/P03-1057`.

Michael Jellinghaus. 2007. *Automatic Acquisition of Semantic Transfer Rules for Machine Translation*. Master's thesis, Universität des Saarlandes.

Taku Kudo, Kaoru Yamamoto, and Yuji Matsumoto. 2004. Applying Conditional Random Fields to Japanese Morphological Analysis. In Dekang Lin and Dekai Wu, editors, *Proceedings of EMNLP*

2004, pages 230–237. Association for Computational Linguistics, Barcelona, Spain.

Adrien Lardilleux and Yves Lepage. 2009. Sampling-based multilingual alignment. In *Proceedings of Recent Advances in Natural Language Processing (RANLP 2009)*, pages 214–218. Borovets, Bulgaria.

Yoshihiro Matsuo, Satoshi Shirai, Akio Yokoo, and Satoru Ikehara. 1997. Direct parse tree translation in cooperation with the transfer method. In Daniel Joneas and Harold Somers, editors, *New Methods in Language Processing*, pages 229–238. UCL Press, London.

Eric Nichols, Francis Bond, Darren Scott Appling, and Yuji Matsumoto. 2007. Combining resources for open source machine translation. In *The 11th International Conference on Theoretical and Methodological Issues in Machine Translation (TMI-07)*, pages 134–142. Skövde.

Franz Josef Och and Hermann Ney. 2003. A systematic comparison of various statistical alignment models. *Computational Linguistics*, 29(1):19–51.

Stephan Oepen, Erik Velldal, Jan Tore Lønning, Paul Meurer, and Victoria Rosen. 2007. Towards hybrid quality-oriented machine translation. on linguistics and probabilities in MT. In *11th International Conference on Theoretical and Methodological Issues in Machine Translation: TMI-2007*, pages 144–153.

Lluís Padró, Miquel Collado, Samuel Reese, Marina Lloberes, and Irene Castellón. 2010. Freeling 2.1: Five years of open-source language processing tools. In *Proceedings of 7th Language Resources and Evaluation Conference (LREC 2010)*. La Valletta. (`http://nlp.lsi.upc.edu/freeling`.

Satoshi Shirai, Kazuhide Yamamoto, and Kazutaka Takao. 2001. Construction of a dictionary to translate japanese phrases into one english word. In *Proceedings of ICCPOL'2001 (19th International Conference on Computer Processing of Oriental Languages*, pages 3–8. Seoul.

Yasuhito Tanaka. 2001. Compilation of a multilingual parallel corpus. In *Proceedings of PACLING 2001*, pages 265–268. Kyushu. (`http://www.colips.org/afnlp/archives/pacling2001/pdf/tanaka.pdf`).

Kiyotaka Uchimoto, Yujie Zhang, Kiyoshi Sudo, Masaki Murata, Satoshi Sekine, and Hitoshi Isahara. 2004. Multilingual aligned parallel treebank corpus reflecting contextual information and its applications. In Gilles Sérasset, editor, *COLING 2004 Multilingual Linguistic Resources*, pages 57–64. COLING, Geneva, Switzerland. URL `http://acl.ldc.upenn.edu/W/W04/W04-2208.bib`.

Masao Utiyama and Mayumi Takahashi. 2003. English-Japanese translation alignment data. `http://www2.nict.go.jp/x/x161/members/mutiyama/align/index.html`.

Andy Way. 1999. A hybrid architecture for robust MT using LFG-DOP. *Journal of Experimental and Theoretical Artificial Intelligence*, 11. Special Issue on Memory-Based Language Processing.

Setsuo Yamada, Kenji Imamura, and Kazuhide Yamamoto. 2002. Corpus-assisted expansion of manual mt knowledge. In *Ninth International Conference on Theoretical and Methodological Issues in Machine Translation: TMI-2002*, pages 199–208. Keihanna, Japan.

Identification and Treatment of Multiword Expressions applied to Information Retrieval

Otavio Costa Acosta, Aline Villavicencio, Viviane P. Moreira
Institute of Informatics
Federal University of Rio Grande do Sul (Brazil)
{ocacosta,avillavicencio,viviane}@inf.ufrgs.br

Abstract

The extensive use of Multiword Expressions (MWE) in natural language texts prompts more detailed studies that aim for a more adequate treatment of these expressions. A MWE typically expresses concepts and ideas that usually cannot be expressed by a single word. Intuitively, with the appropriate treatment of MWEs, the results of an Information Retrieval (IR) system could be improved. The aim of this paper is to apply techniques for the automatic extraction of MWEs from corpora to index them as a single unit. Experimental results show improvements on the retrieval of relevant documents when identifying MWEs and treating them as a single indexing unit.

1 Introduction

One of the motivations of this work is to investigate if the identification and appropriate treatment of Multiword Expressions (MWEs) in an application contributes to improve results and ultimately lead to more precise man-machine interaction. The term "multiword expression" has been used to describe a large set of distinct constructions, for instance support verbs, noun compounds, institutionalized phrases and so on. Calzolari et al. (2002) defines MWEs as a sequence of words that acts as a single unit at some level of linguistic analysis.

The nature of MWEs can be quite heterogeneous and each of the different classes has specific characteristics, posing a challenge to the implementation of mechanisms that provide unified treatment for them. For instance, even if a standard system capable of identifying boundaries between words, i.e. a tokenizer, may nevertheless be incapable of recognizing a sequence of words as an MWEs and treating them as a single unit if necessary (e.g. *to kick the bucket* meaning *to die*). For an NLP application to be effective, it requires mechanisms that are able to identify MWEs, handle them and make use of them in a meaningful way (Sag et al., 2002; Baldwin et al., 2003). It is estimated that the number of MWEs in the lexicon of a native speaker of a language has the same order of magnitude as the number of single words (Jackendoff, 1997). However, these ratios are probably underestimated when considering domain-specific language, in which the specialized vocabulary and terminology are composed mostly by MWEs.

In this paper, we perform an application-oriented evaluation of the inclusion of MWE treatment into an Information Retrieval (IR) system. IR systems aim to provide users with quick access to data they are interested (Baeza-Yates and Ribeiro-Neto, 1999). Although language processing is not vital to modern IR systems, it may be convenient (Sparck Jones, 1997) and in this scenario, NLP techniques may contribute in the selection of MWEs for indexing as single units in the IR system. The selection of appropriate indexing terms is a key factor for the quality of IR systems. In an ideal system, the index terms should correspond to the concepts found in the documents. If indexing is performed only with the atomic terms, there may be a loss of semantic content of the documents. For example, if the query was *pop star* meaning *celebrity*, and the terms were indexed individually, the relevant documents may not be retrieved and the system would return instead irrelevant documents about celestial bodies or carbonated drinks. In order to investigate the effects of indexing of MWEs for IR, the results of queries are analyzed using IR quality metrics.

This paper is structured as follows: in section 2 we discuss briefly MWEs and some of the challenges they represent. This is followed in section 3 by a discussion of the materials and methods employed in this paper, and in section 4 of the evaluation performed. We finish with some conclusions and future work.

2 Multiword Expressions

The concept of Multiword Expression has been widely viewed as *a sequence of words that acts as a single unit at some level of linguistic analysis* (Calzolari et al., 2002), or as *Idiosyncratic interpretations that cross word boundaries (or spaces)* (Sag et al., 2002).

One of the great challenges of NLP is the identification of such expressions, "hidden" in texts of various genres. The difficulties encountered for identifying Multiword Expressions arise for reasons like:

- the difficulty to find the boundaries of a multiword, because the number of component words may vary, or they may not always occur in a canonical sequence (e.g. *rock the boat, rock the seemingly intransigent boat* and *the bourgeois boat was rocked*);
- even some of the core components of an MWE may present some variation (e.g. *throw NP to the lions/wolves/dogs/?birds/?butterflies*);
- in a multilingual perspective, MWEs of a source language are often not equivalent to their word-by-word translation in the target language (e.g. *guarda-chuva* in Portuguese as *umbrella* in English and not as *?store rain*).

The automatic discovery of specific types of MWEs has attracted the attention of many researchers in NLP over the past years. With the recent increase in efficiency and accuracy of techniques for preprocessing texts, such as tagging and parsing, these can become an aid in improving the performance of MWE detection techniques. In terms of practical MWE identification systems, a well known approach is that of Smadja (1993), who uses a set of techniques based on statistical methods, calculated from word frequencies, to identify MWEs in corpora. This approach is implemented in a lexicographic tool called *Xtract*. More recently there has been the release of the *mwetoolkit* (Ramisch et al., 2010) for the automatic extraction of MWEs from monolingual corpora, that both generates and validates MWE candidates. As generation is based on surface forms, for the validation, a series of criteria for removing noise are provided, including some (language independent) association measures such as mutual information, dice coefficient and maximum likelihood. Several other researchers have proposed a number of computational techniques that deal with the discovery of MWEs: Baldwin and Villavicencio (2002) for verb-particle constructions, Pearce (2002) and Evert and Krenn (2005) for collocations, Nicholson and Baldwin (2006) for compound nouns and many others.

For our experiments, we used some standard statistical measures such as mutual information, pointwise mutual information, chi-square, permutation entropy (Zhang et al., 2006), dice coefficient, and t-test to extract MWEs from a collection of documents (i.e. we consider the collection of documents indexed by the IR system as our corpus).

3 Materials and Methods

Based on the hypothesis that the MWEs can improve the results of IR systems, we carried out an evaluation experiment. The goal of our evaluation is to detect differences between the quality of the standard IR system, without any treatment for MWEs, and the same system improved with the identification of MWEs in the queries and in the documents. In this section we describe the different resources and methods used in the experiments.

3.1 Resources and Tools

For this evaluation we used two large newspaper corpora, containing a high diversity of terms:

- Los Angeles Times (Los Angeles, USA - 1994)
- The Herald (Glasgow, Scotland - 1995)

Together, both corpora cover a large set of subjects present in the news published by these newspapers in the years listed. The language used is American English, in the case of the Los Angeles Times and British English, in the case of The Herald. Hereafter, the corpus of the Los Angeles Times will be referred as LA94 and The Herald as GH95. Together, they contain over 160,000 news articles (Table 1) and each news article is considered as a document.

Corpus	Documents
LA94	110.245
GH95	56.472
Total	166.717

Table 1: Total documents

The collection of documents, as well as the query topics and the list of relevance judgments (which will be discussed afterwards), were prepared in the context of the CLEF 2008 (*Cross Language Evaluation Forum*), for the task entitled *Robust-WSD* (Acosta et al., 2008). This task aimed to explore the contribution of the disambiguation of words to bilingual or monolingual IR. The task was to assess the validity of word-sense disambiguation for IR. Thus, the documents in the corpus have been annotated by a disambiguation system. The structure of a document contains information about the identifier of a term in a document (`TERM ID`), the lemma of a term (`LEMA`) and also its morphosyntactic tag (`POS`). In addition, it contains the form in which the term appeared in the text (`WF`) and information of the term in the WordNet (Miller, 1995; Fellbaum, 1998) as `SYNSET SCORE` and `CODE`, both not used for the experiment. An example of the representation of a term in the document is shown in Figure 1.

```
<TERM ID="GH950102-000000-126" LEMA="underworld" POS="NN">
<WF>underworld</WF>
<SYNSET SCORE="0.5" CODE="06120171-n"/>
<SYNSET SCORE="0.5" CODE="06327598-n"/>
</TERM>
```

Figure 1: Structure of a term in the original documents

In this paper, we extracted the terms located in the `LEMA` attribute, in other words, in their canonical form (e.g. *letter bomb* for *letter bombs*). The use of lemmas and not the words (e.g. *write* for *wrote*, *written*, etc.) to the formation of the corpus, avoids linguistic variations that can affect the results of the experiments. As a results, our documents were formed only by lemmas and the next step is the indexing of documents using an IR system. For this task we used a tool called *Zettair* (Zettair, 2008), which is a compact textual search engine that can be used both for the indexing and for querying text collections. Porter's Stemmer (Porter, 1997) as implemented in *Zettair* was also used. Stemming can provide further conflation of related terms. For example, *bomb* and *bombing* were not merged in the lemmatized texts but after stemming they are conflated to a single representation.

After indexing, the next step is the preparation of the query topics. Just as the corpus, only the lemmas of the query topics were extracted and used. The test collection has a total of 310 query topics. The judgment of whether a document is relevant to a query was assigned according to a list of relevant documents, manually prepared and supplied with the material provided by CLEF. We used *Zettair* to generate the ranked list of documents retrieved in response to each query. For each query topic, the 1,000 top scoring documents were selected. We used the cosine metric to calculate the scores and rank the documents.

Finally, to calculate the retrieval evaluation metrics (detailed in Section 3.5) we used the tool *trec eval*. This tool compares the list of retrieved documents (obtained from *Zettair*) against the list of relevant documents (provided by CLEF).

3.2 Multiword Expression as Single Terms

In this work, we focused on MWEs composed of exactly two words (i.e. bigrams). In order to incorporate MWEs as units for the IR system to index, we adopted a very simple heuristics that concatenated together all terms composing an MWE using "_" (e.g. *letter bomb* as *letter_bomb*). Figure 2 exemplifies this concatenation. Each bigram present in a predefined dictionary and occurring in a document is treated as a single term, for indexing and retrieval purposes. The rationale was that documents containing specific MWEs can be indexed more adequately than those containing the words of the expression separately. As a result, retrieval quality should increase.

Original Topic:
- What was the role of the Hubble telescope in proving the existence of black holes?

Modified Topic:
- what be the role of the hubble telescope in prove the existence of black hole ? **black_hole**

Figure 2: Modified query.

3.3 Multiword Expressions Dictionaries

In order to determine the impact of the quality of the dictionary used in the performance of the IR system, we examined several different sources of MWE of varying quality. The dictionaries containing the MWEs to be inserted into the corpus as a single term, are created by a number of techniques involving automatic and manual extraction. Below we describe how these MWE dictionaries were created.

- **Compound Nouns (CN)** - for the creation of this dictionary, we extracted all bigrams contained in the corpus. Since the number of available bigrams was very large (99,744,811 bigrams) we filtered them using the information in the original documents, the morphosyntactic tags. Along with the `LEMA` field, extracted in the previous procedure, we also extracted the value of the field *POS* (*part-of-speech*). In order to make the experiment feasible, we used only bigrams formed by compound nouns, in other words, when the `POS` of both words was NN (*Noun*). Thus, with bigrams consisting of sequences of NN as a preprocessing step to eliminate noise that could affect the experiment, the number of bigrams with MWE candidates was reduced to 308,871. The next step was the selection of bigrams that had the highest frequency in the text, so we chose candidates occurring at least ten times in the whole corpus. As a result, the first list of MWEs was composed by 15,001 bigrams, called *D1*.

- **Best Compound Nouns** - after D1, we refined the list with the use of statistical methods. The methods used were the mutual information and chi-square. It was necessary to obtain frequency values from Web using the search tool *Yahoo!*, because despite the number of terms in the corpus, it was possible that the newspaper genre of our corpus would bias the counts. For this work we used the number of pages in which a term occurs as a measure of frequency. With the association measures based on web frequencies, we generated a ranking in decreasing order of score for each entry. We merged the rankings by calculating the average rank between the positions of each MWE; the first 7,500 entries composed the second dictionary, called *D2*.

- **Worst Compound Nouns** - this dictionary was created from bigrams that have between five and nine occurrences and are more likely to cooccur by chance. It was created in order to evaluate whether the choice of the potentially more noisy MWEs entailed a negative effect in the results of IR, compared to the previous dictionaries. The third dictionary, with 17,328 bigrams, is called *D3*.

- **Gold Standard** - this was created from a sublist of the Cambridge International Dictionary of English (Procter, 1995), containing MWEs. Since this list contains all types of MWEs, it was necessary to further filter these to obtain compound nouns only, using morphosyntactic information obtained by the TreeTagger (Schmid, 1994), which for English is reported to have an accuracy of 96.36%" (Schmid, 1994). Formed by 568 MWEs, the fourth dictionary will be called *D4*.

- **Decision Tree** - created from the use of the J48 algorithm (Witten and Frank, 2000) from *Weka* (Hall et al., 2009), a data mining tool. With this algorithm it is possible to make a MWE classifier in terms of a decision tree. This requires providing training data with true and false examples of MWE. The training set contained 1,136 instances, half true (*D4*) and half false MWEs (taken from *D3*). After combining several statistical methods, the best result for classification was obtained with the use of mutual information, chi-square, pointwise mutual information, and Dice. The model obtained from Weka was applied to test data containing 15,001 MWE candidates (*D1*). The 12,782 bigrams classified as true compose the fifth dictionary, called *D5*.

- **Manual** - for comparative purposes, we also created two dictionaries by manually evaluating the text of the 310 query topics. The first dictionary contained all bigrams which would achieve a different meaning if the words were concatenated (e.g. *space shuttle*). This dictionary, was called *D6* and contains 254 expressions. The other one was created by a specialist (linguist) who classified as true or false a list of MWE candidates from the query topics. The linguist selection of MWEs formed *D7* with 178 bigrams.

3.4 Creating Indices

For the experiments, we needed to manipulate the corpus in different ways, using previously built dictionaries. The MWEs from dictionaries have been inserted in the corpus as single terms, as described before. For each dictionary, an index was created in the IR system. These indices are described below:

1. **Baseline (BL)** - corpus without MWE.
2. **Compound Nouns (CN)** - with 15 MWEs of *D1*.
3. **Best CN (BCN)** - with 7,500 MWEs of *D2*.
4. **Worst CN (WCN)** - with 17,328 MWEs of *D3*.
5. **Gold Standard (GS)** - with 568 MWEs of *D4*.
6. **Decision Tree (DT)** - with 12,782 MWEs of *D5*.
7. **Manual 1 (M1)** - with 254 MWEs of *D6*.
8. **Manual 2 (M2)** - with 178 MWEs of *D7*.

3.5 Evaluation Metrics

To evaluate the results of the IR system, we need to use metrics that estimate how well a user's query was satisfied by the system. IR evaluation is based on recall and precision. Precision (Eq. 1) is the portion of the retrieved documents which is actually relevant to the query. Recall (Eq. 2) is the fraction of the relevant documents which is retrieved by the IRS.

$$Precision(P) = \frac{\#Relevant \bigcap \#Retrieved}{\#Retrieved} \quad (1)$$

$$Recall(R) = \frac{\#Relevant \bigcap \#Retrieved}{\#Relevant} \quad (2)$$

Precision and Recall are set-based measures, therefore, they do not take into consideration the ordering in which the relevant items were retrieved. In order to evaluate ranked retrieval results the most widely used measurement is the *average precision* (*AvP*). AvP emphasizes returning more relevant documents earlier in the ranking. For a set of queries, we calculate the *Mean Average Precision* (MAP) according to Equation 3 (Manning et al., 2008).

$$MAP(Q) = \frac{1}{|Q|}\sum_{j=1}^{|Q|}\frac{1}{m_j}\sum_{k=1}^{m_j}P(R_{jk}) \quad (3)$$

where $|Q|$ is the number of queries, R_{jk} is the set of ranked retrieval results from the top result until document d_k, and m_j is the number of relevant documents for query j.

4 Experiment and Evaluations

The experiments performed evaluate the insertion of MWEs in results obtained in the IR system. The analysis is divided into two evaluations: (A) total set of query topics, where an overview is given of the MWE insertion effects and (B) topics modified by MWEs, where we evaluate only the query topics that contain MWEs.

4.1 Evaluation A

This evaluation investigates the effects of inserting MWEs in documents and queries. After each type of index was generated, MWEs were also included in the query topics, in accordance to the dictionaries used for each index (for Baseline BL, the query topics had no modifications).

With eight corpus variations, we obtained individual results for each one of them. The results presented in Table 2 were summarized by the absolute number of relevant documents retrieved and the MAP for the entire set of query topics. In total, 6,379 relevant documents are returned for the 310 query topics.

Index	Rel. Retrieved	MAP
BL	3,967	0.1170
CN	4,007	0.1179
BCN	3,972	0.1156
WCN	3,982	0.1150
GS	3,980	0.1193
DT	4,002	0.1178
M1	4,064	0.1217
M2	4,044	0.1205

Table 2: Results — Evaluation A.

It is possible to see a small improvement in the results for the indices M1 and M2 in relation to the baseline (BL). This happens because the choice of candidate MWEs was made from the contents of the document topics and not, as with other indices, from the whole corpus. Considering the indices built with MWEs extracted from the corpus, the best result is index GS.In second place, comes the CN index, with a subtle improvement over the Baseline. BL surprisingly got a better result than the Best and Worst CN. The loss in retrieval quality as a result from MWE identification for BCN was not expected.

When comparing the gain or loss in MAP of individual query topics, we can see how the index BCN compares to the Baseline: BCN had better MAP in 149 and worse MAP in 108 cases. However, the average loss is higher than the average gain, this explains why BL obtains a better result overall. In order do decide if one run is indeed superior to another, instead of using the absolute MAP value, we chose to calculate a margin of 5%. The intuition behind this is that in IR, a difference of less than 5% between the results being compared is not considered significant (Buckley and Voorhees, 2000). To be considered as gain the difference between the values resulting from two different indices for the same query topic should be greater than 5%. Differences of less than 5% are considered ties. This way, MAP values of 0.1111 and 0.1122 are considered ties. Given this margin, we can see in Tables 3 and 4 that the indices BCN and WCN are better compared to the baseline. In the case of BCN, the gain is almost 20% of cases and the WCN, the difference between gain and loss is less than 2%.

Gain	60	19.35%
Loss	35	11.29%
Ties	215	69.35%
Total	310	100.00%
Difference between Gain and Loss		8,06%

Table 3: BCN x Baseline

Gain	26	8.39%
Loss	21	6.77%
Ties	263	84.84%
Total	310	100.00%
Difference between Gain and Loss		1.61%

Table 4: WCN x Baseline

Finally, this first experiment guided us toward a deeper evaluation of the query topics that have MWEs, because there is a possibility that the MWE insertions in documents can decrease the accuracy of the system on topics that have no MWE.

4.2 Evaluation B

This evaluation studies in detail the effects on the document retrieval in response to topics in which there were MWEs. For this purpose, we used the same indices used before and we performed an individual evaluation of the topics, to obtain a better understanding on where the identification of MWEs improves or degrades the results.

As each dictionary was created using a different methodology, the number of expressions contained in each dictionary is also different. Thus, for each method, the number of query topics considered as having MWEs varies according to the dictionary used. Table 5 shows the number of query topics containing MWEs for each dictionary used, and as a consequence, the percentage of modified query topics over the complete set of 310 topics.

First, it is interesting to observe the values of MAP for all topics that have been altered by the identification of MWEs. These values are shown in Table 6.

As shown in Table 6 we verified that the GS index obtained the best result compared to others. This

Index	Topics with MWEs	% Modified
BL	0	0.00%
CN	75	24.19%
BCN	41	13.23%
WCN	28	9.03%
GS	9	2.90%
DT	51	16.45%
M1	195	62.90%
M2	152	49.03%

Table 5: Topics with MWEs

Index	MAP
CN	0.1011
BCN	0.0939
WCN	0.1224
GS	0.2393
DT	0.1193
M1	0.1262
M2	0.1236

Table 6: Results - Evaluation B

was somewhat expected since the MWEs in that dictionary are considered "real" MWEs. After GS, best results were obtained from the manual indices M1 and M2. The index that we consider as containing the lowest confident MWEs (WCN), obtained better results than Decision Trees, Nominal Compounds and Best Nominal Compounds, in this order. One possible reason for this to happen is that the number of MWEs inserted is higher than in the other indices. Compared with the BL, all indices with MWE insertion have improved more than degraded the results, in quantitative terms. Our largest gain was with the index GS, where 55.56% of the topics have improved, but the same index showed the highest percentage of loss, 22.22%. Analyzing the WCN, we can identify that this index has the lowest gain compared to all other indices: 32.14%, although having also the lowest loss. But, 60.71 % of the topics modified had no significant differences compared to the Baseline. Thus, we can conclude that the WCN index is the one that modifies the least the result of a query. The indices CN and BCN had a similar result, and knowing that a dictionary used to create BCN is a subset of the dictionary CN, we can conclude that the gain values, choosing the best MWE candidates, does not affect the accuracy, which only improves subtly. But the computational cost for the insertion of these MWEs in the corpus was reduced by half. In terms of gain percentage, indices M1 and M2 were superior only to WCN, but they are close to other results, including the DT index, which obtained an intermediate result between manual dictionaries and CN. Analyzing some topics in depth, like topic 141 (Figure 3), the best the result among all the indices was obtained by the CN.

```
<num>141</num>
<title>
letter bomb for kiesbauer find information on the explosion of a letter
bomb in the studio of the tv channel pro7 presenter arabella kiesbauer .
letter_bomb letter_bomb tv_channel
</title>
```

Figure 3: Topic #141

Table 7 shows the top ten scoring documents retrieved for query topic 141 in the baseline. The relevant document (in bold) is the fourth position in the Baseline. After inserting the expression *letter bomb* twice (because it occurs twice in the original topic), and *tv channel* that were in dictionary D1 used by the CN index, the relevant document is scored higher and as a consequence is returned in the first position of the ranking(Table 8) . The MAP of this topic has increased 75 percentage points, from 0.2500 in Baseline to 1.000 in the CN index. We see also that the document that was in first position in the Baseline ranking, has its score decreased and was ranked in fourth position in the ranking given by the CN. This document contained information on a "small bomb located outside the of the Russian embassy" and has is not relevant to topic 141, being properly relegated to a lower position.

An interesting fact about this topic is that only the MWE *letter bomb* influences the result. This was verified as in the index BCN, whose dictionary does not have this MWE, the topic was changed only because of the MWE *tv channel* and there was no gain or loss for the result.

The second highest gain was of M1 index, in topic 173. The gain was of 28 percentage points. On the other hand, we found a downside in M1 and M2 indices, although they improved results on average, they have reached very high values of loss in some topics.

Position	Document	Score
P1	LA043094-0230	0.470900
P2	GH950823-000105	0.459994
P3	GH951120-000182	0.439536
P4	**GH950610-000164**	**0.430784**
P5	GH950614-000122	0.428766
P6	LA091894-0425	0.428429
P7	GH950829-000082	0.422941
P8	GH950220-000162	0.411968
P9	GH950318-000131	0.406006
P10	GH950829-000037	0.402806

Table 7: Ranking for Topic #141 - Baseline

Position	Document	Score
P1	**GH950610-000164**	**0.457950**
P2	GH950614-000122	0.436753
P3	GH950823-000105	0.423938
P4	LA043094-0230	0.421757
P5	GH951120-000182	0.400123
P6	GH950829-000082	0.393195
P7	LA091894-0425	0.386613
P8	GH950705-000100	0.384116
P9	GH950220-000162	0.382157
P10	GH950318-000131	0.380471

Table 8: Ranking for Topic #141 - CN

In sum, the MWEs insertion seems to improve retrieval bringing more relevant documents, due to a more precise indexing of specific terms. However, the use of these expressions also brought a negative impact for some cases, because some topics require a semantic analysis to return relevant documents (as for example topic 130, which requires relevant documents to mention the causes of the death of Kurt Cobain — documents which mention his death without mentioning the causes were not considered relevant).

5 Conclusions and Future Work

This work consists in investigating the impact of Multiword Expressions on applications, focusing on compound nouns in Information Retrieval systems, and whether a more adequate treatment for these expressions can bring possible improvements in the indexing these expressions. MWEs are found in all genres of texts and their appropriate use is being targeted for study, both in linguistics and computing, due to the different characteristic variations of this type of expression, which ends up causing problems for the success of computational methods that aim their processing.

In this work we aimed at achieving a better understanding of several important points associated with the use of Multiword Expressions in IR systems. In general, the MWEs insertion improves the results of retrieval for relevant documents, because the indexing of specific terms makes it easier to retrieve specific documents related to these terms. Nevertheless, the use of these expressions made the results worse in some c]ases, because some topics require a semantic analysis to return relevant documents. Some of these documents are related to the query, but do not satisfy all criteria in the query topic. We conclude also that the quality of MWEs used directly influenced the results.

For future work, we would like to use other MWE types and not just compound nouns as used in this work. Other methods of extraction and a further study in Named Entities are good themes to complement this subject. A variation of corpora, different from newspaper articles, because each domain has a specific terminology, can also be an interesting subject for further evaluation.

References

Otavio Acosta, Andre Geraldo, Viviane Moreira Orengo, and Aline Villavicencio. 2008. Ufrgs@clef2008: Indexing multiword expressions for information retrieval. Aarhus, Denmark. Working Notes of the Workshop of the Cross-Language Evaluation Forum - CLEF.

Ricardo Baeza-Yates and Berthier Ribeiro-Neto. 1999. *Modern Information Retrieval*. ACM Press / Addison-Wesley.

Timothy Baldwin and Aline Villavicencio. 2002. Extracting the unextractable: A case study on verb-particles. Sixth Conference on Computational Natural Language Learning - CoNLL 2002.

Timothy Baldwin, C. Bannard, T. Tanaka, and D. Widdows. 2003. An empirical model of multiword expression decomposability. ACL 2003 Workshop on Multiword Expressions: Analysis, Acquisition and Treatment.

Chris Buckley and Ellen M. Voorhees. 2000. Evaluating evaluation measure stability. In *SIGIR '00: Proceedings of the 23rd annual international ACM SIGIR conference on Research and development in information retrieval*, pages 33–40, New York, NY, USA. ACM.

Nicoletta Calzolari, Charles Fillmore, Ralph Grishman, Nancy Ide, Alessandro Lenci, Catherine MacLeod, and Antonio Zampolli. 2002. Towards best practice for multiword expressions in computational lexicons. Third International Conference on Language Resources and Evaluation - LREC.

Stefan Evert and Brigitte Krenn. 2005. Using small random samples for the manual evaluation of statistical association measures. Computer Speech & Language - Special Issue on Multiword Expression - Volume 19, Issue 4, p. 450-466.

Christiane Fellbaum. 1998. *WordNet: An Electronic Lexical Database*. MIT Press, Cambridge, MA.

Mark Hall, Eibe Frank, Geoffrey Holmes, Bernhard Pfahringer, Peter Reutemann, and Ian H. Witten. 2009. The weka data mining software: An update.

Ray Jackendoff. 1997. The architecture of the language faculty. MIT Press.

Christopher D. Manning, Prabhakar Raghavan, and Hinrich Schtze. 2008. *Introduction to Information Retrieval*. Cambridge University Press. 1394399.

George A. Miller. 1995. Wordnet: a lexical database for english. *Commun. ACM*, 38:39–41, November.

Jeremy Nicholson and Timothy Baldwin. 2006. Interpretation of compound nominalisations using corpus and web statistic. Workshop on Multiword Expressions: Identifying and Exploiting Underlying Properties.

Darren Pearce. 2002. A comparative evaluation of collocation extraction techniques. Third International Conference on Language Resources and Evaluation.

Martin F. Porter. 1997. An algorithm for suffix stripping. pages 313–316, San Francisco, CA, USA. Morgan Kaufmann Publishers Inc.

Paul Procter. 1995. *Cambridge international dictionary of English*. Cambridge University Press, Cambridge, New York.

Carlos Ramisch, Aline Villavicencio, and Christian Boitet. 2010. Multiword expressions in the wild? the mwetoolkit comes in handy. In *Coling 2010: Demonstrations*, pages 57–60, Beijing, China, August. Coling 2010 Organizing Committee.

Ivan Sag, Timothy Baldwin, Francis Bond, Ann Copestake, and Dan Flickiger. 2002. Multiword expressions. a pain in the neck for nlp. Third International Conference on Computational Linguistics and intelligent Text Processing.

Helmut Schmid. 1994. Probabilistic part-of-speech tagging using decision trees. In *Proceedings of the International Conference on New Methods in Language Processing*.

Frank Smadja. 1993. Retrieving collocations from text: Xtract. Computational Linguistics.

Karen Sparck Jones. 1997. What is the role of nlp in text retrieval? University of Cambridge.

Ian H. Witten and Eibe Frank. 2000. *Data Mining: Practical Machine Learning Tools and Techniques with Java Implementations*. Morgan Kaufmann, San Francisco.

Zettair. 2008. The zettair search engine. (disponível via WWW em http://www.seg.rmit.edu.au/zettair).

Yi Zhang, Valia Kordoni, Aline. Villavicencio, and Marco Idiart. 2006. Automated multiword expression prediction for grammar engineering. COLING/ACL 2006 Workshop on Multiword Expressions: Identifying and Exploiting Underlying Properties.

Stepwise Mining of Multi-Word Expressions in Hindi

R. Mahesh K. Sinha
Indian Institute of Technology, Kanpur, India
sinharmk@gmail.com

Abstract

Multi-word expressions (MWEs) play an important role in all tasks that involve natural language processing. MWEs in Hindi are quite varied and many of these are of the types that are not encountered in English. In this paper, we examine different types of MWEs encountered in Hindi. Many of these have not received adequate attention of investigators. For example, 'vaalaa' constructs, doublets (word-pairs), replication, and a variety of verb group forms have not been explored *as MWEs*. We examine these MWEs from machine translation viewpoint. Many of these are frequently used in day-to-day conversations and informal communication but are not that frequently encountered in a formal textual corpus. Most of the conventional statistical methods for MWE identification use corpus with limited linguistic cues. These are found to be inadequate for detecting all types of MWEs that exist in real life. In this paper, we present a stepwise methodology for mining Hindi MWEs using linguistic knowledge. Interpretation and representation for some of these from machine translation perspective have also been explored.

1 Introduction

The identification and interpretation of multi-word expressions (MWEs) find application in almost all NLP tasks such as machine translation, information retrieval, question-answering etc. These are particularly helpful in parsing where the sequence of words forming the MWE is treated as a single word with a single part of speech (POS) tag. MWE information has been used for word alignment task (Venkatapathy et al., 2006). This is useful to lexicographers for deciding entry into the dictionary.

MWEs in Hindi are quite varied and many of these are of the types that are not encountered in English. No comprehensive work has been reported on Hindi MWE. In the following section a brief survey of related work is given. This is followed by a section on types of Hindi MWEs. Aspects of MWE identification, extraction and interpretation for Hindi are presented in section 4. Section 5 presents details of experimentation with results and section 6 concludes our investigation.

2 Related work

Baldwin et al. (2010) is an excellent review covering almost all aspects of MWEs. MWEs are characterized by non-compositionality, non-substitutability and non-modifiability (Brundage et al. 1992). Another definition of MWE is that it is 'any phrase that is not *entirely* predictable on the basis of standard grammar rules and lexical entries' (http://mwe.stanford.edu/reading-group.html). The design of a general purpose automated MWE extractor is dominated by using association measures such as point-wise mutual information and other statistical hypothesis tests (Church et al. 1990; Smadja 1993; Pecina 2008). Superior results have been reported when a supervised classifier is used with multiple association measures (Pecina 2008). The association measure is extended to include substitution to test semantic and statistical idiomaticity (Lin 1999). Moiron et al. (2006) use translation ambiguity to determine non-compositionality of MWEs.

For Hindi, there have been limited investigations on MWE extraction. Venkatapathy et al. (2005) considered N-V collocation extraction problem using MaxEnt classifier with certain syntactic and semantic features. Mukerjee et al. (2006) used POS projection from English to Hindi with corpus alignment for extracting complex predicates. Chakrabarti et al. (2008) present a method for extracting Hindi V+V compound verbs using linguistic features. Kunchukuttan et al. (2008) present a method for extracting compound nouns in Hindi using statistical co-occurrence. Sinha (2009b) use linguistic property of light verbs in extracting complex predicates using Hindi-English parallel corpus. All of these works have considered only limited aspects of Hindi MWE. In this paper, we have considered almost all types of MWEs in Hindi and present method for their identification using linguistic features.

3 Types of MWEs in Hindi

Multi-word expressions appear in a variety of forms in Hindi. The primary criterion used in defining a MWE in this work is non-compositionality i.e. the meaning of MWE is not composed purely on the meanings of the constituent words (Baldin et al. 2002). From machine translation perspective, non-compositionality is of primary concern. In the following subsections, we enumerate different types of MWEs in Hindi.

3.1 Replicating words

All South Asian languages have replicating word feature (Abbi 1975, Abbi 1992) that exhibit non-compositionality property of MWE. This is found for all parts of speech. Some examples from Hindi (Sinha et. al. 2005) are: *ghar ghar* {house house} 'every house' ; *ruk ruk* {stop stop}'after stopping'; *baRii baRii* {big big} 'quite big'; *ek ek* {one one}; 'every one' or 'one by one'; *dhiire dhiire* {slow slow} '(quite) slowly' or 'gradually'; Replicating words may also have a particle in between and the meaning changes. Example: *paani hi paani* (water only water) 'water all over'. Another class of MWE is where the replicating word is in singular form of the preceding word. An example is: *dinon-din* (days-day) 'day by day' or 'gradually'.

It should be noted here that not all replications make an MWE (see section 4).

3.2 Doublets / pair of words, Samaas and Sandhi

A pair of words that are antonym of each other may form an MWE. Example: *din-raat* (day night) 'all the time'. Yet another class is where the meaning of the doublet is usually a hyponym or a near synonym of the pair of the words. Example: *roji-roti* (job bread) 'employment'. When there is a change of gender in the pair of words, it may represent a group. Example: *betaa-betii* (son daughter) 'issues'. When the second word in the pair of words is a non-sensical word providing rhythm to the group, the meaning is hyponym of the preceding word. Examples: *chaay-vaaya* {tea vaaya} 'snacks'; *taix-viax* {tax viax} 'tax etc'.

Samaas (N+N, A+N) and Sandhi (means joining or fusion of words) are Hindi grammatical constructs at the morphological level and are borrowed concepts from Sanskrit. In Samaas, while combining the two words, the intervening postposition markers are deleted. Samaas are of different kinds depending upon the semantics of the constituent words involved and their importance (head word) in the resulting combined word. Examples: *rasoi* (cooking) +*ghar*(house) = *rasoighar* (house <u>for</u> cooking = kitchen); *ganga* (Ganges)+*jal*(water) = *gangajal* (water <u>from</u> Ganges). Sandhi is a process by which two words in Hindi get co-joined to yield a single word. This process could be recursively applied and quite complex compositions with multiple words are possible. The words formed by the process of Sandhi and some of the Samaas, result in a single word and as such cannot be called an MWE. However, they are very large in number in Hindi with innumerable combination of words. It is not practical to store all of them in a dictionary. Hence algorithms are designed to decompose the word into constituent words for interpretation. Thus, in a sense, it is the reverse process of MWE.

3.3 Vaalaa morpheme constructs

The 'vaalaa' Hindi morpheme may appear in different morphological forms as 'vaalaa', 'vaalii', 'vaale' or 'vaalo.M'. All the constructs involving 'vaalaa' are candidates for MWE. The multi-word may involve just the preceding word or both preceding and following words. The morpheme 'vaalaa' as such has no meaning. Examples (Sinha 2009a): *jaane vaalaa* (go vaalaa) 'about to go'; *doodh vaalii balti* (milk vaalii bucket) 'bucket filled with milk'; *lohe vaalii balti* (iron vaalii bucket) 'bucket made of iron'; *dilli vaalii gaadii* (Delhi vaalii train) 'train to/from Delhi'; *nahaane vaalaa sabun* (bathe vaalaa soap) 'soap used for bathing'; *sabzii vaalaa* (vegetable vaalaa) 'vegetable seller'.

3.4 Complex and Compound Verbs

The complex predicates and compound verb forms as MWEs have been widely studied (Hook, 1974; Abbi, 1992; Mohanan, 1994; Butt, 1995; Venkatapathy et.al., 2005; Mukerjee et. al., 2006; Chakrabarti et. al., 2008; Sinha 2009b). A complex predicate is a multi-word expression (MWE) where a noun, a verb or an adjective is followed by a light verb (LV) and the MWE behaves as a single verb unit. LV (Sinha 2009b) can also be a main verb. A compound verb form has the main verb in its root/stem form followed by conjugated light verbs. In Hindi compound verbs, the primary meaning of the light/helping verbs are often completely lost and may lead to a different semantic interpretation or result in affecting tense, aspect and modality of the compound verb. A few illustrative examples (light verbs are shown underlined): *daan denaa* (donation give) 'to donate'; *mukka maaranaa* (fist kill/beat) 'to punch'; *mukka de maaranaa* (fist give kill/beat) 'to blow punch'; *mukka maaraa gaya* (fist kill/beat went) 'was punched'; *mukka maaraa gaya thaa* (fist kill/beat went was) 'had been punched'; *mukka maaraa jaa rahaa thaa* (fist kill/beat go continue was) 'was being punched'; *mukka paRaa* (fist lie)'got punched '; *ruka jaao* (stop go) 'stop'; *aa jaao* (come go) 'come'; *galati kara baiThanaa* (mistake do sit); 'commit mistake (unintentional)'.

There are innumerable numbers of such MWEs in Hindi. However not all verb forms are MWEs.

3.5 Acronyms and Abbreviations

The acronyms and abbreviations in Hindi differ from their English counterparts. For example, the name 'Mohandas Karamchand Gandhi' may be abbreviated as 'ma. ka. gaandhii' (taking the first letter) or 'mo. ka. gaandhii' (taking the first letter with associated vowel modifier) or 'ema. ke. gaandhii' (taking the English alphabet letter). Similarly, the Hindi acronym for 'Bharatiya Janata Party' could be 'bee. je. pii.' (first English characters with dots) or 'beejepii.' (first English characters with no dots) or 'bhaa. ja. paa.' (first Hindi character with associated vowel modifier with dots) or 'bhaajapaa' (first Hindi character with associated vowel modifier with no dots). Although acronyms without dots are single words but they represent MWEs.

3.6 MWEs with foreign words and terms

It is often a common practice to mix foreign words and terms in day-to-today conversation in Hindi (Sinha et al. 2005b). Sometimes there are morphological variations to these as per Hindi grammar. These may appear as MWEs with arbitrary combinations. Some of these are institutionalized MWEs. Examples: *skilda* (skilled) *mainegaron* (managers); *spektram* (spectrum) *laaiisenson* (licenses). Here, the words *mainegaron* and *laaiisenson* are plural forms of the transliterated English words 'manager' and 'license' respectively, but the morphological changes are as per the Hindi pluralization rule. Since the foreign root word may undergo morphological variation as per Hindi grammar or may retain its English form, a cross morphological analysis is required to be done to extract the root word. Further, the transliteration of foreign word has a number of phonetic variations which needs to be considered before a look up into the English dictionary is performed. This class of MWE is not focused in this study.

4 Identification, extraction and interpretation of MWEs in Hindi

In this paper, we have considered only those MWEs that are particularly applicable to Hindi. The general characteristics of these MWEs have been outlined in the preceding section. We use these very characteristics in extracting the MWEs from the corpus. The extraction of MWEs that are more generally based on collocation and co-occurrence, require exhaustive and representative corpus to succeed which is not available for Hindi.

For identifying MWEs, we use multiple strategies and resources depending upon the class of the MWEs. The process of identification is semi-automatic. The automatic process generates the probable MWEs and then filtered manually. In future, the process can be fully automated using this tagged data through machine learning. A monolingual corpus and a lexical database (dictionary) are used in all the cases. In addition, a bilingual English-Hindi corpus and a Hindi wordnet are used for identifying some. We attempt to provide limited interpretation for some of these. Our method is mostly based on linguistic knowledge. We also show how these interpretations are engineered for a machine translation task by making appropriate substitutions in the source text.

For identification, there is a preferred order in which we mine them as it helps in further processing. At a broad level, the processes are: sentence boundary identification; POS tagging;

morphological analysis; identification of acronym and abbreviation with dots; Hindi chunker and verb-phrase form separation; identification of replicating class; identification of doublet class; identification of *vaalaa* morpheme construct class; complex predicates and compound verb identification; identification of acronym (with no dots); and identification of named-entities.

After the sentence boundary identification, POS tagging and the morphological analysis, the identification of acronyms and abbreviations that have dots associated with them, is carried out using a rule base. Next, chunking is performed. Chunking is a process of performing shallow parsing of the sentence where the words having affinity with each other at a syntactic level are grouped together. An example (chunks are shown within curly parentheses and English equivalent is enclosed within parentheses):{*bhagawaan raam ke haathon*}(by Lord Ram) {*mahaabalii raavana*}(mighty Ravan) {*yuddha bhoomi men*}(in battlefield) {*maara daalaa gayaa thaa*}(had been killed). In chunking, firstly the verb group is identified. Since Hindi is a verb ending language, a finite state machine (FSM) is designed which starts scanning the words from the rear end (right to left) for possible inclusion in the verb group based on the POS tag and the morphemes (Gune et al. 2010) of the words. A Hindi complex verb group may consist of auxiliaries, light verbs, predicate verbs and intensifiers besides the main verb. Such verb groups make an MWE because of its non-compositionality. In the above example, the last chunk which is the verb group chunk, is reproduced with meanings:{*maara* (kill) *daalaa* (put) *gayaa* (went) *thaa* (was)} (had been killed). Here main verb is *maara* (kill), *daalaa* (put) is a light verb making *maara daalaa* a predicate verb, *gayaa* (went) is an intensifier and *thaa* (was) is an auxiliary verb. The sequence of words that constitute the verb group could be quite long and is usually delimited by a postposition, a punctuation mark or a noun that does not form part of a predicate verb.

Identification of replicating words with a space, hyphen or a particle in between, and with plural-singular combination are searched within a chunk as identified in the earlier stage. The chunker creates a surface linear parse structure for the sentence and so is useful in eliminating false groupings of the replicating words. Replicating words (exact match) with a hyphen in between are definite MWEs while those without hyphen may not be so. In general, their identification and interpretation depends upon the associated POS and semantic role. Given below is an example rule (Sinha et al. 2005a) :

If the replicative verb has a suffix –te and the
main verb is of the 'resultive:psych' type
then <verb_x-te><verb_x-te> =>
due to|of <verb_x>+ing

This rule when applied to the Hindi sentence, *vah daurate daurate thak gayaa* (he run run tire went), yields the interpretation as 'He got tired of running'. For machine translation, the replicating words 'daurate daurate' is substituted by a dummy variable (say 'dv1') with POS as an adverb and its value will be stored as 'of running'. The Hindi sentence is modified to '*vah dv1 thak gayaa*' for machine translation. This kind of strategy is applied for all interpretations. The ambiguity resolution, if any, is left to the translation engine to tackle.

Hindi wordnet (Narayan et al., 2002) is used for checking antonym, hyponym and near synonym relationships in the pair of words. The doublets with hyphens are sure candidates of MWE but the doublets without hyphen are considered MWEs if they belong to the same chunk. In a semi-onomatopoeia combination, the second word is usually an unknown word and its suffix provides a rhythmic companionship. This is what is used in their identification. For example, in "*chaaya vaaya*". '*vaaya*' is an unknown word and the suffix '*aaya*' is common to the two words. The interpretation of the semi-onomatopoeia combination is usually the hyponym of the first word. Thus "*chaaya* (tea) *vaaya*" is interpreted as 'snacks'.

Since all 'vaalaa' constructs are MWEs, the mere presence of 'vaalaa' morpheme facilitates their identification. The major issue is that of determining the adjoining words that form the MWE. For this a number of rules are devised based on the semantic interpretation of the MWE. Given below is an illustration (Sinha 2009a):

> "If 'vaalaa' is preceded by a verb in infinitive form and followed by an auxiliary verb, then it represents a future event (about to action representing the verb). The verb+vaalaa is a MWE."

A number of such rules are devised using semantic relationships obtained through wordnet or a lexical database.

For identification of compound verb, we use a list of 30 light verbs (Sinha 2009b). When a verb in its stem form, is followed by a light verb, it is identified as a compound verb (strategy used is similar to Chakrabarti et al. 2008). This rule is applied recursively to make a larger group.

For the identification of complex predicates, we use a parallel aligned Hindi-English corpus. A simple heuristic of the absence of the light verb translated into English in the parallel corpus is taken as the complex predicate (Sinha 2009b).

We use an in-house named-entity recognizer. All the forms of the names as outlined in section 2.11 are detected and interpreted accordingly. All the unknown word sequences are considered probable candidates for MWEs. A name gazetteer is used to identify the named entities and the rest are checked for being acronyms. A majority of acronyms without dots in Hindi are mappings of English acronyms. Therefore, the individual Roman alphabet character mapping to Hindi is utilized to detect these. The names that are also valid dictionary words do not get identified.

5 Experimentation and Results

As a general corpus is very sparse in terms of occurrences of each type of MWE, we created corpus consisting of instances of different types sampled from various sources such as news articles, grammar books and corpora available at http://www.cfilt.iitb.ac.in/hin_corp_unicode.tar, www.cdacnoida.in/snlp/digital_library/gyan_nidhi.asp. The sampling was mostly done through an automatic process where templates of patterns were supplied with randomly picking up words from a list of frequent words created by an analysis of a Hindi corpus. These were further clubbed into six different classes of MWEs where each class consisted of similar MWE type. This helped us in taking care of sparseness to some extent to make our study more meaningful. Our sample space for each class consisted of approximately 5000 words.

Table 1 shows the results of our experimentation. The f-score varied from 27% to 97%. The identification of named entities is poor as it is based on a gazetteer and unknown words. The performance of the MWEs identification in the doublet class is affected due to inadequacy of the Hindi wordnet that has been used for some of its subclasses. The Hindi wordnet is not complete and many of the antonyms, hypernyms/hyponyms and ontological classification are not present.

Table 1: Experimental results

MWE Type	F-score
acronym and abbreviation with dots	92.2%
replicating class	97.4%
doublet class	73.6%
'vaala' construct class	90.7%
Complex predicates and compound verbs	77.2%
acronym (with no dots) and named entity	27.5%

6 Conclusions and Discussions

In this paper, we have provided comprehensive details and characteristics of the MWEs that are specific to Hindi. Many of these characteristics are generic in nature in the sense that it is not based on any statistical inference but it is the linguistic property that helps in MWE extraction. For example, all replicating words irrespective of their POS, all doublets with plural-singular form combinations, 'vaala' forms, complex verb forms etc are all strong candidates for MWEs in Hindi irrespective of whether these have earlier been encountered in the corpus or not. This means that even the low frequency MWEs can be captured. All the statistical approaches require the corpus to be representative and exhaustive in order to be able to yield reliable results (limitations: Kunchukuttan et al., 2008). Moreover, most of the idiosyncrasies of the language surface in informal conversations and are rarely available in regular textual corpora (Baldwin et al., 2010). The statistical approach will anyway be needed to mine other types of MWEs and discover new and institutionalized MWEs (mostly domain specific) that keep getting added (Baldwin et al., 2010). However, our stepwise methodology of filtering MWEs in stages provides a reduced sample space for searching the MWEs. Thus the size of the bag of the context words (Katz, 2006) needed for their identification and interpretation gets reduced. One of the primary aims of this study is to collect MWEs of different types in a semi-automatic way for use by the lexicographers for possible entry in the dictionary and stepwise mining is helpful.

Our contribution lies in presenting a comprehensive study of all types of MWEs encountered in Hindi and devise methods for their mining. We have not been able to present a detailed description of our method due to space constraints. In future work, we would like to hybridize rule based and statistical methods with bootstrapping of the data obtained for different classes.

References

Amitabh Mukerjee, A. Soni, and A. Raina. 2006. Detecting Complex Predicates in Hindi using POS Projection across Parallel corpora. ACL Workshop on Multiword Expressions

Anoop Kunchukuttan and Om P. Damani. 2008. A System for Compound Noun Multiword Expression Extraction for Hindi. Proceedings of International Conference on Natural Language Processing (ICON2008)

Anvita Abbi. 1992. Reduplication in South Asian Languages: An Areal, Typological and Historical Study. Allied Publishers, New Delhi.

Anvita Abbi. 1975. Reduplication in Hindi: A Generative Semantic Study. Dissertation Abstracts Internacional, Vol. 36, University of NY (1975).

Anvita Abbi. 1992. The explicator compound verb:some definitional issues and criteria for identification. Indian Linguistics, 53, 27-46.

B. V. Moiron and J. Tiedemann. 2006. Identifying idiomatic expressions using automatic word alignment. EACL 2006 Workshop on Multiword Expressions in a multilingual context.

Debasri Chakrabarti, Hemang Mandalia, Ritwik Priya, Vaijayanthi Sarma and Pushpak Bhattacharyya.2008. Hindi Compound Verbs and their Automatic Extraction, Computational Linguistics (COLING08), Manchester, UK.

D. Lin. 1999. Automatic identification of noncompositional phrases. ACL-1999.

D. Narayan, D. Chakrabarti, P. Pandey, and P.Bhattacharyya. 2002. An experience in building the IndoWordNet - a WordNet for Hindi. Global WordNet Conference.

G. Katz and E. Giesbrechts. 2006. Automatic identification of noncompositional multi-word expressions using Latent Semantic Analysis. ACL Workshop on Multiword Expressions.

Harshada Gune, Mugdha Bapat, Mitesh Khapra and Pushpak Bhattacharyya. 2010. Verbs are where all the Action Lies: Experiences of Shallow Parsing of a Morphologically Rich Language, Computational Linguistics Conference (COLING 2010), Beijing, China.

I. A. Sag,, T. Baldwin, F. Bond, A. C-opestake, and D. Flickinger. 2002. Multiword expressions: A pain in the neck for NLP. In Proceedings of the 3rd International Conference on Intelligent Text Processing and Computational Linguistics (CICLing-2002), Mexico City, Mexico. 1–15

Jennifer Brundage, M. Kresse, U. Schwall and A. Storrer. 1992. Multiword lexemes: A monolingual and contrastive typology for natural language processing and machine translation. Technical Report 232, Institut fuer Wissensbasierte Systeme, IBM Deutschland GmbH, Heidelberg.

K. Church and P. Hanks. 1990. Word association norms, mutual information, and lexicography. Computational Linguistics. 16(1).

Miriam Butt. 1995. The Structure of Complex Predicates in Urdu. CSLI Publications.

P. Pecina. 2008. Lexical Association Measures. Ph. D. thesis, Charles University.

Peter Edwin Hook. 1974. The Compound Verb in Hindi. Center for South and Southeast Asian Studies: The University of Michigan.

R. Mahesh K. Sinha. 2009a. Learning Disambiguation of Hindi Morpheme 'vaalaa' with a Sparse Corpus, The Eighth International Conference on Machine Learning and Applications (ICMLA 2009), Miami, Florida, USA

R. Mahesh K. Sinha. 2009b. Mining Complex Predicates In Hindi Using Parallel Hindi-English Corpus, ACL-IJCNLP 2009 Workshop on Multi Word Expression (MWE 2009), Singapore.

R. M. K. Sinha and Anil Thakur. 2005a. Dealing with Replicative Words in Hindi for Machine Translation to English, 10th Machine Translation summit (MT Summit X), Phuket, Thailand., 157-164.

R. M. K. Sinha and Anil Thakur. 2005b. Machine Translation of Bi-lingual Hindi-English (Hinglish) Text, 10th Machine Translation summit (MT Summit X), Phuket, Thailand.. 149-156.

Sriram Venkatapathy and A. Joshi. 2006. Using information about multi-word expressions for the word alignment task. In Proceedings of the COLING/ACL Workshop on Multiword Expressions: Identifying and Exploiting Underlying Properties, Sydney, Australia, 53–60.

Sriram Venkatapathy and Aravind K. Joshi, 2005. Relative compositionality of multi-word expressions: a study of verb-noun (V-N) collocations, In Proceedings of International Joint Conference on Natural Language Processing - 2005, Jeju Island, Korea, 553-564.

Tara Mohanan. 1994. Argument Structure in Hindi. CSLI Publications, Stanford, California.

Timothy Baldwin and F. Bond. 2002. Multiword expressions: Some problems for Japanese NLP. In Proceedings of the 8th Annual Meeting of the Association for Natural Language Processing (Japan), Keihanna, Japan, 379–382.

Timothy Baldwin and Su Nam Kim. 2010. Multiword Expressions, in Nitin Indurkhya and Fred J. Damerau (eds.) Handbook of Natural Language Processing, Second Edition, CRC Press, Boca Raton, USA. 267-292.

Detecting noun compounds and light verb constructions: a contrastive study

Veronika Vincze[1], **István Nagy T.**[2] and **Gábor Berend**[2]
[1]Hungarian Academy of Sciences, Research Group on Artificial Intelligence
vinczev@inf.u-szeged.hu
[2]Department of Informatics, University of Szeged
{nistvan,berendg}@inf.u-szeged.hu

Abstract

In this paper, we describe our methods to detect noun compounds and light verb constructions in running texts. For noun compounds, dictionary-based methods and POS-tagging seem to contribute most to the performance of the system whereas for light verb constructions, the combination of POS-tagging, syntactic information and restrictions on the nominal and verbal component yield the best result. However, focusing on deverbal nouns proves to be beneficial for both types of MWEs. The effect of syntax is negligible on noun compound detection whereas it is unambiguously helpful for identifying light verb constructions.

1 Introduction

Multiword expressions are lexical items that can be decomposed into single words and display idiosyncratic features (Sag et al., 2002; Calzolari et al., 2002; Kim, 2008). They are frequent in language use and they usually exhibit unique and idiosyncratic behavior, thus, they often pose a problem to NLP systems. A compound is a lexical unit that consists of two or more elements that exist on their own. Light verb constructions are verb and noun combinations in which the verb has lost its meaning to some degree and the noun is used in one of its original senses (e.g. *have a walk* or *give advice*).

In this work, we aim at identifying *nominal compounds* and *light verb constructions* by using rule-based methods. Noun compounds belong to the most frequent MWE-classes (in the Wikipedia corpus we developed for evaluation (see 3.2), about 75% of the annotated multiword expressions were noun compounds) and they are productive, i.e. new nominal compounds are being formed in language use all the time, which yields that they cannot be listed exhaustively in a dictionary (as opposed to e.g. prepositional compounds). Their inner syntactic structure varies: they can contain nouns, adjectives and prepositions as well.

Light verb constructions are semi-productive, that is, new light verb constructions might enter the language following some patterns (e.g. *give a Skype call* on the basis of *give a call*). On the other hand, they are less frequent in language use (only 9.5% of multiword expressions were light verb constructions in the Wikipedia database) and they are syntactically flexible, that is, they can manifest in various forms: the verb can be inflected, the noun can occur in its plural form and the noun can be modified. The nominal and the verbal component may not even be adjacent in e.g. passive sentences.

Our goal being to compare how different approaches perform in the case of the different types of multiword expressions, we have chosen these two types of MWEs that are dissimilar in several aspects.

2 Related work

There are several applications developed for identifying MWEs, which can be classified according to the methods they make use of (Piao et al., 2003). First, statistical models rely on word frequencies, co-occurrence data and contextual information in deciding whether a bigram or trigram (or even an n-gram) of words can be labeled as a multiword expression or not. Such systems are used for several languages and several types of multiword expressions, see e.g. Bouma (2010). The advantage of statistical systems is that they can be easily adapted to other languages and other types of multiword expressions, however, they are not able to identify rare multiword expressions (as Piao et al. (2003) emphasize, 68% of multiword expressions occur at most twice in their corpus).

Some hybrid systems make use of both statistical and linguistic information as well, that is, rules based on syntactic or semantic regularities are also incorporated into the system (Evert and Kermes, 2003; Bannard, 2007; Cook et al., 2007; Al-Haj and Wintner, 2010). This results in better coverage of multiword expressions. On the other hand, these methods are highly language-dependent because of the amount of linguistic rules encoded, thus, it requires much effort to adapt them to different languages or even to different types of multiword expressions. However, the combination of different methods may improve the performance of MWE-extracting systems (Pecina, 2010).

Several features are used in identifying multiword expressions, which are applicable to different types of multiword expressions to various degrees. Co-occurrence statistics and POS-tags seem to be useful for all types of multiword expressions, for instance the tool `mwetoolkit` (Ramisch et al., 2010a) makes use of such features, which is illustrated through the example of identifying English compound nouns (Ramisch et al., 2010b).

Caseli et al. (2010) developed an alignment-based method for extracting multiword expressions from parallel corpora. This method is also applied to the pediatrics domain (Caseli et al., 2009). Zarrieß and Kuhn (2009) argue that multiword expressions can be reliably detected in parallel corpora by using dependency-parsed, word-aligned sentences. Sinha (2009) detects Hindi complex predicates (i.e. a combination of a light verb and a noun, a verb or an adjective) in a Hindi–English parallel corpus by identifying a mismatch of the Hindi light verb meaning in the aligned English sentence. Van de Cruys and Moirón (2007) describe a semantic-based method for identifying verb-preposition-noun combinations in Dutch, which relies on selectional preferences for both the noun and the verb. Cook et al. (2007) differentiate between literal and idiomatic usages of verb and noun constructions in English. They make use of syntactic fixedness of idioms when developing their unsupervised method. Bannard (2007) also seeks to identify verb and noun constructions in English on the basis of syntactic fixedness. Samardžić and Merlo (2010) analyze English and German light verb constructions in parallel corpora. They found that linguistic features (i.e. the degree of compositionality) and the frequency of the construction both have an effect on aligning the constructions.

3 Experiments

In order to identify multiword expressions, simple methods are worth examining, which can serve as a basis for implementing more complex systems and can be used as features in machine learning settings. Our aim being to compare the effect of different methods on the identification of noun compounds and light verb constructions, we considered it important to develop methods for both MWE types that make use of their characteristics and to adapt those methods to the other type of MWE – in this way, the efficacy and the MWE-(in)dependence of the methods can be empirically evaluated, which can later have impact on developing statistical MWE-detectors.

Earlier studies on the detection of light verb constructions generally take syntactic information as a starting point (Cook et al., 2007; Bannard, 2007; Tan et al., 2006), that is, their goal is to classify verb + object constructions selected on the basis of syntactic pattern as literal or idiomatic. However, we do not aim at classifying LVC candidates filtered by syntactic patterns but at identifying them in running text without assuming that syntactic information is necessarily available. In our investigations, we will pay distinctive attention to the added value of syntactic features on the system's performance.

3.1 Methods for MWE identification

For identifying noun compounds, we made use of a list constructed from the English Wikipedia. Lowercase n-grams which occurred as links were collected from Wikipedia articles and the list was automatically filtered in order to delete non-English terms, named entities and non-nominal compounds etc. In the case of the method 'Match', a noun compound candidate was marked if it occurred in the list. The second method we applied for noun compounds involved the merge of two possible noun compounds: if A B and B C both occurred in the list, A B C was also accepted as a noun compound ('Merge'). Since the methodology of dictionary building was not applicable for collecting light verb constructions (i.e. they do not function as links in Wikipedia), we could not apply these two methods to them.

In the case of 'POS-rules', a noun compound candidate was marked if it occurred in the list and its POS-tag sequence matched one of the previously defined patterns (e.g. `JJ (NN|NNS)`). For light verb constructions, the POS-rule method meant that each n-gram for which the pre-defined patterns (e.g. `VB.?  (NN|NNS)`) could be applied was accepted as light verb constructions. For POS-tagging, we used the Stanford POS Tagger (Toutanova and Manning, 2000). Since the methods to follow rely on morphological information (i.e. it is required to know which element is a noun), matching the POS-rules is a prerequisite to apply those methods to identify MWEs.

The 'Suffix' method exploited the fact that many nominal components in light verb constructions are derived from verbs. Thus, in this case only constructions that contained nouns ending in certain derivational suffixes were allowed and for nominal compounds the last noun had to have this ending.

The 'Most frequent' (MF) method relied on the fact that the most common verbs function typically as light verbs (e.g. *do*, *make*, *take*, *have* etc.) Thus, the 15 most frequent verbs typical of light verb constructions were collected and constructions where the stem of the verbal component was among those of the most frequent ones were accepted. As for noun compounds, the 15 most frequent nouns in English were similarly collected[1] and the lemma of the last member of the possible compound had to be among them.

The 'Stem' method pays attention to the stem of the noun. In the case of light verb constructions, the nominal component is typically one that is derived from a verbal stem (*make a decision*) or coincides with a verb (*have a walk*). In this case, we accepted only candidates that had the nominal component / the last noun whose stem was of verbal nature, i.e. coincided with a stem of a verb.

Syntactic information can also be exploited in identifying MWEs. Typically, the syntactic relation between the verb and the nominal component in a light verb construction is `dobj` or `prep` – using Stanford parser (Klein and Manning, 2003)). The relation between the members of a typical noun compound is `nn` or `amod` in attributive constructions. The 'Syntax' method accepts candidates among whose members these syntactic relations hold.

We also combined the above methods to identify noun compounds and light verb constructions in our databases (the union of candidates yielded by the methods is denoted by $\cup$ while the intersection is denoted by $\cap$ in the respective tables).

3.2 Results

For the evaluation of our models, we developed a corpus of 50 Wikipedia articles, in which several types of multiword expressions (including nominal compounds and light verb constructions) and Named Entities were marked. The database contains 2929 occurrences of nominal compounds and 368 occurrences of light verb constructions and can be downloaded under the Creative Commons licence at `http://www.inf.u-szeged.hu/rgai/mwe`.

Table 1 shows the results of our experiments. Methods were evaluated on the token level, i.e. each occurrence of a light verb construction had to be identified in text. It can be seen that the best result for noun compound identification can be obtained if the three dictionary-based methods are combined. We also evaluated the method of POS-rules without taking into account dictionary matches (POS-rules w/o dic), which result serves as the baseline for comparing the effect of LVC-specific methods on noun compound detection.

As can be seen, by adding any of the LVC-specific features, the performance of the system declines, i.e. none of them can beat the baseline. While the feature 'Stem' (and its combinations) improve precision, recall severely falls back: especially 'Most frequent noun' (MFN) has an extremely poor effect on it. This was expected since the lexical constraint on the last part of the compound heavily restricts the scope of the noun compounds available. On the

[1] as listed at `http://en.wikipedia.org/wiki/Most\_common\_words\_in\_English`

other hand, the 15 most frequent nouns in English are not derived from verbs hence they do not end in any of the pre-defined suffixes, thus, the intersection of the features 'MFN' and 'Suffix' does not yield any noun compound (the intersection of all the three methods also behaves similarly). It must be mentioned, however, that the union of all features yields the best recall as expected and the best F-measure can be achieved by the union of 'Suffix' and 'Stem'.

The effect of adding syntactic rules to the system is not unequivocal. In many cases, the improvement is marginal (it does not exceed 1% except for the POS-rules w/o dic method) or the performance even degrades. The latter is most obvious in the case of the combination of dictionary-based rules, which is mainly caused by the decline in recall, however, precision improves. The overall decline in F-score may thus be related to possible parsing errors.

In the case of light verb constructions, the recall of the baseline (POS-rules) is high, however, its precision is low (i.e. not all of the candidates defined by the POS patterns are light verb constructions). The 'Most frequent verb' (MFV) feature proves to be the most useful: the verbal component of the light verb construction is lexically much more restricted than the noun, which is exploited by this feature. The other two features put some constraints on the nominal component, which is typically of verbal nature in light verb constructions: 'Suffix' simply requires the noun to end in a given n-gram (without exploiting further grammatical information) whereas 'Stem' allows nouns derived from verbs. When combining a verbal and a nominal feature, union results in high recall (the combinations typical verb + non-deverbal noun or atypical verb + deverbal noun are also found) while intersection yields high precision (typical verb + deverbal noun combinations are found only).

We also evaluated the performance of the 'Syntax' method without directly exploiting POS-rules. Results are shown in Table 2. It is revealed that the feature `dobj` is much more effective in identifying light verb constructions than the feature `prep`, on the other hand, `dobj` itself outperforms POS-rules. If we combine the `dobj` feature with the best LVC-specific feature (namely, MFV), we can achieve an F-measure of 26.46%. The feature `dobj` can achieve a recall of 59.51%, which suggests

Method	**P**	**R**	**F**
Dobj	10.39	59.51	17.69
Prep	0.46	7.34	0.86
Dobj ∪ Prep	2.09	38.36	3.97
Dobj ∩ MFV	31.46	22.83	**26.46**
Prep ∩ MFV	3.24	5.12	4.06
Dobj ∪ Prep ∩ MFV	8.78	19.02	12.02

Table 2: Results of syntactic methods for light verb constructions in terms of precision (P), recall (R) and F-measure (F). Dobj: verb + object pairs, Prep: verb + prepositional complement pairs, MFV: the verb is among the 15 most frequent light verbs.

that about 40% of the nominal components in our database are not objects of the light verb. Thus, approaches that focus on only verb-object pairs (Cook et al., 2007; Bannard, 2007; Tan et al., 2006) fail to identify a considerable part of light verb constructions found in texts.

The added value of syntax was also investigated for LVC detection as well. As the results show, syntax clearly helps in identifying LVCs – its overall effect is to add up to 4% to the F-score. The best result, again, is yielded by the MFV method, which is about 30% above the baseline.

4 Discussion

When contrasting results achieved for light verb constructions and noun compounds, it is revealed that the dictionary-based method applying POS-rules yields the best result for noun compounds and the MFV feature combined with syntactic information is the most useful for LVC identification. If no dictionary matches were taken into consideration, the combination of the features 'Suffix' and 'Stem' achieved the best result, however, 'Stem' alone can also perform similarly. Since 'Stem' identifies deverbal nouns, that is, nouns having an argument structure, it is not surprising that this feature is valuable in noun compound detection because the first part in the compound is most probably an argument of the deverbal noun (as in *noun compound detection* the object of *detection* is *noun compound*, in other words, we detect noun compounds). Thus, it will be worth examining how the integration of the 'Stem' feature can improve dictionary-based models.

Making use of only POS-rules does not seem to

Method	Noun compounds			NC + syntax			LVC			LVC + syntax		
	P	R	F	P	R	F	P	R	F	P	R	F
Match	37.7	54.73	44.65	49.64	48.31	48.97	-	-	-	-	-	-
Merge	40.06	57.63	47.26	51.69	47.86	49.70	-	-	-	-	-	-
POS-rules	55.56	49.98	52.62	59.18	46.39	**52.02**	-	-	-	-	-	-
Combined	59.46	52.48	**55.75**	62.07	45.81	**52.72**	-	-	-	-	-	-
POS-rules w/o dic	28.33	66.23	**39.69**	29.97	64.18	40.87	9.35	72.55	**12.86**	7.02	76.63	16.56
Suffix	27.02	8.91	13.4	28.58	8.84	13.5	9.62	16.3	12.1	11.52	15.22	13.11
MF	12.26	1.33	2.4	12.41	1.29	2.34	33.83	55.16	**41.94**	40.21	51.9	**45.31**
Stem	29.87	37.62	**33.3**	31.69	36.63	33.99	8.56	50.54	14.64	11.07	47.55	17.96
Suffix∩MF	0	0	0	-	-	-	44.05	10.05	16.37	11.42	54.35	18.88
Suffix∪MF	23.36	10.24	14.24	24.50	10.13	14.34	19.82	61.41	29.97	23.99	57.88	33.92
Suffix∩Stem	28.4	6.49	10.56	30.03	6.42	10.58	10.35	11.14	11.1	12.28	11.14	11.68
Suffix∪Stem	29.35	**40.05**	**33.87**	31.12	39.06	**34.64**	8.87	57.61	15.37	11.46	54.35	18.93
MF∩Stem	9.16	0.41	0.78	9.6	0.41	0.79	39.53	36.96	38.2	46.55	34.78	39.81
MF∪Stem	29.13	38.55	**33.18**	31.85	36.04	33.81	10.42	68.75	18.09	13.36	64.67	22.15
Suffix∩MF∩Stem	0	0	0	-	-	-	**47.37**	7.34	12.7	50.0	6.79	11.96
Suffix∪MF∪Stem	28.68	**40.97**	33.74	30.33	39.95	34.48	10.16	**72.28**	17.82	13.04	68.2	21.89

Table 1: Experimental results in terms of precision (P), recall (R) and F-measure (F). Match: dictionary match, Merge: merge of two overlapping noun compounds, POS-rules: matching of POS-patterns, Combined: the union of Match, Merge and POS-rules, POS-rules w/o dic: matching POS-patterns without dictionary lookup, Suffix: the (head) noun ends in a given suffix, MF: the head noun/verb is among the 15 most frequent ones, Stem: the (head) noun is deverbal.

be satisfactory for LVC detection. However, the most useful feature for identifying LVCs, namely, MFV/MFN proves to perform poorly for noun compounds, which can be explained by the fact that the verbal component of LVCs usually comes from a well-defined set of frequent verbs, thus, it is lexically more restricted than the parts of noun compounds. The feature 'Stem' helps improve recall and this feature can be further enhanced since in some cases, the Porter stemmer did not render the same stem to derivational pairs such as *assumption – assume*. For instance, derivational information encoded in wordnet relations might contribute to performance.

Concerning syntactic information, it has clearly positive effects on LVC identification, however, this influence is ambiguous in the case of noun compounds. Since light verb constructions form a syntactic phrase and noun compounds behave syntactically as one unit (having an internal syntactic hierarchy though), this result suggests that for noun compound detection, POS-tagging provides enough information while for light verb constructions, syntactic information is expected to improve the system.

5 Conclusions

In this paper, we aimed at identifying noun compounds and light verb constructions in running texts with rule-based methods and compared the effect of several features on detecting those two types of multiword expressions. For noun compounds, dictionary-based methods and POS-tagging seem to contribute most to the performance of the system whereas for light verb constructions, the combination of POS-tagging, syntactic information and restrictions on the nominal and verbal component yield the best result. Although the effect of syntax is negligible on noun compound detection, it is unambiguously helpful for identifying light verb constructions. Our methods can be improved by extending the set and scope of features and refining POS- and syntactic rules and they can be also adapted to other languages by creating language-specific POS-rules, lists of suffixes and light verb candidates.

For higher-level of applications, it is necessary to know which tokens form one (syntactic or semantic) unit, thus, we believe that our results in detecting noun compounds and light verb constructions can be fruitfully applied in e.g. information extraction or machine translation as well.

Acknowledgments

This work was supported in part by the National Innovation Office of the Hungarian government within the framework of the project MASZEKER.

References

Hassan Al-Haj and Shuly Wintner. 2010. Identifying multi-word expressions by leveraging morphological and syntactic idiosyncrasy. In *Proceedings of Coling 2010*, Beijing, China, August.

Colin Bannard. 2007. A measure of syntactic flexibility for automatically identifying multiword expressions in corpora. In *Proceedings of the Workshop on a Broader Perspective on Multiword Expressions*, MWE '07, pages 1–8, Morristown, NJ, USA. ACL.

Gerlof Bouma. 2010. Collocation extraction beyond the independence assumption. In *Proceedings of the ACL 2010 Conference Short Papers*, pages 109–114, Uppsala, Sweden, July. ACL.

Nicoletta Calzolari, Charles Fillmore, Ralph Grishman, Nancy Ide, Alessandro Lenci, Catherine MacLeod, and Antonio Zampolli. 2002. Towards best practice for multiword expressions in computational lexicons. In *Proceedings of LREC-2002*, pages 1934–1940, Las Palmas.

Helena de Medeiros Caseli, Aline Villavicencio, André Machado, and Maria José Finatto. 2009. Statistically-driven alignment-based multiword expression identification for technical domains. In *Proceedings of the Workshop on Multiword Expressions: Identification, Interpretation, Disambiguation and Applications*, pages 1–8, Singapore, August. ACL.

Helena de Medeiros Caseli, Carlos Ramisch, Maria das Graças Volpe Nunes, and Aline Villavicencio. 2010. Alignment-based extraction of multiword expressions. *Language Resources and Evaluation*, 44(1-2):59–77.

Paul Cook, Afsaneh Fazly, and Suzanne Stevenson. 2007. Pulling their weight: exploiting syntactic forms for the automatic identification of idiomatic expressions in context. In *Proceedings of the Workshop on a Broader Perspective on Multiword Expressions*, pages 41–48, Morristown, NJ, USA. ACL.

Stefan Evert and Hannah Kermes. 2003. Experiments on candidate data for collocation extraction. In *Proceedings of EACL 2003*, pages 83–86.

Su Nam Kim. 2008. *Statistical Modeling of Multiword Expressions*. Ph.D. thesis, University of Melbourne, Melbourne.

Dan Klein and Christopher D. Manning. 2003. Accurate unlexicalized parsing. In *Proceedings of the 41st Annual Meeting on Association for Computational Linguistics*, ACL '03, pages 423–430, Stroudsburg, PA, USA. Association for Computational Linguistics.

Pavel Pecina. 2010. Lexical association measures and collocation extraction. *Language Resources and Evaluation*, 44(1-2):137–158.

Scott S. L. Piao, Paul Rayson, Dawn Archer, Andrew Wilson, and Tony McEnery. 2003. Extracting multiword expressions with a semantic tagger. In *Proceedings of the ACL 2003 workshop on Multiword expressions: analysis, acquisition and treatment*, pages 49–56, Morristown, NJ, USA. ACL.

Carlos Ramisch, Aline Villavicencio, and Christian Boitet. 2010a. Multiword Expressions in the wild? The mwetoolkit comes in handy. In *Coling 2010: Demonstrations*, Beijing, China, August.

Carlos Ramisch, Aline Villavicencio, and Christian Boitet. 2010b. Web-based and combined language models: a case study on noun compound identification. In *Coling 2010: Posters*, Beijing, China, August.

Ivan A. Sag, Timothy Baldwin, Francis Bond, Ann Copestake, and Dan Flickinger. 2002. Multiword Expressions: A Pain in the Neck for NLP. In *Proceedings of CICLing-2002*, pages 1–15, Mexico City, Mexico.

Tanja Samardžić and Paola Merlo. 2010. Cross-lingual variation of light verb constructions: Using parallel corpora and automatic alignment for linguistic research. In *Proceedings of the 2010 Workshop on NLP and Linguistics: Finding the Common Ground*, pages 52–60, Uppsala, Sweden, July. ACL.

R. Mahesh K. Sinha. 2009. Mining Complex Predicates In Hindi Using A Parallel Hindi-English Corpus. In *Proceedings of the Workshop on Multiword Expressions: Identification, Interpretation, Disambiguation and Applications*, pages 40–46, Singapore, August. ACL.

Yee Fan Tan, Min-Yen Kan, and Hang Cui. 2006. Extending corpus-based identification of light verb constructions using a supervised learning framework. In *Proceedings of the EACL Workshop on Multi-Word Expressions in a Multilingual Contexts*, pages 49–56, Trento, Italy, April. ACL.

Kristina Toutanova and Christopher D. Manning. 2000. Enriching the knowledge sources used in a maximum entropy part-of-speech tagger. In *Proceedings of EMNLP 2000*, pages 63–70, Stroudsburg, PA, USA. ACL.

Tim Van de Cruys and Begoña Villada Moirón. 2007. Semantics-based multiword expression extraction. In *Proceedings of the Workshop on a Broader Perspective on Multiword Expressions*, MWE '07, pages 25–32, Morristown, NJ, USA. ACL.

Sina Zarrieß and Jonas Kuhn. 2009. Exploiting Translational Correspondences for Pattern-Independent MWE Identification. In *Proceedings of the Workshop on Multiword Expressions: Identification, Interpretation, Disambiguation and Applications*, pages 23–30, Singapore, August. ACL.

jMWE: A Java Toolkit for Detecting Multi-Word Expressions

Nidhi Kulkarni & Mark Alan Finlayson
Computer Science and Artificial Intelligence Laboratory
Massachusetts Institute of Technology
Cambridge, MA, 02139, USA
{nidhik,markaf}@mit.edu

Abstract

jMWE is a Java library for implementing and testing algorithms that detect Multi-Word Expression (MWE) tokens in text. It provides (1) a detector API, including implementations of several detectors, (2) facilities for constructing indices of MWE types that may be used by the detectors, and (3) a testing framework for measuring the performance of a MWE detector. The software is available for free download.

jMWE is a Java library for constructing and testing Multi-Word Expression (MWE) token detectors. The original goal of the library was to detect tokens (instances) of MWE types in a token stream, given a list of types such as those that can be extracted from an electronic dictionary such as WordNet (Fellbaum, 1998). The purpose of the library is not to discover new MWE types, but rather find instances of a set of given types in a given text. The library also supports MWE detectors that are not list-based.

The functionality of the library is basic, but it is a necessary foundation for any system that wishes to use MWEs in later stages of language processing. It is a natural complement to software for discovering MWE types, such as `mwetoolkit` (Ramisch et al., 2010) or the NSP package (Banerjee and Pedersen, 2003). jMWE is available online for free download (Finlayson and Kulkarni, 2011a).

1 Library Facilities

Detector API The core of the library is the detector API. The library defines a detector interface which provides a single method for detecting MWE tokens in a list of individual tokens; anyone interested in taking advantage of jMWE's testing infrastructure or writing their own MWE token detection algorithm need only implement this interface. jMWE provides several baseline MWE token detection strategies. Also provided are detector filters, which apply a specific constraint to, or resolve conflicts in, the output another detector.

MWE Index jMWE also provides classes for constructing, storing, and accessing indices of valid MWE types. An MWE index allows an algorithm to retrieve a list of MWE types given a single word token and part of speech. The index also lists how frequently, in a particular concordance, a set of tokens appears as a particular MWE type rather than as independent words. To facilitate construction of indices, jMWE provides bindings to the MIT Java Wordnet Interface (JWI) (Finlayson, 2008b) and JSemcor (Finlayson, 2008a), as well as classes which extract all MWE types from those resources and write them to disk.

Test Harness The linchpin of jMWE's testing infrastructure is a test harness that runs an MWE detector over a given corpus and measures its precision and recall. The library comes with default bindings for running detectors over the Semcor corpus or any other corpus that can be mounted with the JSemcor library. Nevertheless, jMWE is not restricted to running tests over Semcor, or even restricted to using JSemcor for interfacing with a corpus: a detector can be run over any corpus whose MWE instances have been marked can be analyzed, merely by implementing four interfaces. Also included in the testing infrastructure are a number of error detectors, which analyze the detailed output of the test harness to identify common MWE token detection errors. The library includes implementation for twelve standard error types.

2 Detection Algorithms

Preprocessing To run an MWE detector over a text the text must, at a minimum, be tokenized. jMWE does not include facilities to do this; tokenization must be done via an external library. Most detection strategies also require tokens to be tagged with a part of speech and lemmatized. This information is also not provided directly by jMWE, but there are bindings in the library for using JWI and the Stanford POS Tagger (Toutanova et al., 2003) to tag and lemmatize a set of texts, provided those texts can be accessed via the JSemcor library.

2.1 Detector Types

MWE token Detectors can be split into at least three types: *Basic Detectors*, *Filters*, and *Resolvers*. Performance of selected combinations of these detectors are given in Table 1.

Basic Detectors that fall into this category use an MWE index, or other source of information, to detect MWE tokens in a stream of tokens. jMWE includes several implementations of basic detectors, including the following:
(1) *Exhaustive:* Given a MWE type index, finds all possible MWE tokens regardless of inflection, order, or continuity.
(2) *Consecutive:* Given a MWE type index, finds all MWE tokens whose constituent tokens occur without other tokens interspersed.
(3) *Simple Proper Noun:* Finds all continuous sequences of proper noun tokens, and marks them as proper noun MWE tokens.

Filters These MWE detectors apply a particular filter to the output of another, wrapped, detector. Only MWE tokens from the wrapped detector that pass the filter are returned. Examples of implemented filters are:
(1) *In Order:* Only returns MWE tokens whose constituent tokens are in the same order as the constituents listed in the MWE type's definition.
(2) *No Inflection:* Removes inflected MWE tokens.
(3) *Observed Inflection:* Returns base form MWEs, as well as those whose inflection has been observed in a specified concordance.
(4) *Pattern Inflection:* Only return MWE tokens whose inflection matches a pre-defined set of part of speech patterns. We used the same rules as those found in (Arranz et al., 2005) with two additional rules related to Verb-Particle MWEs.

Resolvers Like filters, these wrap another MWE detector; they resolve conflicts between identified MWE tokens. A conflict occurs when two identified MWE tokens share a constituent. Examples include:
(1) *Longest-Match-Left-to-Right:* For a set of conflicting MWE tokens, picks the one that starts earliest. If all of the conflicting MWE tokens start at the same point, picks the longest.
(2) *Observed Probability:* For a set of conflicting MWE tokens, picks the one whose constituents have most often been observed occurring as an MWE token rather than as isolated words.
(3) *Variance Minimizing:* For a set of conflicting MWE tokens, picks the MWE token with the fewest interstitial spaces.

Detector	**F$_1$ (precision/recall)**
Exhaustive +Proper Nouns	0.197_{F_1} (0.110_p/0.919_r)
Consecutive +Proper Nouns	0.631_{F_1} (0.472_p/0.950_r)
Consecutive +Proper Nouns +No Inflection +Longest-Match-L-to-R	0.593_{F_1} (0.499_p/0.731_r)
Consecutive +Proper Nouns +Pattern Inflection +More Frequent As MWE	0.834_{F_1} (0.835_p/0.832_r)

Table 1: F-measures for select detectors, run over Semcor 1.6 brown1 and brown2 concordances using MWEs drawn from WordNet 1.6. The code for generating this table is available at (Finlayson and Kulkarni, 2011b)

Acknowledgments

This work was supported in part by the AFOSR under grant number A9550-05-1-0321, and DARPA under award FA8750-10-1-0076.

References

Victoria Arranz, Jordi Atserias, and Mauro Castillo. 2005. Multiwords and word sense disambiguation. In Alexander Gelbukh, editor, *Proceedings of the Sixth International Conference on Intelligent Text Processing and Computational Linguistics (CICLING 2005)*, volume 3406 in Lecture Notes in Computer Science (LNCS), pages 250–262, Mexico City, Mexico. Springer-Verlag.

Satanjeev Banerjee and Ted Pedersen. 2003. The design, implementation, and use of the ngram statistics package. In Alexander Gelbukh, editor, *Proceedings of the Fourth International Conference on Intelligent Text Processing and Computational Linguistics (CICLING 2003)*, volume 2588 in Lecture Notes in Computer Science (LNCS), pages 370–381, Mexico City, Mexico. Springer-Verlag. `http://ngram.sourceforge.net.`

Christiane Fellbaum. 1998. *Wordnet: An Electronic Lexical Database*. MIT Press, Cambridge, MA.

Mark Alan Finlayson and Nidhi Kulkarni. 2011a. jMWE:, version 1.0.0. `http://projects.csail.mit.edu/jmwe` `http://hdl.handle.net/1721.1/62793.`

Mark Alan Finlayson and Nidhi Kulkarni. 2011b. Source code and data for MWE'2011 papers. `http://hdl.handle.net/1721.1/62792.`

Mark Alan Finlayson. 2008a. JSemcor, version 1.0.0. `http://projects.csail.mit.edu/jsemcor.`

Mark Alan Finlayson. 2008b. JWI: The MIT Java Wordnet Interface, version 2.1.5. `http://projects.csail.mit.edu/jwi.`

Carlos Ramisch, Aline Villavicencio, and Christian Boitet. 2010. Multiword expressions in the wild? the mwetoolkit comes in handy. In Chu-Ren Huang and Daniel Jurafsky, editors, *Proceedings of the Twenty-Third International Conference on Computational Linguistics (COLING 2010): Demonstrations*, volume 23, pages 57–60, Beijing, China. `http://mwetoolkit.sourceforge.net.`

Kristina Toutanova, Daniel Klein, Christopher D. Manning, and Yoram Singer. 2003. Feature-rich part-of-speech tagging with a cyclic dependency network. In *Proceedings of the Human Language Technology Conference of the North American Chapter of the Association for Computational Linguistics (HLT-NAACL)*, pages 252–259, Edmonton, Canada.

FipsCoView: On-line Visualisation of Collocations Extracted from Multilingual Parallel Corpora

Violeta Seretan
School of Informatics
University of Edinburgh
violeta.seretan@gmail.com

Eric Wehrli
Language Technology Laboratory
University of Geneva
eric.wehrli@unige.ch

Abstract

We introduce FipsCoView, an on-line interface for dictionary-like visualisation of collocations detected from parallel corpora using a syntactically-informed extraction method.

1 Introduction

Multilingual (parallel) corpora—e.g., Europarl (Koehn, 2005)—represent a valuable resource for tasks related to language production that is exploitable in a wide variety of settings, such as second language learning, lexicography, as well as human or automatic translation. We focus on lexicographic exploitation of such resources and present a system, called FipsCoView,[1] which is specifically aimed at supporting the work of lexicographers who compile multilingual collocation resources.

Collocation, a rather ill-defined linguistic concept referring to a large and heterogeneous sub-class of multi-word expressions, is understood here as a combination of words that produces natural-sounding speech and writing (Lea and Runcie, 2002) and that has syntactic and semantic properties which cannot be entirely predicted from those of its components and therefore has to be listed in a lexicon (Evert, 2004). Collocations are particularly interesting from a translation point of view, and our system can also be used to facilitate the task of translators looking for the right translation of a word in context.

The usage scenario is the following. Given a word, like *money*, our system provides a concise and intuitive presentation of the list of collocations with that word, which have previously been detected in the source language version of the parallel corpus. By selecting one of the items in this list, e.g., *money laundering*, users will be able to see the contexts of that item, represented by the sentences in which it occurs. In addition, users can select a target language from the list of other languages in which the multilingual corpus is available[2] and visualise the target language version of the source sentences.

This presentation enables users to find potential translation equivalents for collocations by inspecting the target sentences. Thus, in the case of French, the preferred equivalent found is *blanchiment d'argent*, lit., 'money whitening', rather than the literal translation from English, **lavage d'argent*. In the case of Italian, this is *riciclaggio di denaro*, lit., 'recycling of money', rather than the literal translation *?lavaggio di soldi*, also possible but much less preferred. Access to target sentences is important as it allows users to see how the translation of a collocation vary depending on the context. Besides, it provides useful usage clues, indicating, *inter alia*, the allowed or preferred morphosyntactic features of a collocation.

In this paper, we present the architecture of FipsCoView and outline its main functionalities. This system is an extension of FipsCo, a larger fully-fledged off-line system, which, in turn, is integrated into a complex framework for processing multi-word expressions (Seretan, 2009). While the off-line system finds direct applicability in our on-going projects of large-scale multilingual syntac-

[1] Available at http://tinyurl.com/FipsCoView.

[2] Europarl includes 11 languages: French, Italian, Spanish, Portuguese, English, Dutch, German, Danish, Swedish, Greek, Finnish. Note that our tool is not tailored to this specific corpus.

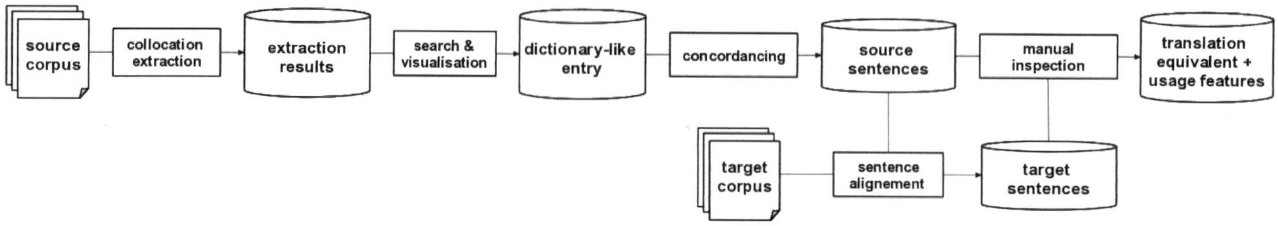

Figure 1: FipsCoView: System architecture.

tic parsing (Wehrli, 2007) and syntax-based machine translation (Wehrli et al., 2009), the on-line version is designed to offer access to the derived collocation resources to a broader community.

2 Architecture and Main Functionalities

Figure 1 shows the architecture of FipsCoView. The main system modules are the *collocation extraction* module, the *search & visualisation* module, the *concordancing* and the *sentence alignment* modules.

The processing flow is pipelined. The key module of the system, *collocation extraction*, relies on a syntax-based methodology that combines lexical statistics with syntactic information provided by Fips, a deep symbolic parser (Wehrli, 2007). This methodology is fully described and evaluated in Seretan (2011). In principle, the extraction takes place only once, but new corpora can be processed later and results are cumulated. The *sentence alignment* (Nerima et al., 2003) is performed partially, i.e., only for the sentences actually displayed by the concordancing module. It is done on the fly, thus eliminating the need of pre-aligning the corpora.

The role of the *concordancing* module is to present the sentence contexts for a selected collocation (cf. scenario described in §1). The words in this collocation are highlighted for readability. The list of sentences is displayed in the order given by the syntactic variation of collocations, that is, the collocation instances for which the distance between the components is larger are displayed first. This functionality is designed to support the work of users inspecting the syntactic properties of collocations.

The *search & visualisation* module takes as input the word entered by the user in the system interface, performs a search in the database that stores the collocation extraction results, and provides a one-page presentation of the collocational information related to the sought word. Users can set visualisation parameters such as the minimal frequency and association score, which limit the displayed results according to the number of occurrences in the corpus and the "association strength" between the component words, as given by the lexical association measure used to extract collocations. The measure we typically use is log-likelihood ratio (Dunning, 1993); see Pecina (2008) for an inventory of measures.

Depending on these parameters, the automatically created collocation entry is more or less exhaustive (the output adapts to the specific user's purpose). A different sub-entry is created for each part of speech of the sought word (for instance, *report* can either be a noun or a verb). Under each sub-entry, collocations are organised by syntactic type, e.g., adjective-noun (*comprehensive report*), noun-noun (*initiative report*), subject-verb (*report highlights*), verb-object (*produce a report*). To avoid redundancy, only the collocating words are shown. The sought word is understood and is replaced by a tilde character, in a paper dictionary style. Unlike in paper dictionary presentations, the online presentation benefits from the HTML environment by using colours, adapting the font size so that it reflects the association strength (the most important combinations are more visually salient), displaying additional information such as score and frequency, and using hyper-links for navigating from one word to another.

With respect to similar systems (Barlow, 2002; Scott, 2004; Kilgarriff et al., 2004; Charest et al., 2007; Rayson, 2009; Fletcher, 2011), our system uniquely combines parallel concordancing with collocation detection based on deep syntactic processing. It is available for English, French, Spanish and Italian and it is being extended to other languages.

Acknowledgement

This work is partly supported by the Swiss National Science Foundation (grant no. PA00P1_131512).

References

Michael Barlow. 2002. Paraconc: Concordance software for multilingual parallel corpora. In *Proceedings of the Third International Conference on Language Resources and Evaluation. Workshop on Language Resources in Translation Work and Research*, pages 20–24, Las Palmas, Spain.

Simon Charest, Éric Brunelle, Jean Fontaine, and Bertrand Pelletier. 2007. Élaboration automatique d'un dictionnaire de cooccurrences grand public. In *Actes de la 14e conférence sur le Traitement Automatique des Langues Naturelles (TALN 2007)*, pages 283–292, Toulouse, France, June.

Ted Dunning. 1993. Accurate methods for the statistics of surprise and coincidence. *Computational Linguistics*, 19(1):61–74.

Stefan Evert. 2004. *The Statistics of Word Cooccurrences: Word Pairs and Collocations*. Ph.D. thesis, University of Stuttgart.

William H. Fletcher. 2011. Phrases in english: Online database for the study of English words and phrases. `http://phrasesinenglish.org`. Accessed March, 2011.

Adam Kilgarriff, Pavel Rychly, Pavel Smrz, and David Tugwell. 2004. The Sketch Engine. In *Proceedings of the Eleventh EURALEX International Congress*, pages 105–116, Lorient, France.

Philipp Koehn. 2005. Europarl: A parallel corpus for statistical machine translation. In *Proceedings of The Tenth Machine Translation Summit (MT Summit X)*, pages 79–86, Phuket, Thailand, September.

Diana Lea and Moira Runcie, editors. 2002. *Oxford Collocations Dictionary for Students of English*. Oxford University Press, Oxford.

Luka Nerima, Violeta Seretan, and Eric Wehrli. 2003. Creating a multilingual collocation dictionary from large text corpora. In *Companion Volume to the Proceedings of the 10th Conference of the European Chapter of the Association for Computational Linguistics (EACL'03)*, pages 131–134, Budapest, Hungary.

Pavel Pecina. 2008. *Lexical Association Measures: Collocation Extraction*. Ph.D. thesis, Charles University in Prague.

Paul Rayson. 2009. Wmatrix: a web-based corpus processing environment. `http://ucrel.lancs.ac.uk/wmatrix`. Accessed March, 2011.

Mike Scott. 2004. *WordSmith Tools version 4*. Oxford University Press, Oxford.

Violeta Seretan. 2009. An integrated environment for extracting and translating collocations. In Michaela Mahlberg, Victorina González-Díaz, and Catherine Smith, editors, *Proceedings of the Corpus Linguistics Conference CL2009*, Liverpool, UK.

Violeta Seretan. 2011. *Syntax-Based Collocation Extraction*. Text, Speech and Language Technology. Springer, Dordrecht.

Eric Wehrli, Luka Nerima, and Yves Scherrer. 2009. Deep linguistic multilingual translation and bilingual dictionaries. In *Proceedings of the Fourth Workshop on Statistical Machine Translation*, pages 90–94, Athens, Greece. Association for Computational Linguistics.

Eric Wehrli. 2007. Fips, a "deep" linguistic multilingual parser. In *ACL 2007 Workshop on Deep Linguistic Processing*, pages 120–127, Prague, Czech Republic.

The StringNet Lexico-Grammatical Knowledgebase and its Applications

David Wible **Nai-Lung Tsao**
National Central University
No.300, Jhongda Rd.
Jhongli City, Taoyuan County 32001, Taiwan
wible@stringnet.org beaktsao@stringnet.org

Abstract

This demo introduces a suite of web-based English lexical knowledge resources, called StringNet and StringNet Navigator (http://nav.stringnet.org), designed to provide access to the immense territory of multiword expressions that falls between what the lexical entries encode in lexicons on the one hand and what productive grammar rules cover on the other. StringNet's content consists of 1.6 billion hybrid n-grams, strings in which word forms and parts of speech grams can co-occur. Subordinate and super-ordinate relations among hybrid n-grams are indexed, making StringNet a navigable web rather than a list. Applications include error detection and correction tools and web browser-based tools that detect patterns in the webpages that a user browses.

1 Introduction and Background

This demo introduces a suite of web-based English lexical knowledge resources, called StringNet and StringNet Navigator (http://nav.stringnet.org), which have been designed to give lexicographers, translators, language teachers and language learners direct access to the immense territory of multiword expressions, more specifically to the lexical patterning that falls in the gap between dictionaries and grammar books.

MWEs are widely recognized in two different research communities as posing persistent problems, specifically in the fields of computational linguistics and human language learning and pedagogy.

In computational linguistics, MWEs are notorious as a "pain in the neck" (Sag et al 2002; Baldwin et al 2004; Villavicencio et al 2005; inter alia). The high proportion of MWEs with non-canonical structures lead to parse failures and their non-compositional or only partially compositional semantics raise difficult choices between which ones to store whole and which ones to construct as needed. Perhaps above all, this massive family of expressions resists any unified treatment since they constitute a heterogeneous mix of regularity and idiomicity (Fillmore et al 1988).

The other area where they famously cause difficulties is in human language learning and teaching, and largely for reasons parallel to those that make them hard for NLP. They resist understanding or production by general rules or composition, and they constitute an unpredictable mix of productivity and idiomicity.

The StringNet lexico-grammatical knowledge-base has been designed to capture this heterogeneity of MWEs by virtue of its unique content and structure. These we describe in turn below.

2 StringNet Content: Hybrid N-grams

The content of StringNet consists of a special breed of n-grams which we call hybrid n-grams (Tsao and Wible 2009; Wible and Tsao 2010). Unlike traditional n-grams, there are four different categories of gram type. From specific to general (or abstract) these four are: specific word forms (*enjoyed* and *enjoys* would be two distinct word forms); lexemes (**enjoy**, including all its inflectional variations, *enjoyed*, *enjoys*, etc); rough POS categories (V, N, etc); and fine-grained POS categories (verbs are distinguished as VVn, VVd, VVt, etc.). A hybrid n-gram can consist of any sequence from any of these four categories with our stipulation that one of the grams must be a word form or lexeme (to insure that all hybrid n-grams are lexically anchored). A traditional bi-gram such as *enjoyed hiking* can be described by 16 distinct hybrid n-grams, such as *enjoyed VVg*, ***enjoy*** *VVg*, ***enjoy hike***, and so on. A traditional 5-gram, such as *kept a close eye on* has 1024 hybrid n-gram variants (4^5), e.g., *keep a close eye on*; *kept a [Adj] eye on*; *keep a close [N][Prep]*; and so on. We have extracted all hybrid n-grams ranging in length from bigrams to 8-grams that are attested at least five times in BNC. StringNet's content thus consists of 1.6 billion hybrid n-grams (including traditional n-grams), each indexed to its attested instances in BNC.

3 Structure and Navigation

Rather than a list of hybrid n-grams, StringNet is a structured net. Hybrid n-grams can stand in sub-ordinate or super-ordinate relation to each other (we refer to these as parent/child relations). For example, the hybrid tri-gram *consider yourselves lucky* has among its many parents the more inclusive *consider [prn rflx] lucky*; which in turn has among its parents the even more general *consider [prn rflx] [Adj]* and *[V] [prn rflx] lucky* and so on. We index all of these relations within the entire set of hybrid n-grams.

StringNet Navigator is the Web interface (shown in Figure 1) for navigating this massive, structured lexico-grammatical knowledgebase of English MWEs. Queries are as simple as submitting a Google query. A query of the noun *trouble* immediately shows users (say, language learners) subtle but important patterns such as *take the trouble [to-V]* and *go to the trouble of [VVg]* (shown in Figure 2). Submitting *mistake* yields *make the mistake of [VVg]* and *it would be a mistake [to-V]*. StringNet Navigator also accepts multiword queries, returning all hybrid n-grams where the submitted words or the submitted words and POSs co-occur. For all queries, clicking on any pattern given in the results will display all the attested example sentences with that pattern from BNC. Each listed pattern for a query also gives links to that pattern's parents and children or to its expansion (longer version) or contraction (shorter version) (See Figure 2).

4 Some Applications

Among the many sorts of knowledge that StringNet renders tractable is the degree of frozenness or substitutability available for any MWE. Thus, not only does a query of the noun *eye* yield the string *keep a close eye on.* Navigating upward reveals that *close* and *eye* in this string can be replaced (*keep a close watch on*; *keep a careful eye on*; *keep a tight grip on*; *keep a firm hold on*, etc), but also that, in this same frame *keep a [Adj][N] on*, the verb slot occupied by *keep* is basically unsubstitutable, essentially serving as a lexical anchor to this expression. Thus, due to its structure as a net, StringNet makes it possible to glean the degree and location(s) of the frozenness or substitutability of an MWE.

4.1 Error Checking

Automatic error detection and correction is a rapidly growing area of application in computational linguistics (See Leacock et al 2010 for a recent book-length review). StringNet supports a novel approach to this area of work. The flexibility afforded by hybrid n-grams makes it possible to capture patterns that involve subtle combinations of lexical specificity or generality for different grams within the same string. For example, running StringNet on BNC data shows that 'enjoy hiking' is best captured as an instance of the lexeme **enjoy** followed by a verb in –ing form: ***enjoy*** *Vvg*. For error checking this makes it possible to overcome sparseness. Thus, while BNC has no tokens of either 'enjoy spelunking' or 'enjoy to spelunk,' we can distinguish between them nevertheless and detect that the former is correct and the latter is an error. The wide range of error types that can be handled by a single algorithm run on StringNet will be shown in the demo.

4.2 Browser-based Tools

Other tools include a toolbar that can be installed on the user's own web browser (Wible et al 2011), from which the system can detect lexical patterns in the text of the web pages the user freely browses. A "Query Doctor" on the toolbar detects errors in multiword queries (submitting 'in my point of view' triggers the suggestion: 'from my point of view').

Figure 1: StringNet Navigator front page.

No.	Chunks	Frequency	Examples	Parents	Children	Expand	Contract
1	**take** the trouble [to-vb]	153					
2	**go** to the trouble of [v-ing]	42					

Figure 2: Top 2 search results for "trouble"

5 Conclusion

Future areas of application for StringNet include machine translation (e.g., detecting semi-compositional constructions); detection of similar and confusable words for learners, document similarity using hybrid n-grams as features, and StringNet Builder for generating StringNets from corpora of languages other than English and from domain-specific corpora.

Acknowledgments

The work described in this paper was partially supported by the grants from the National Science Council, Taiwan (Project Nos. 99-2631-H-008-004- and 98-2511-S-008-002-MY2).

References

Timothy Baldwin, Emily M. Bender, Dan Flickinger, Ara Kim and Stephan Oepen. 2004. Road-testing the English Resource Grammar over the British National Corpus. In *Proceedings of the Fourth International Conference on Language Resources and Evaluation (LREC 2004)*, Lisbon, Portugal, pp. 2047-2050.

Charles J. Fillmore, Paul Kay, and Mary Katherine O'Connor. 1988. Regularity and Idiomaticity in Grammatical Constructions: the Case of *Let Alone. Language* 64: 501–538.

Claudia Leacock, Martin Chodorow, Michael Gamon, and Joel Tetreault, 2010. *Automated Grammatical Error Detection for Language Learners*. Morgan and Claypool Publishers.

Ivan Sag, Timothy Baldwin, Francis Bond, Ann Copestake, Dan Flickinger. 2002. Multiword expressions: A pain in the neck for NLP. In *Proceedings of the 3rd International Conference on Intelligent Text Processing and Computational Linguistics (CICLing-2002)*, Mexico City, Mexico, pp. 1-15.

Nai-Lung Tsao and David Wible. 2009. A Method for Unsupervised Broad-Coverage Lexical Error Detection and Correction. *The NAACL Workshop on Innovative Use of NLP for Building Educational Applications*, Boulder, Colorado, June 2009.

Aline Villavicencio, Francis Bond, Anna Korhonen, and Diana McCarthy. 2005. Introduction to the Special Issue on Multiword Expressions: Having a Crack at a Hard Nut. *Computer Speech & Language* 19(4): 365-377.

David Wible and Nai-Lung Tsao. 2010. StringNet as a Computational Resource for Discovering and Investigating Linguistic Constructions. *The NAACL Workshop on Extracting and Using Constructions in Computational Linguistics*, Los Angeles, June 2010.

David Wible, Anne Li-E Liu and Nai-Lung Tsao. 2011. A Browser-based Approach to Incidental Individualization of Vocabulary Learning. *Journal of Computer Assisted Learning*, in press, early view.

The Ngram Statistics Package (Text::NSP) - A Flexible Tool for Identifying Ngrams, Collocations, and Word Associations

Ted Pedersen*
Department of Computer Science
University of Minnesota
Duluth, MN 55812

Satanjeev Banerjee
Twitter, Inc.
795 Folsom Street
San Francisco, CA 94107

Bridget T. McInnes
College of Pharmacy
University of Minnesota
Minneapolis, MN 55455

Saiyam Kohli
SDL Language Weaver, Inc.
6060 Center Drive, Suite 150
Los Angeles, CA 90045

Mahesh Joshi
Language Technologies Institute
Carnegie Mellon University
Pittsburgh, PA 15213

Ying Liu
College of Pharmacy
University of Minnesota
Minneapolis, MN 55455

Abstract

The Ngram Statistics Package (Text::NSP) is freely available open-source software that identifies ngrams, collocations and word associations in text. It is implemented in Perl and takes advantage of regular expressions to provide very flexible tokenization and to allow for the identification of non-adjacent ngrams. It includes a wide range of measures of association that can be used to identify collocations.

1 Introduction

The identification of multiword expressions is a key problem in Natural Language Processing. Despite years of research, there is still no single best way to proceed. As such, the availability of flexible and easy to use toolkits remains important. Text::NSP is one such package, and includes programs for counting ngrams (count.pl, huge-count.pl), measuring the association between the words that make up an ngram (statistic.pl), and for measuring correlation between the rankings of ngrams created by different measures (rank.pl). It is also able to identify n-th order co-occurrences (kocos.pl) and pre–specified compound words in text (find-compounds.pl).

This paper briefly describes each component of NSP. Additional details can be found in (Banerjee and Pedersen, 2003) or in the software itself, which is freely available from CPAN [1] or Sourceforge [2].

*Contact author : tpederse@d.umn.edu. Note that authors Banerjee, McInnes, Kohli and Joshi contributed to Text::NSP while they were at the University of Minnesota, Duluth.

[1] http://search.cpan.org/dist/Text-NSP/

[2] http://sourceforge.net/projects/ngram/

2 count.pl

The program **count.pl** takes any number of plain text files or directories of such files and counts the total number of ngrams as well their marginal totals. It provides the ability to define what a token may be using regular expressions (via the `--token` option). An ngram is an ordered sequence of n tokens, and under this scheme tokens may be almost anything, including space separated strings, characters, etc. Also, ngrams may be made up of nonadjacent tokens due to the `--window` option that allows users to specify the number of tokens within which an ngram must occur.

Counting is done using hashes in Perl which are memory intensive. As a result, NSP also provides the **huge-count.pl** program and various other **huge-*.pl** utilities that carry out count.pl functionality using hard drive space rather than memory. This can scale to much larger amounts of text, although usually taking more time in the process.

By default count.pl treats ngrams as ordered sequences of tokens; *dog house* is distinct from *house dog*. However, it may be that order does not always matter, and a user may simply want to know if two words co-occur. In this case the **combig.pl** program adjusts counts from count.pl to reflect an unordered count, where *dog house* and *house dog* are considered the same. Finally, **find-compounds.pl** allows a user to specify a file of already known multiword expressions (like place names, idioms, etc.) and then identify all occurrences of those in a corpus before running count.pl

3 statistic.pl

The core of NSP is a wide range of measures of association that can be used to identify interesting ngrams, particularly bigrams and trigrams. The measures are organized into families that share common characteristics (which are described in detail in the source code documentation). This allows for an object oriented implementation that promotes inheritance of common functionality among these measures. Note that all of the Mutual Information measures are supported for trigrams, and that the Log-likelihood ratio is supported for 4-grams. The measures in the package are shown grouped by family in Table 1, where the name by which the measure is known in NSP is in parentheses.

Table 1: Measures of Association in NSP

Mutual Information (MI)
(ll) Log-likelihood Ratio (Dunning, 1993)
(tmi) *true* MI (Church and Hanks, 1990)
(pmi) Pointwise MI (Church and Hanks, 1990)
(ps) Poisson-Stirling (Church, 2000)
Fisher's Exact Test (Pedersen et al., 1996)
(leftFisher) left tailed
(rightFisher) right tailed
(twotailed) two tailed
Chi-squared
(phi) Phi Coefficient (Church, 1991)
(tscore) T-score (Church et al., 1991)
(x2) Pearson's Chi-Squared (Dunning, 1993)
Dice
(dice) Dice Coefficient (Smadja, 1993)
(jaccard) Jaccard Measure
(odds) Odds Ratio (Blaheta and Johnson, 2001)

3.1 rank.pl

One natural experiment is to compare the output of statistic.pl for the same input using different measures of association. **rank.pl** takes as input the output from statistic.pl for two different measures, and computes Spearman's Rank Correlation Coefficient between them. In general, measures within the same family correlate more closely with each other than with measures from a different family. As an example *tmi* and *ll* as well as *dice* and *jaccard* differ by only constant terms and therefore produce identical rankings. It is often worthwhile to conduct exploratory studies with multiple measures, and the rank correlation can help recognize when two measures are very similar or different.

4 kocos.pl

In effect **kocos.pl** builds a word network by finding all the n-th order co-occurrences for a given literal or regular expression. This can be viewed somewhat recursively, where the 3-rd order co-occurrences of a given target word are all the tokens that occur with the 2-nd order co-occurrences, which are all the tokens that occur with the 1-st order (immediate) co-occurrences of the target. kocos.pl outputs chains of the form `king -> george -> washington`, where *washington* is a second order co-occurrence (of *king*) since both *king* and *washington* are first order co-occurrences of *george*. kocos.pl takes as input the output from count.pl, combig.pl, or statistic.pl.

5 API

In addition to command line support, Test::NSP offers an extensive API for Perl programmers. All of the measures described in Table 1 can be included in Perl programs as object–oriented method calls (Kohli, 2006), and it is also easy to add new measures or modify existing measures within a program.

6 Development History of Text::NSP

The Ngram Statistics Package was originally implemented by Satanjeev Banerjee in 2000-2002 (Banerjee and Pedersen, 2003). Amruta Purandare incorporated NSP into SenseClusters (Purandare and Pedersen, 2004) and added huge-count.pl, combig.pl and kocos.pl in 2002-2004. Bridget McInnes added the log-likelihood ratio for longer ngrams in 2003-2004 (McInnes, 2004). Saiyam Kohli rewrote the measures of association to use object-oriented methods in 2004-2006, and also added numerous new measures for bigrams and trigams (Kohli, 2006). Mahesh Joshi improved cross platform support and created an NSP wrapper for Gate in 2005-2006. Ying Liu wrote find-compounds.pl and rewrote huge-count.pl in 2010-2011.

References

S. Banerjee and T. Pedersen. 2003. The design, implementation, and use of the Ngram Statistics Package. In *Proceedings of the Fourth International Conference on Intelligent Text Processing and Computational Linguistics*, pages 370–381, Mexico City, February.

D. Blaheta and M. Johnson. 2001. Unsupervised learning of multi-word verbs. In *ACL/EACL Workshop on Collocations*, pages 54–60, Toulouse, France.

K. Church and P. Hanks. 1990. Word association norms, mutual information and lexicography. *Computational Linguistics*, pages 22–29.

K. Church, W. Gale, P. Hanks, and D. Hindle. 1991. Using statistics in lexical analysis. In U. Zernik, editor, *Lexical Acquisition: Exploiting On-Line Resources to Build a Lexicon*. Lawrence Erlbaum Associates, Hillsdale, NJ.

K. Church. 1991. Concordances for parallel text. In *Seventh Annual Conference of the UW Centre for New OED and Text Research*, Oxford, England.

K. Church. 2000. Empirical estimates of adaptation: The chance of two noriegas is closer to p/2 than p2. In *Proceedings of the 18th International Conference on Computational Linguistics (COLING-2000)*, pages 180–186, Saarbrücken, Germany.

T. Dunning. 1993. Accurate methods for the statistics of surprise and coincidence. *Computational Linguistics*, 19(1):61–74.

S. Kohli. 2006. Introducing an object oriented design to the ngram statistics package. Master's thesis, University of Minnesota, Duluth, July.

B. McInnes. 2004. Extending the log-likelihood ratio to improve collocation identification. Master's thesis, University of Minnesota, Duluth, December.

T. Pedersen, M. Kayaalp, and R. Bruce. 1996. Significant lexical relationships. In *Proceedings of the Thirteenth National Conference on Artificial Intelligence*, pages 455–460, Portland, OR, August.

A. Purandare and T. Pedersen. 2004. Word sense discrimination by clustering contexts in vector and similarity spaces. In *Proceedings of the Conference on Computational Natural Language Learning*, pages 41–48, Boston, MA.

F. Smadja. 1993. Retrieving collocations from text: Xtract. *Computational Linguistics*, 19(1):143–177.

Fast and Flexible MWE Candidate Generation with the `mwetoolkit`

Vitor De Araujo♠ **Carlos Ramisch**♠ ♡ **Aline Villavicencio**♠
♠ Institute of Informatics, Federal University of Rio Grande do Sul, Brazil
♡ GETALP – LIG, University of Grenoble, France
{vbuaraujo, ceramisch, avillavicencio}@inf.ufrgs.br

Abstract

We present an experimental environment for computer-assisted extraction of Multiword Expressions (MWEs) from corpora. Candidate extraction works in two steps: generation and filtering. We focus on recent improvements in the former, for which we increased speed and flexibility. We present examples that show the potential gains for users and applications.

1 Project Description

The `mwetoolkit` was presented and demonstrated in Ramisch et al. (2010b) and in Ramisch et al. (2010a), and applied to several languages (Linardaki et al., 2010) and domains (Ramisch et al., 2010c). It is a downloadable open-source[1] set of command-line tools mostly written in Python. Our target users are researchers with a background in computational linguistics. The system performs language- and type-independent candidate extraction in two steps[2]:

1. Candidate generation
   - Pattern matching[3]
   - n-gram counting
2. Candidate filtering
   - Thresholds, stopwords and patterns
   - Association measures, classifiers

[1] `sf.net/projects/mwetoolkit`

[2] For details, see previous papers and documentation

[3] The following attributes, if present, are supported for patterns: surface form, lemma, POS, syntactic annotation.

The main contribution of our tool, rather than a novel approach to MWE extraction, is an environment that systematically integrates the functionalities found in other tools, that is, sophisticated corpus queries like in CQP (Christ, 1994) and Manatee (Rychlý and Smrz, 2004), candidate generation like in Text::NSP (Banerjee and Pedersen, 2003), and filtering like in UCS (Evert, 2004). The pattern matching and n-gram counting steps are the focus of the improvements described in this paper.

2 An Example

Our toy corpus, consisting of the first 20K sentences of English Europarl v3[4], was POS-tagged and lemmatized using the TreeTagger[5] and converted into XML. [6] As MWEs encompass several phenomena (Sag et al., 2002), we define our target word sequences through the *patterns* shown in figure 1. The first represents sequences with an optional (?) determiner DET, any number (*) of adjectives A and one or more (+) nouns N. This shallow pattern roughly corresponds to noun phrases in English. The second defines expressions in which a repeated noun is linked by a preposition PRP. The `backw` element matches a previous word, in this example the same lemma as the noun identified as `noun1`.

After corpus indexing and n-gram pattern matching, the resulting unique candidates are returned. Examples of candidates captured by the first pattern

[4] `statmt.org/europarl`

[5] `http://www.ims.uni-stuttgart.de/projekte/corplex/TreeTagger`

[6] For large corpora, XML imposes considerable overhead. As corpora do not require the full flexibility of XML, we are currently experimenting with plain-text, which is already in use with the new C indexing routines.

```
<pat id="1">
   <pat repeat="?"><w pos="DET"/></pat>
   <pat repeat="*"><w pos="A"/></pat>
   <pat repeat="+"><w pos="N"/></pat>
</pat>
<pat id="2">
   <w pos="N" id="noun1"/>
   <w pos="PRP"/>
   <backw lemma="noun1" pos="noun1"/>
</pat>
```

Figure 1: Pattern 1 matches NPs, pattern 2 matches sequences N_1 PRP N_1.

are *complicated administrative process*, *the clock*, *the War Crimes Tribunal*. The second pattern captures *hand in hand*, *eye to eye*, *word for word*. [7]

3 New Features

Friendlier User Interface In the previous version, one needed to manually invoke the Python scripts passing the correct options. The current version provides an interactive command-based interface which allows simple commands to be run on data files, while keeping the generation of intermediary files and the pipelining between the different phases of MWE extraction implicit. At the end, a user may want to save the session and restart the work later.[8]

Regular Expression Support While in the previous version only wildcard words were possible, now we support all the operators shown in figure 1 plus repetition interval (2,3), multiple choice (`either`) and in-word wildcards like *writ** matching *written*, *writing*, etc. All these extensions allow for much more powerful candidate patterns to be expressed. This means that one can also use syntax annotation if the text is parsed: if two words separated by n words share a syntactic head, they are extracted. Multi-attribute patterns are correctly handled during pattern matching, in spite of individual per-attribute indices. Some scripts may fuse the individual indices on the fly, producing a combined index (e.g. n-gram counting).

Faster processing Candidate generation was not able to deal with large corpora such as Europarl and the BNC. The first optimization concerns pattern matching: instead of using the XML corpus and external matching procedures, now we match candidates using Python's builtin regular expressions directly on the corpus index. On a small corpus the current implementation takes about 72% the original time to perform pattern-based generation. On the BNC, extraction of the two example patterns shown before took about 4.5 hours and 1 hour, respectively. The second optimization concerns the creation of the index. The previous script allowed a static index to be created from the XML corpus, but it was not scalable. Thus, we have rewritten index routines in C. We still assume that the index must fit in main memory, but the new routines provide faster indexing with reasonable memory consumption, proportional to the corpus size. These scripts are still experimental and need extensive testing. With the C index routines, indexing the BNC corpus took about 5 minutes per attribute on a 3GB RAM computer.

4 Future Improvements

Additionally to evaluation on several tasks and languages, we intend to develop several improvements to the tool. First, we would like to rewrite the pattern matching routines in C to speed the process up and reduce memory consumption. Second, we would like to test several heuristics to handle nested candidates (current strategy returns all possible matches). Third, we would like to perform more tests on using regular expressions to extract candidates based on their syntax annotation. Fourth, we would like to improve candidate filtering (not emphasized in this paper) by testing new association measures, filters, context-based measures, etc. Last but most important, we are planning a new release version and therefore we need extensive testing and documentation.

References

Satanjeev Banerjee and Ted Pedersen. 2003. The design, implementation, and use of the Ngram Statistic Package. In *Proceedings of the Fourth International Conference on Intelligent Text Processing and Com-*

[7] Currently only contiguous n-grams can be captured; non-contiguous extraction (e.g., verb-noun pairs, with intervening material, not part of the expression) is planned.

[8] Although it is not a graphical interface some users request, it is far easier to use than the previous version.

putational Linguistics, pages 370–381, Mexico City, Mexico, Feb.

Oli Christ. 1994. A modular and flexible architecture for an integrated corpus query system. In *COMPLEX 1994*, Budapest, Hungary.

Stefan Evert. 2004. *The Statistics of Word Cooccurrences: Word Pairs and Collocations*. Ph.D. thesis, Institut für maschinelle Sprachverarbeitung, University of Stuttgart, Stuttgart, Germany.

Evita Linardaki, Carlos Ramisch, Aline Villavicencio, and Aggeliki Fotopoulou. 2010. Towards the construction of language resources for greek multiword expressions: Extraction and evaluation. In Stelios Piperidis, Milena Slavcheva, and Cristina Vertan, editors, *Proc. of the LREC Workshop on Exploitation of multilingual resources and tools for Central and (South) Eastern European Languages*, pages 31–40, Valetta, Malta. May.

Carlos Ramisch, Aline Villavicencio, and Christian Boitet. 2010a. Multiword expressions in the wild? the mwetoolkit comes in handy. In *Proc. of the 23rd COLING (COLING 2010) — Demonstrations*, pages 57–60, Beijing, China, Aug. The Coling 2010 Organizing Committee.

Carlos Ramisch, Aline Villavicencio, and Christian Boitet. 2010b. mwetoolkit: a framework for multiword expression identification. In *Proc. of the Seventh LREC (LREC 2010)*, Malta, May. ELRA.

Carlos Ramisch, Aline Villavicencio, and Christian Boitet. 2010c. Web-based and combined language models: a case study on noun compound identification. In *Proc. of the 23rd COLING (COLING 2010)*, pages 1041–1049, Beijing, China, Aug. The Coling 2010 Organizing Committee.

Pavel Rychlý and Pavel Smrz. 2004. Manatee, bonito and word sketches for czech. In *Proceedings of the Second International Conference on Corpus Linguisitcs*, pages 124–131, Saint-Petersburg, Russia.

Ivan Sag, Timothy Baldwin, Francis Bond, Ann Copestake, and Dan Flickinger. 2002. Multiword expressions: A pain in the neck for NLP. In *Proc. of the 3rd CICLing (CICLing-2002)*, volume 2276/2010 of *LNCS*, pages 1–15, Mexico City, Mexico, Feb. Springer.

How Many Multiword Expressions do People Know?

Kenneth Church
HLT COE
Johns Hopkins University
Kenneth.Church@jhu.edu

Abstract

What is a multiword expression (MWE) and how many are there? What is a MWE? What is many? Mark Liberman gave a great invited talk at ACL-89 titled "how many words do people know?" where he spent the entire hour questioning the question. Many of these same questions apply to multiword expressions. What is a word? What is many? What is a person? What does it mean to know? Rather than answer these questions, this paper will use these questions as Liberman did, as an excuse for surveying how such issues are addressed in a variety of fields: computer science, web search, linguistics, lexicography, educational testing, psychology, statistics, etc.

1 How many words do people know?

One can find all sorts of answers on the web:

- **Very low**: Apparently I only knew 7,000 words when I was seven and 14,000 when I was fourteen. I learned from exposure. Now things are not that easy in a second language, but it just shows that the brain can absorb information from sheer input.[1]
- **Low**: 12,000 – 20,000 words[2]
- **Higher**: 988,968[3]
- **Even higher**: 13,588,391[4]

2 Motivation

As mentioned in the abstract, Liberman used his ACL-89 invited talk to survey how various fields approach these issues. He started his ACL-89 invited talk by questioning every word in the title of his talk: *How many words do people know?*

1. What is a word? Is a word defined in terms of meaning? Sound? Syntax? Spelling? White space? Distribution? Etymology? Learnability?
2. What is a person? Child? Adult? Native speaker? Language Learner?
3. What does it mean to know something? Active knowledge is different from passive knowledge. What is (Artificial) Intelligence? Is vocabulary size a measure of intelligence? (Terman, 1918)
4. What do we mean by many? Is there a limit like 20,000 or 1M or 13.6M or does vocabulary size (V) keep growing with experience (larger corpora → larger V)?

The original motivation for Liberman's talk came from a very practical business concern. At the time, Liberman was running a speech synthesis effort at AT&T Bell Labs. As the manager of this effort, Liberman would receive questions from the business asking how large the synthesizer's dictionary would have to be for such and such commercial application.

Vocabulary size was also a hot topic in many other engineering applications. How big does the dictionary have to be for X? X can be anything from parsing, part of speech tagging, spelling correction, machine translation, word breaking for Chinese and Japanese (and English), speech recog-

1 http://thelinguist.blogs.com/how_to_learn_english_and/2009/02/how-many-words-do-you-know-how-many-have-you-looked-up-in-a-dictionary.html

2 http://answers.yahoo.com/question/index?qid=20061105205054AA5YL0B

3 http://www.independent.co.uk/news/world/americas/english-language-nears-the-one-millionword-milestone-473935.html

4 Franz and Brants (2006)

nition, speech synthesis, web search or some other application.

3 Dictionary Estimates

These questions reminded Liberman of similar questions that his colleagues in lexicography were receiving from their marketing departments. Many dictionaries and other reference books lead with a marketing pitch such as: "Most comprehensive: more than 330,000 words and phrases [MWEs]…" (Kipfer, 2001).

The very smallest dictionaries are called "gems." They typically contain 20,000 words. Unabridged collegiate dictionaries have about 500,000 words.[5] The Oxford English Dictionary (OED) has 600,000 entries.[6]

All of these dictionaries limit themselves to what is known as general vocabulary, words that would be expected to be understood by a general audience. General vocabulary is typically contrasted with technical terminology, words that would only be understood by domain experts in a particular topic. There are reference books that specialize on place names (Gazetteers), surnames, technical terminology, quotations, etc., but standard dictionaries of general vocabulary tend to avoid proper nouns, complex nominals (e.g., "staff meeting"), abbreviations, acronyms, technical terminology, digit sequences, street addresses, trademarks, product numbers, etc.[7] Even the largest dictionaries may not have all that much coverage because in practice, one often runs into texts that go well beyond general vocabulary.

4 Broder's Taxonomy of Web Queries

Obviously, the web goes well beyond general vocabulary. Web queries tend to be short phrases (MWEs), often a word or two such as a product number. Broder (2002) introduced a taxonomy of queries that has become widely accepted. His percentage estimates were estimated from AltaVista query logs and could use updating.

- Naviational (20%)
- Informational (48%)
- Transactional (30%)

Navigational queries are extremely common these days, perhaps even more common than 20%. The user intent is to navigate to a particular url:

- google → www.google.com
- Greyhound Bus → www.greyhound.com
- American Airlines → www.aa.com

Broder's examples of informational queries are: *cars, San Francisco, normocytic anemia, Scoville heat units*. The user intent is to research a particular information need. The user expects to read one or more *static* web pages in order to address the information need. Broder italicized "static" to distinguish informational queries from transactional queries. Transactional queries are intended to reach a site where further (non-static) action will take place: shopping, directions, web-mediated services, medical advice, gaming, downloading music, pictures, videos, etc.

5 User Intent & One Sense Per Query

I prefer a two-way distinction between

1. Navigational queries: user knows where she wants to go, and
2. Non-navigational queries: user is open to suggestions.

Google, for example, offers the following "related search" suggestions for "camera:" *digital camera, video camera, history of the camera, sony camera, ritz camera, Nikon camera, camera brands, camera reviews, camera store, beach camera, canon, photography, bestbuy, camara, cannon, circuit city. camero. Olympus, camcorder, b&h.* These kinds of suggestions can be very successful when the user is open to suggestions, but not for navigational queries. There are a number of other mechanisms for making suggestions such as ads and did-you-mean spelling suggestions.

[5] http://www.collinslanguage.com/shop/english-dictionary-landing.aspx
[6] http://www.oed.com/public/about
[7] See Sproat (1994) and references therein for more on complex nominals. See Coker et al (1990) for coverage statistics on surnames. See Liberman and Church (1991) for more on abbreviations, acronyms, digit sequences and more. See Dagan and Church (1994) for more on technical terminology.

Pitler and Church (2009) used click logs to classify queries by intent (CQI). Consider five types of clicks. Some types of clicks are evidence that the user knows where she wants to go, and some are evidence that the user is open to suggestions.

1. Algo: clicks on the so-called 10 blue links
2. Paid: clicks on commercial ads
3. Wikipedia: clicks on Wikipedia entries
4. Spelling Corrections: did you mean …?
5. Other suggestions from search engine

Many queries are strongly associated with one type of click (more than others).

- Commercial queries → clicks on ads
- Non-commercial queries → Wikipedia.

There is a one-sense-per-X constraint (Gale et al, 1992; Yarowsky, 1993). It is unlikely that the same query will be ambiguous with both commercial and non-commercial senses. Indeed, the click logs show that both ads and Wikipedia are effective, but they have complementary distributions. There are few queries with both clicks on ads and clicks on Wikipedia entries. For a commercial query like, "JC Penney," it is ok for Google to return an ad and a store locator map, but Google shouldn't return a Wikipedia discussion of the history of the company.

Although the click logs are very large, they are never large enough. How do we resolve the user intention when the click logs are too sparse to resolve the ambiguity directly? Pitler suggested using word sense disambiguation methods. For example, her method labels the ambiguous query "designer trench" as commercial because it is closer (in random walk distance) to a couple of stores than to a Wikipedia discussion of trench warfare during World War I.

More generally, random walk methods (like word sense disambiguation) can be used to resolve all sorts of hidden variables such as gender, age, location, political orientation, user intent, etc. Did the user mean X? Does the user know what she wants, or is she open to suggestions?

5.1 User Intent & Spelling Correction

Spelling correction is an extreme case where it is often relatively easy for the system to determine user intent. On the web, spelling correction has become synonymous with did-you-mean. The synonymy makes it clear that the point of spelling correction is to get at what users mean as opposed to what they say.

> *Then you should say what you mean,' the March Hare went on.*
> *`I do,' Alice hastily replied; `at least--at least I mean what I say--that's the same thing, you know.'*
> *`Not the same thing a bit!' said the Hatter.* (Lewis Carroll, 1865)

See Kukich (1992) for a comprehensive survey on spelling correction. Boswell (2004) is a nice research exam; it is short and crisp and recent.

I've worked on Microsoft's spelling correction products in two different divisions: Office and Web Search. One might think that correcting documents in Microsoft Word would be similar to correcting web queries, but in fact, the two applications have remarkably little in common. A dictionary of general vocabulary is essential for correcting documents and nearly useless for correcting web queries. General vocabulary is more important in documents than web queries.

The surveys mentioned above are more appropriate for correcting documents than web queries. Cucerzan and Brill (2004) propose an iterative process that is more appropriate for web queries. In Table 1, they show a number of (mis)spellings of Albert Einstein's name from a query log, sorted by frequency: *albert einstein* (4834), *albert einstien* (525), *albert einstine* (149), *albert einsten* (27), *albert einsteins* (25), etc. Their method takes a web query that may or may not be misspelled and considers nearby corrections with higher frequencies. The method continues to iterate in this way until it converges at a fixed point. The iteration makes it possible to correct multiple errors. For example, *anol scwartegger* → *arnold schwartznegger* → *arnold schwarznegger* → *arnold schwarzenegger*. They find that context is often very helpful. In general, it is easier to correct the combination of the first name and the last name together than separately. So too, it is probably easier to correct MWEs as a combination than to correct each of the parts separately.

5.2 User Intent & Spoken Queries

Queries often depend on context in complex and unexpected ways. It has been said that there is no there there on the web, but queries from cell phones are often looking for stuff that has a "there" (a location), and moreover the location is often near the user (e.g., restaurants, directions).

Users now have the option to enter queries by voice in addition to the keyboard. Kamvar and Beeferman (2010) found voice was relatively popular on mobile devices with "compressed" (hard-to-use) keyboards. They also found some topics were relatively more likely to be spoken:

- Food & Drink: *Starbucks, tuna fish, Mexican food*
- Business Listings: *Starbucks Holmdel NJ, Lake George*
- Properties relating to places: *weather Holmdel NJ, best gas prices*
- Shopping & Travel: *Rapids Water Park coupons, black Converse shoes, Costco, Walmart*

Other topics such as adult queries are relatively less likely to be spoken, presumably because users don't want to be overheard. Privacy is more of a concern for some topics and less for others.

6 What is "large"?

The term "large vocabulary" has been a moving target. Vocabulary sizes have been increasing with advances in technology. Around the time of Liberman's ACL-89 talk, the speech recognition community was working really hard on a 20,000-word task. Since it was so hard at the time to scale up recognizers to such large vocabularies, some researchers were desperately hoping that 20,000 words would be sufficient to achieve broad coverage of unrestricted language.

At that time, I gave a workshop talk that used a much larger vocabulary of 400,000 words (Church and Gale, 1989). A leading researcher pulled me aside and begged me to tell him that I had made a mistake and there was no need to go beyond 20,000 words.

Similar questions came up when Google released their ngram counts over a trillion word corpus (Franz and Brants, 2006). There was considerable pushback from the community over the size of the vocabulary (13,588,391). Norvig (personal communication) called me up to ask if their estimate of 13.6 million seemed unreasonable.

While I had no reason to question Google's estimate, I was reluctant to make a strong statement, given Efron and Thisted (1976). Efron and Thisted studied a similar question: How many words did Shakespeare know (but didn't use)? They conclude that one can extrapolate corpus size a little bit (e.g., a factor of two) but not too much (e.g., an order of magnitude). Since Google is working with corpora that are many orders of magnitude larger than what I had the opportunity to work with, it would require way too much extrapolation to answer Norvig's question based on my relatively limited experience.

7 Vocabulary Grows with Experience

Many people share the (mistaken) intuition that there is an upper bound on the size of the vocabulary. Marketing pitches such "330,000 words" (above) suggest that there is a reasonable upper bound that a person could hope to master (something considerably more manageable than Google's estimate of 13.6 million).

In fact, the story is probably worse than that. At ACL-1989, Liberman showed plots like those below.[8] These plots make it clear that vocabulary (V) is going up and up and up with corpus size (N). There appears to be no end in sight. It is unlikely that there is an upper bound. 20k isn't enough. Nor is 400k, or even 13.6 million…

The different curves call out differences in what counts as a word. Do we consider morphologically related forms to be one word or two? How about

[8] Plots borrowed with permission from Language Log: http://itre.cis.upenn.edu/~myl/languagelog/archives/005514.html

upper and lower case? MWEs? The different curves correspond to different choices.

No matter how we define a word, we find that vocabulary grows (rapidly) with corpus size for as far as we can see. This observation appears to hold across a broad set of conditions (languages, definitions of word/ngram, etc.) Vocabulary becomes larger and larger with experience. Similar comments apply to ngrams and MWEs.

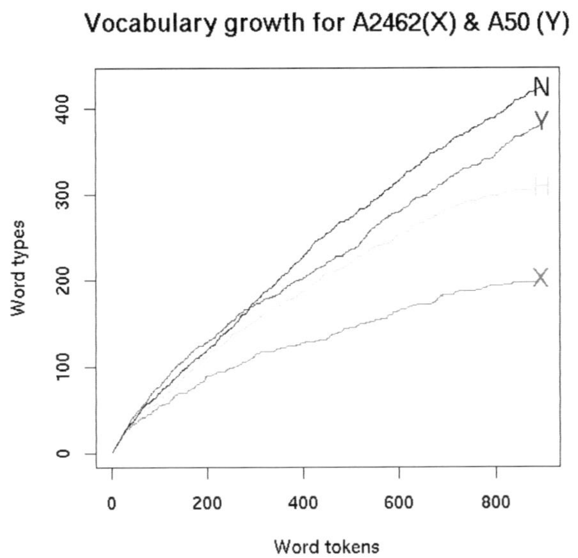

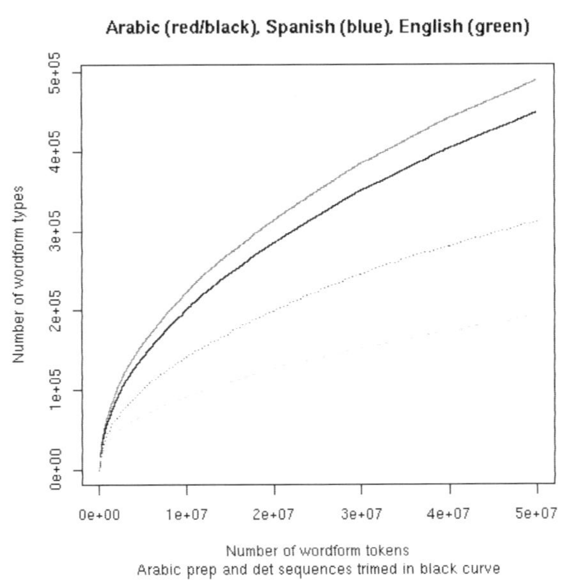

There is wide agreement that there's no data like more data (Mercer, 1985).[9] Google quoted Mercer in their announcement of ngram counts (Franz and Brants, 2006).

Banko and Brill (2001) observed that performance goes up and up and up with experience (data). In the plot below, they note that the differences between lines (learners) are small compared to the gains to be had by simply collecting more data. Based on this observation, Brill has suggested (probably in jest) that we should fire everyone and spend the money on collecting data.

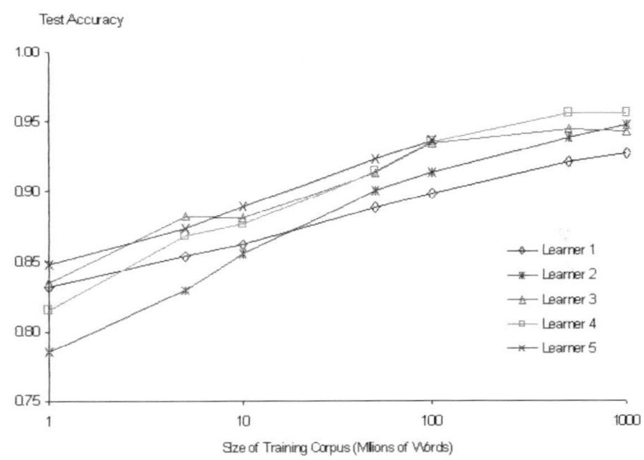

Another interpretation is that experience improves performance on a host of tasks. This pattern might help account for the large correlation (0.91) in Terman (1918). Terman suggests that vocabulary size should not be viewed as a measure of intelligence but rather a measure of experience. He uses the term "mental age" for experience, and measures "mental age" by performance on a standardized test. After adjusting for the large correlation between vocabulary size and experience, there is little evidence of a connection between vocabulary size and intelligence (or much of anything else). Terman also considers a number of other factors such as gender and the language spoken at home (and testing errors), but ultimately concludes that experience dominates all of these alternative factors.

[9] Jelinek (2004) attributes this position to Mercer (1985) http://www.lrec-conf.org/lrec2004/doc/jelinek.pdf.

8 What is a Word? MWE?

We tend to think that white space makes it pretty easy to tokenize English text into words. Obviously, white space makes the task much easier than it would be otherwise. There is a considerable literature on word breaking in Chinese and Japanese which is considerably more challenging than English largely because there is no white space in Chinese and Japanese. There are a number of popular dictionary-based solutions such as ChaSen[10] and Juman.[11] Sproat *et al* (1996) proposed an alternative solution based on distributional statistics such as mutual information.

The situation may not be all that different in English. English is full of multiword expressions. An obvious example involves words that look like prepositions: *up, in, on, with.* A great example is often attributed to Winston Churchill: *This is the sort of arrant nonsense up with which I will not put.*[12] One could argue that "put up with" is a phrasal verb and therefore it should be treated more like a fixed expression (or a word) than a stranded preposition.

8.1 Preventing Bloopers

Almost any high frequency verb (*go, make, do, have, give, call*) can form a phrase with almost any high frequency function word (*it, up, in, on, with, out, down, around, over*), often with non-compositional (taboo) semantics.

This fact led to a rather entertaining failure mode with a word sense program that was trained on a combination of Roget's Thesaurus and Grolier's Encyclopedia (Yarowsky, 1992). Yarowsky's program had a tendency to label high frequency words incorrectly with taboo senses due to a mismatch between Groliers and Roget's. Groliers was written for the parents of middle-American school children and therefore avoided taboo language, whereas Roget's was edited by Chapman, an authority on American Slang (taboo language). The mismatch was particularly nasty for high frequency words, which are very common in Groliers, but unlikely to be mentioned in Roget's, except when the semantics are non-compositional (taboo). Consequently, there was an embarrassingly high probability that Yarowsky's program would find embarrassing interpretations of benign texts.

While some of these mistakes are somewhat understandable and even somewhat amusing in a research prototype, such mistakes are no laughing matter in a commercial product. The testers at Microsoft worked really hard to make sure that their products don't make inappropriate suggestions. Despite their best efforts, there have been a few highly publicized mistakes[13] and there will probably be more unless we find better ways to prevent bloopers.

8.2 Complex Nominals and What is a Word?

Complex nominals are probably more common than phrasal verbs. Is "White House" one word or two? Is a word defined in terms of spelling? White space?

These days, among computational linguists, there would be considerable sympathy for using distributional statistics such as word frequency and mutual information to find MWEs. Following Firth (1957), we know a word by the company that it keeps. In Church and Hanks (1990), we suggested using pointwise mutual information as a heuristic to look for pairs of words that have non-compositional distributional statistics. That is, if the joint probability, P(x,y), of seeing two words together in a context (e.g., window of 5 words) is much higher than chance, P(x)P(y), then there is probably a hidden variable such as meaning that is causing the deviation from chance. In this way, we are able to discover lots of word associations (e.g., *doctor…nurse*), collocates, fixed expressions, etc.

If the list of MWEs becomes too large and too unmanageable, one could turn to a method like Stolcke pruning to cut back the list as necessary. Stolcke pruning is designed to prune ngram models so they fit in a manageable amount of memory. Suppose we have an ngram model with too many

[10] http://chasen.naist.jp/hiki/ChaSen/
[11] http://nlp.kuee.kyoto-u.ac.jp/nl-resource/juman-e.html
[12] For a discussion of the source of this quotation, see http://itre.cis.upenn.edu/~myl/languagelog/archives/002670.html .

[13] http://www.zdnet.co.uk/news/it-strategy/1999/07/01/microsoft-sued-for-racist-application-2072468/

ngrams and we have to drop some of them. Which ones should we drop? Stolcke pruning computes a loss in terms of relative entropy for dropping each ngram in the model. The method drops the ngram that minimizes loss.

When an ngram is dropped from the model, that sequence is modeled with a backed off estimate from other ngrams. Stolcke pruning can be thought of as introducing compositionality assumptions. Suppose, for example, that "nice house" has more compositional statistics than "white house." That is, Pr(*nice house*) ≈ Pr(*nice*) Pr(*house*) whereas Pr(*white house*) >> Pr(*white*) Pr(*house*). In this case, Stolcke pruning would drop "nice house" before it drops "white house."

8.3 Linguistic Diagnostics

Linguists would feel more comfortable with defining word in terms of sound (phonology) and meaning (semantics). It is pretty clear that "White House" has non-compositional sound and meaning. The "White House" does not refer to a house that happens to be white, which is what would be expected under compositional semantics. It is accented on the left (the WHITE house) in contrast with the general pattern where adjective-noun complex nominals are typically accented on the right (a nice HOUSE), though there are many exceptions to this rule (Sproat 1994).[14]

Linguists would also feel comfortable with diagnostic tests based on paraphrases and transformations. Fixed expressions are fixed. One can't paraphrase a "red herring" as "*herring that is red." They resist regular inflection: "*two red herrings." In Bergsma *et al* (2011), we use a paraphrase diagnostic to distinguish [N & N] N from N & [N N]:

- [*dairy and meat*] *production*
  - *meat and dairy production*
  - *production of meat and dairy*
  - *production de produits* [*laitiers et de viand*] (French)
- *asbestos and* [*polyvinyl chloride*]
  - *polyvinyl chloride and asbestos*
  - *asbestos and chloride*
  - *l'asbesto e il* [*polivinilcloruro*] (Italian)

The first three paraphrases make it clear that "dairy and meat" is a constituent whereas the last three paraphrases make it clear that "polyvinyl chloride" is a constituent. Comparable corpora can be viewed as a rich source of paraphrase data, as indicated by the French and Italian examples above.

9 Conclusions

How many multiword expressions (MWEs) do people know? The question is related to how many words do people know. 20k? 400k? 1M? 13M? Is there a bound or does vocabulary size increase with experience (corpus size)? Is vocabulary size a measure of intelligence or just experience?

Dictionary sizes are just a lower bound because they focus on general vocabulary and avoid much of what matters on the web. Spelling correction is not the same for documents of general vocabulary and web queries.

One can use Stolcke pruning and other compositionality tricks to cut down on the number of the number of multiword units that people must know. But obviously, the number they must know is just a lower bound on the number they may know.

There are lots of engineering motivations for wanting to know how many words and MWEs people know. How big does the dictionary have to be for X (where X is parsing, tagging, spelling correction, machine translation, word breaking for Chinese and Japanese (and English), speech recognition, speech synthesis or some other application)?

Rather than answer these questions, this paper used these questions as Liberman did, as an excuse for surveying how such issues are addressed in a variety of fields: computer science, web search, linguistics, lexicography, educational testing, psychology, statistics, etc.

[14] Sproat has posted a list of 7831 English binary noun compounds with hand assigned accent labels at: http://www.cslu.ogi.edu/~sproatr/newindex/ap90nominals.txt

References

Harald Baayen (2001) *Word Frequency Distributions*. Kluwer, Dordrecht.

Michele Banko and Eric Brill. (2001) "Scaling to very very large corpora for natural language disambiguation," ACL.

Shane Bergsma, David Yarowsky and Kenneth Church (2011), "Using Large Monolingual and Bilingual Corpora to Improve Coordination Disambiguation," ACL.

Dustin Boswell (2004) "Speling Korecksion: A Survey of Techniques from Past to Present," http://dustwell.com/PastWork/SpellingCorrectionResearchExam.pdf

Andrei Broder. 2002. A taxonomy of web search. *SIGIR Forum* 36, 2 (September 2002), 3-10.

Lewis Carroll, 1865, Alice's Adventures in Wonderland.

Kenneth Church and William Gale (1989) "Enhanced Good-Turing and Cat-Cal: two new methods for estimating probabilities of English bigrams." HLT.

Kenneth Church and Patrick Hanks. (1990) "Word association norms, mutual information, and lexicography." CL.

Cecil Coker, Kenneth Church and Mark Liberman (1990) "Morphology and rhyming: two powerful alternatives to letter-to-sound rules for speech synthesis," In ESCA Workshop on Speech Synthesis *SSW1-1990*, 83-86.

Silviu Cucerzan and Eric Brill (2004) "Spelling Correction as an Iterative Process that Exploits the Collective Knowledge of Web Users, EMNLP.

Ido Dagan and Kenneth Church. (1994) "Termight: identifying and translating technical terminology," ANLC.

William Gale, Kenneth Church and David Yarowsky. (1992) "One sense per discourse," HLT.

Bradley Efron and Ronald Thisted, (1976) "Estimating the number of unseen species: How many words did Shakespeare know?" *Biometrika*, 63, 3, pp. 435-447.

John Firth, (1957) "A Synopsis of Linguistic Theory 1930-1955," in Studies in Linguistic Analysis, Philological Society, Oxford; reprinted in Palmer, F. (ed.) 1968 Selected Papers of J. R. Firth, Longman, Harlow.

Alex Franz and Thorsten Brants (2006) http://googleresearch.blogspot.com/2006/08/all-our-n-gram-are-belong-to-you.html.

Fred Jelinek (2004) "Some of my Best Friends are Linguists," LREC.

Maryan Kamvar and Doug Beeferman, (2010) "Say What? Why users choose t speak their web queries," Interspeech.

Barbara Kipfer (ed.) (2001) Roget's Thesaurus, Sixth Edition, HarperCollins, NY, NY, USA.

Karen Kukich. 1992. Techniques for automatically correcting words in text. *ACM Comput. Surv.* 24, 4.

Mark Liberman (1989) "How many words do people know?" *ACL*.

Mark Liberman and Kenneth Church (1991). "Text analysis and word pronunciation in text-to-speech synthesis." In *Advances in Speech Signal Processing*, edited by S. Furui and M. Sondhi.

Frederick Mosteller and David Wallace. *Inference and Disputed Authorship: the Federalist*, Addison-Wesley, 1964.

Emily Pitler and Kenneth Church. (2009) "Using word-sense disambiguation methods to classify web queries by intent," EMNLP.

Richard Sproat, William Gale, Chilin Shih, and Nancy Chang. 1996. A stochastic finite-state word-segmentation algorithm for Chinese, CL.

Richard Sproat (1994) "English noun-phrase accent prediction for text-to-speech," Computer Speech and Language, 8, pp. 79-94.

Andreas Stolcke (1998) "Entropy-based Pruning of Backoff Language Models" Proc. DARPA News Transcription and Understanding Workshop.

Lewis Terman, (1918) "The vocabulary test as a measure of intelligence," *Journal of Educational Psychology*, Vol 9(8), pp. 452-466.

David Yarowsky. 1993. One sense per collocation, HLT.

Author Index

Association for Computational Linguistics
209 N. Eighth Street
Stroudsburg, Pennsylvania 18360

CURRAN ASSOCIATES INC
proceedings.com